THINK LIKE A CHAMPION

Dr Rudi Webster was a champion track and field athlete at school in Barbados. He studied medicine at Edinburgh University in Scotland and became the sportsman of the year while he was there. In his debut first-class game – Scotland against the MCC – he established a unique record by getting a wicket with the first ball he bowled in each innings. He also played cricket for Warwickshire County in England.

Dr Webster did pioneering work in the mental component of performance and the mental conditioning of athletes in Australia and helped many of its top teams and athletes to give their best performance. He also worked with the national cricket teams of West Indies, Sri Lanka and India.

He was the manager of the West Indies team in Kerry Packer's World Series of Cricket and witnessed first-hand the birth and development of that champion team.

From 1986 to 1990 Dr Webster worked with the prime minister of Barbados and later became Barbados' ambassador to the US.

He was the mental skills coach to the Kolkata Knight Riders who won the championship in the 2012 IPL season.

He is the author of *Winning Ways: In Search of Your Best Performance.*

THINK LIKE A CHAMPION

RUDI V. WEBSTER

*Interviews with Wasim Akram, M.S. Dhoni, Jacques Kallis,
Rahul Dravid, V.V.S. Laxman, Clive Lloyd, Sir Garfield Sobers,
Greg Norman and more.*

Harper
Sport

First published in India in 2013 by Harper Sport
An imprint of HarperCollins *Publishers* India

ISBN: 978-93-5029-665-3

2 4 6 8 10 9 7 5 3 1

HarperCollins *Publishers*
A-53, Sector 57, Noida, Uttar Pradesh 201301, India
77-85 Fulham Palace Road, London W6 8JB, United Kingdom
Hazelton Lanes, 55 Avenue Road, Suite 2900, Toronto, Ontario M5R 3L2
and 1995 Markham Road, Scarborough, Ontario M1B 5M8, Canada
25 Ryde Road, Pymble, Sydney, NSW 2073, Australia
31 View Road, Glenfield, Auckland 10, New Zealand
10 East 53rd Street, New York NY 10022, USA

Typeset in 11/14 Adobe Caslon Pro at
Inosoft Systems

Printed and bound at
Thomson Press (India) Ltd.

For all the sportsmen and sportswomen
around the world

CONTENTS

ACKNOWLEDGEMENTS

I wish to acknowledge books, periodicals and other reference material consulted. These are listed in the bibliography.

Recognition must be given to all the sports teams and sportspersons with whom I worked in Australia, West Indies, Sri Lanka, India and the United States of America.

Recognition must also go to Jim Keogh and Ian Frazer in Australia, to Tony Fraser in Trinidad and Tobago and to my sister Elaine Kaps in Switzerland, for their help and suggestions during the writing of the manuscript.

Extra special thanks must be given to Clive Lloyd and his champion cricket team. As manager of that team during Kerry Packer's World Series of Cricket I saw first-hand the birth, growth and development of a champion team that dominated world cricket for more than fifteen years; a team that has been heralded as one of the best sports teams in the history of sport. I am indebted to the players and to Kerry Packer for giving me the opportunity to take part in that development process.

I am grateful to Gamini Dissanayake and the Board for Cricket Control in Sri Lanka for inviting me to Sri Lanka to work with their players. My visits to Sri Lanka were important and highly educational. The lessons that I learnt from the Buddhist priests and the people of Sri Lanka had a great impact on my thinking and my attitude towords life.

I had a wonderful experience working with the Indian cricket team on two occasions. I learned a lot from the players and I am particularly thankful to the Board of Control for Cricket in India (BCCI) for giving me this opportunity.

I learned valuable lessons about the mental component of the game from the Australian Rules football clubs with whom I worked when I was living in Melbourne. They allowed me to do pioneering work in the mental conditioning of their players and their teams and I thank them, their players, coaches, support staff and administrators.

I was invited to work with the US Power Soccer Team in 2010. All the members of that team had severe physical disabilities and played the game in special wheelchairs. There, I saw a level of courage and mental toughness that I had never seen before, and I learned about the awesome power of the human spirit and the human will to overcome and conquer. I wish to thank the coach and team members for this exposure.

Very special thanks must go to M.S. Dhoni, Rahul Dravid and V.V.S. Laxman from India, Wasim Akram from Pakistan, Jacques Kallis from South Africa, Sir Garfield Sobers and Clive Lloyd from the West Indies, and Dennis Lillee, Greg Norman, Peter Thomson, Peter Brock and Ian and Greg Chappell from Australia for taking part in the interviews and sharing their knowledge, experience and wisdom with the readers.

I must also thank my wife Lyndi for her constant support and priceless contributions.

FOREWORD

Dr Rudi Webster has rare gifts.

On the one hand, his academic prowess is undoubted and he has a number of specialist degrees in medicine to prove that.

On the other hand, he is possessed of that most uncommon commodity – common sense. This allows him to convey very technical information to laymen, especially to sportsmen and sportswomen, in simple and clear terms. He has a way of illustrating his instructions with examples and anecdotes (often humorous) that make the concept that he is trying to convey very understandable.

As manager of the West Indies cricket team in Kerry Packer's World Series Cricket he became a mental skills coach to many of the players who, under Clive Lloyd and later Viv Richards, dominated world cricket for over fifteen years.

Rudi is truly a pioneer in the mental preparation and mental conditioning of athletes and soon became known as the 'guru' in Australian sporting circles.

In Australian Rules football his impact on the game and his influence with the coaches were such that during the quarter-time break in a finals game in Melbourne two head coaches fought with each other over him; a sensational incident that stunned the 80,000 spectators at the ground and the millions of TV viewers around Australia.

In 1984 Rudi wrote his first book, *Winning Ways: In Search of Your Best Performance*.

Around that time I was indeed in search of my best performance, as a 'privateer' driver in professional saloon car racing in Australia, and

Rudi helped me to find it inter alia by teaching me techniques which allowed me to control my thought processes, both in preparation for races, and in the high-speed pressure situations which confronted me in most races. By this means I was able to produce my best performance on a regular basis. He did similar things for other sportsmen and sportswomen, and for politicians, businessmen, administrators, doctors and medical students.

Rudi later became Barbados' ambassador to the US and Barbados' ambassador to the Organization of American States (OAS) and despite his worldwide success he retains his common touch and his 'wicked' sense of humour.

In his new book *Think Like a Champion* the sections on motivation, concentration, mastery of the basics and coping with pressure are important and revealing and will be of great benefit to the athlete. Fascinating are his techniques, including visualization, for training the mind to remove mental limitations and self-imposed barriers to performance, as well as his methods for tapping into the secret of success that is already within us. These will no doubt be a handy reference for those training to be mental skills coaches in sport.

Interviews with great sportsmen like Sir Garfield Sobers, Clive Lloyd, Greg Norman, Jacques Kallis, Wasim Akram and Rahul Dravid provide a rare and intimate insight into their minds. His conversation with Clive Lloyd is truly revealing and gives a long-awaited account of the birth, development and triumph of Lloyd's champion West Indies cricket team.

In his book *Greg Norman: My Story* (Harrap Publishers), Greg described how Rudi got him out of a performance slump and turned his golfing career around. He claimed that his phone call to Dr Webster from London was probably the best investment he ever made. Norman subsequently went on to be the world's number one golfer for many years until Tiger Woods came on the scene.

Read this book, and refer to it often. It contains the secrets of success, and it applies as much to most forms of life's endeavour as it does to sport.

−Jim Keogh
Melbourne, Australia

INTRODUCTION

The ancient Greeks were great lovers of sport and believed that games were a metaphor of life. They paid enormous attention to winners and bestowed great wealth and status on them. Not so with the losers. At the time, poets and philosophers were eagerly studying athletes' performance to discover the root causes of victory and defeat.

For instance, the Greek poet Pindar recognized the positive impact of dedication, discipline, hard work, and mental control on performance, while Plato and Pythagoras observed the negative effects of fear, confusion and mental weakness.

These poets and philosophers felt that the secret of success lies within the athlete, and thought that bad habits, self-doubts and other negative mental forces cloud that secret. They hinted that the athlete's worst enemy is himself, not his opponent, and that self-sabotage is one of the greatest threats to performance.

It is only in recent years that mental conditioning and the science of sports psychology have become a public part of sport, but it is untrue to say that they have not been used privately and in an unstructured way for more than a thousand years. Richie Benaud, a former cricket captain of Australia, points out that throughout the ages successful athletes, captains and leaders in sport have given due importance to the mental component and ended up successful.

Many years ago, when I was playing cricket for Warwickshire

County in England, I used to spend hours in the pavilion listening to the wise advice of 'Tiger' Smith, an old Warwickshire and England player who represented his country from 1911 to 1914. He continually stressed the importance of the mind in performance and tried to teach me simple methods to improve my mental skills; techniques that he had learned from his predecessors who played in the late 19th century. He described mind techniques that today's sports psychologists have cleverly packaged and repackaged to enhance the performance of their players.

He spoke about the dangers of mental and physical tension and the advantages of having a clear, calm and inventive mind. He talked about positive and negative thinking, goal setting, motivation, concentration, self-confidence, self-belief and pressure, as well as the importance of good planning, preparation and execution. He even spoke about debriefing after the game. He was very keen on positive imagery and acquainted me with visualization and mental rehearsal techniques that he used during his career.

Today's technologies have revolutionized sport and have brought enormous benefits to the game, but they have also brought a few negatives. For instance, players and some captains have become so dependent on technology and their coaches that they have lost some of their self-reliance and the ability to think independently and creatively. We must not allow knowledge and speed to replace wisdom and good judgement. In this techno-environment, imagination, common sense and honesty with self are often forgotten factors in performance.

Some coaches now place greater emphasis on information gathering, analysis and diagnosis than on good execution. This is a troubling development since execution is a key to successful performance. Plans and strategies amount to nothing unless they are well executed. Moreover, the skills of acquiring knowledge and information are very different from those of doing. Both are needed for good performance. Unfortunately, many coaches and players, mistakenly believe that once they have information and knowledge, execution would be easy and automatic.

In recent years there has been a tendency to play down the

importance of the basics of the game. This is unfortunate because the basics form the fabric of your performance. If you ignore them or execute them poorly, your performance will suffer. They are most important when the pressure is greatest and the odds are stacked against you, or when you are in good form and become overconfident. The stronger the impulse to disregard the basics, the greater is the need to stick to them.

Performance in sport is built on four interconnected pillars – physical fitness, physical skills, tactics and strategies, and mental skills. In *Think Like a Champion*, a few of the world's best sportsmen discuss their own recipes for success. They point out the importance of those pillars and highlight the need to be strong in all four of them. But they claim that at the highest levels of sport, the mental pillar is most important because it determines how well the other components are combined and executed.

What Napoleon Bonaparte, the French general, said a few hundred years ago about the importance of the mind in battle reinforces that last point. He stated that in his war campaigns, the psychological was to the physical, what two is to one.

Athletes who value the advice of these champions and who pay attention to the principles that are expressed in the chapters on performance, leadership and teamwork, self-confidence, concentration, and pressure will give themselves a great chance of lifting their performance to a higher level.

These principles are not just relevant to sport. They can be used to improve performance in other professions and in other areas of our lives.

In today's complex and rapidly changing world we must modify our thinking and strategies to fit the varying demands and requirements that we face. Albert Einstein recognized this need many years ago when he said, 'The world that we have made as a result of the level of thinking we have done thus far creates problems that we cannot solve at the same level as they were created.'

We need to design a new performance model that combines the finest of the old with the best of the new. It should focus on clear vision, inventive thinking, mastery of self, and mastery of the basics. It should also focus on good execution, good teamwork, cooperative and productive relationships; continuous learning and training; and respect for the beliefs, values and rights of other people.

Let's take a hint from Pindar, Pythagoras and Plato: remove the obstacles that are holding us back and use our imagination to awaken and set free the secret of success that already lies within us. The thoughts and pictures that you embed into your mind today determine what you become tomorrow.

ATHLETES INTERVIEWED

WASIM AKRAM

Wasim Akram the Pakistan cricketer is one of the best fast bowlers in the history of cricket. He developed and perfected the art of reverse swing bowling and confused batsman all over the world with his guile and swing.

Wasim was the master of swing bowling and could bowl equally well from both sides of the wicket. He and Waqar Younis were known as the 'Sultans of Swing'. He bowled with great speed and hostility and intimidated many international batsmen.

Brian Lara the great West Indies batsman once said, 'Over fifteen or sixteen years of playing international cricket in Tests and One Day Internationals, Wasim Akram is definitely the most outstanding bowler I've ever faced.'

Wasim captained Pakistan and his County Lancashire that in 1998 won the ECB trophy, the Benson and Hedges Cup and the AXA League under his shrewd leadership.

In the 1992 Cricket World Cup Final, Pakistan defeated England and Wasim won the Man of the Match Award for his outstanding performance.

Wasim played 104 Tests and captured 414 wickets at an average of 23.62 and in 356 One Day Internationals he got 502 wickets at 23.62. He won seventeen Man of the Match Awards in 104 Tests – one every six Tests. He was the first bowler to take more than 400 wickets in both Tests and One Day Internationals(ODI).

Wasim was Wisden Cricketer of the Year in 1993. He is currently the bowling coach for the Kolkata Knight Riders in the Indian Premier League.

INTERVIEWED IN KOLKATA, INDIA, 28 APRIL 2012

MAHENDRA SINGH DHONI

Mahendra Singh Dhoni is a captain with one of the coolest heads in cricket. Of pressure he once said, 'A lot of negative things are said about pressure. To me, pressure is just added responsibility. How can it be pressure when God gives you an opportunity to be a hero for your team and your country?

Dhoni is India's most successful cricket captain. Under his captaincy, India won the 2007 ICC World Twenty 20 CB Series, the Border-Gavaskar Trophy in 2008 and 2010 against Australia and the 2011 World Cup. Dhoni also led the Indian team to the number one position in the ICC rankings in Test cricket, the first time that India has had that honour. His Test and ODI record is so far the best among all captains of India. Dhoni captains India in all three forms of the game – Twenty 20, One Day Internationals and Tests.

Dhoni has also captained Chennai Super Kings to victory in the 2011 IPL and in the Champions League.

Dhoni is a flamboyant and destructive batsman and a good wicketkeeper. In the final of the 2011 World Cup he hit ninety-one not out off just seventy-one balls to lead India to victory and was given the Man of the Match Award for his outstanding performance.

Dhoni has been the recipient of many other awards. He was the first Indian to receive the ICC ODI Player of the Year in two consecutive years, 2008 and 2009. He received the Rajiv Gandhi Khel Ratna Award, India's highest honour for achievement in sports and the Padma Shri Award, India's fourth highest civilian honour, in 2009. He was named the captain of the ICC World Test and ODI teams in 2009.

Time magazine listed him in the 'Time 100' list of the 100 most influential people of 2011.

INTERVIEWED IN DOMINICA, WEST INDIES, 9 JULY 2011

JACQUES KALLIS

South African Jacques Kallis is one of the greatest all-rounders ever to play the game. He is a right hand bat and a right hand fast/medium bowler. He is the only player in the history of the game to score more than 12,000 runs and capture 250 wickets in both Tests and One Day Internationals. In 2005 he was ICC Player of the Year and in 2008 he was the Wisden Leading Cricketer in the World and the ICC Test Player of the Year.

Along with Sir Donald Bradman, Mohammad Yousuf and Gautam Gambhir he is the only person to make a century in five consecutive matches. In 2007 he was the fourth person to score five centuries in four Tests; the others being Sir Donald Bradman, Ken Barrington and Matthew Hayden.

So far, Kallis has played in 156 Tests and has scored 12,837 runs including forty-four centuries at an average of 57.30. He has taken 260 Test wickets at an average of 32.73. He has so far played 319 One Day Internationals and has scored 11,481 runs at an average of 45.55 and has taken 267 wickets at an average of 31.76.

Kallis is the epitome of the quiet achiever.

INTERVIEWED IN KOLKATA, INDIA, 12 MAY 2012

RAHUL DRAVID

Rahul Dravid is one of India's best ever batsmen and around the world he is one of the most respected and admired players. Known as the 'Wall of Indian Cricket' because of his strong technique, he has been the backbone of the batting unit in the Indian team.

Dravid has been a member of the Indian team since 1996 and was its captain from 2005 to 2007. He was one of Wisden's Top Five Cricketers of the Year in 2000 and was the ICC Player of the Year and the ICC Test Player of the Year in 2004.

He is the only Indian batsman apart from Sachin Tendulkar to score over 12,000 runs in Test cricket, and is the third international player to do so.

Dravid has played in 157 Tests and has scored thirty-five centuries in Test cricket, including five double centuries, at an average of 53.00,

One of his greatest innings was played in the second Test against Australia at Kolkata in 2001 when he and V.V.S. Laxman produced one of the greatest comeback victories in the history of the game. Following on, the pair put on 376 runs for the fifth wicket in the second innings of the match. Dravid scored 180 and Laxman 281.

Dravid holds the record for the highest number of catches in Test cricket.

Dravid's greatest strength was in his mind – his mental toughness, his clear thinking, his enormous powers of concentration and his ability to handle pressure. Nowhere was this better demonstrated than in the 2011 Test Series in England when he was the only Indian batsman to play really well.

INTERVIEWED IN DOMINICA, WEST INDIES, 8 JULY 2011

VANGIPURAPU VENKATA SAI LAXMAN

V.V.S. Laxman has been one of India's most elegant and attractive batsmen. Ian Chappell a former captain of Australia once described him as a very, very special batsman.

Laxman is noted for his exquisite timing and his ability to play spin. His supple wrists allow him to hit against the spin and to flick balls to all parts of the leg side.

Laxman saved his best performances for the games against Australia in both Tests and One Day Internationals. He has scored six of his sixteen Test hundreds, and four of his six ODI hundreds against Australia. Two of those Test centuries were double centuries, 281 in Kolkata in 2000-01 and 200 in Delhi in 2008-09.

With Rahul Dravid he played one of his greatest Test innings against Australia at Kolkata in 2001 when the pair grabbed victory from the jaws of defeat by putting on 376 runs in the second innings. Laxman scored 281.

Laxman has played some extraordinary Test innings under pressure.

He says that he loves to play in tough situations where the odds are stacked against him and adds that in those situations he rises to the occasion and gets the best out of himself.

Laxman turned defeat into victory in another match against Australia in Mohali when India was 124 for 8 chasing 216 to win. Batting with a runner because of a bad back, Laxman and number ten batsman Ishant Sharma put on eighty-one runs to take the score to 205 before Sharma fell. Laxman who scored seventy-three not out, and last man Pragyan Ojha knocked off the remaining runs and India won the game.

Laxman was also involved in a historic Indian victory in December 2010 against South Africa in Durban. When Dhoni joined Laxman the score was 94 for 5. Together with Dhoni and the tail-end batsmen Laxman took the Indian lead to 302 runs of which he scored a match-winning ninety-six.

Like Rahul Dravid, Laxman's strength is his mental toughness and concentration.

Laxman has so far played in 127 Tests with a batting average of 46.27.

Laxman was captain of the Deccan Chargers in the first year of the IPL. He has been a recipient of the Padma Shri Award, India's fourth highest civilian award.

INTERVIEWED IN DOMINICA, WEST INDIES, 10 JULY 2011

SIR GARFIELD SOBERS

Sir Garfield Sobers is the greatest all-round cricketer in the history of the game. He was about the best in every area of the game. According to Richie Benaud, a former Australian captain, 'Sobers is the greatest all-round cricketer the world has seen. He was a brilliant batsman, splendid fielder, particularly close to the wicket, and a bowler of extraordinary skill, whether bowling with the new ball, providing orthodox left-arm spin or over-the-wrist spin.'

He took over the captaincy of the West Indies team from Frank Worrell in the 1964-65 series against Australia and held it until 1973.

Sobers at one time held the record for the highest number of Test runs, 8032 runs, the highest Test innings, 365 not out, and the highest number of runs in a six-ball over, thirty-six.

Sobers was elected Wisden Cricketer of the Year in 1964 and was awarded the Wisden Leading Cricketer in the World title (retrospectively) eight times in thirteen years.

In January 1972, in the third (unofficial) Test between Australia and the Rest of the World XI at the Melbourne Cricket Ground, Sobers played an innings of 254 which was described by Don Bradman as 'the greatest exhibition of batting ever seen in Australia'.

Sobers played in ninety-three Tests, scored twenty-six centuries and had a Test average of 57.58. He took 235 Test wickets at an average of 34.03 and held 109 catches.

Sobers was knighted in 1975 by Queen Elizabeth II for his services to cricket.

INTERVIEWED IN AUSTRALIA, 23 AUGUST 1983

CLIVE LLOYD

Clive Lloyd captained the West Indies team between 1974 and 1985. Under his leadership West Indies became the dominant Test-playing nation, a position that was only relinquished in the latter half of the 1990s. He captained the team in seventy-four Test matches more than any other person in the history of Test cricket.

Clive is one of the most successful Test captains of all time: during his captaincy the side had a run of twenty-seven matches without defeat, which included eleven wins in succession.

Lloyd captained the West Indies team that won the first World Cup in 1975 in which he scored a century and the second World Cup in 1979. His team was expected to win the 1983 World Cup but it was surprisingly beaten by India in the Final.

Lloyd was named Wisden Cricketer of the Year in 1971 for his performances in the previous twelve months when he scored 1,600 runs for Lancashire.

Lloyd was one of the best fielders in the game and was nicknamed 'Super Cat' for his speed, agility, flexibility and catlike movements. He was a flamboyant and devastating left hand bat and holds the record for the fastest double hundred in first-class cricket, 201 in just 120 minutes against Glamorgan in 1976.

Lloyd played 110 Tests and has a batting average of 46.67.

Clive Lloyd's greatest achievement was bringing together a diverse collection of talented individuals who lacked direction, focus, discipline and common purpose and transforming them into a highly professional and all-conquering unit that dominated world cricket for fifteen consecutive years. That team is regarded as one of the most successful teams in the history of sport.

INTERVIEWED IN ST LUCIA, WEST INDIES, 13 OCTOBER 2011

DENNIS LILLEE

Dennis Lillee is a former Australian cricketer who was rated not just as the most outstanding fast bowler of his generation but the best fast bowler of all time. Enormous ability coupled with a fiery temperament, consistent hostility, and a 'never-say-die' attitude propelled him to the very top of his profession. At his peak no one was faster, more competitive or more menacing. He and Jeff Thompson formed one of the most lethal and frightening fast-bowling combinations ever seen. In 1975, the University of Western Australia timed Lillee's bowling at 154.8 km/h. Dennis played in seventy Tests and took 355 wickets at an average of 23.92.

In the early part of his career Lillee had four stress fractures in his back that almost ended his career. But he took on a strict rehabilitation programme, worked extremely hard and demonstrated unbelievable tenacity and persistence to overcome his crippling injuries.

By the time he retired from international cricket in 1984 he was holder of the world record for most Test wickets (355) even though he had missed nearly four years of Test cricket because of injury and participation in World Series cricket. By that time he was firmly established as one of the most recognizable and renowned Australian sportsmen of all time.

Dennis Lillee has done great service to the art of fast bowling by contributing immensely at the MRF Pace Foundation in Chennai, India. On 17 December 2009, Lillee was inducted into the ICC Cricket Hall of Fame.

INTERVIEWED IN AUSTRALIA, 23 FEBRUARY 1983

IAN CHAPPELL

Ian Chappell captained Australia between 1970-71 and 1975 and Australia's World Series team from 1977 to 1979 and gained the reputation of being one of the greatest captains in the game. He captained Australia in thirty Tests, lost the first two and was never beaten again.

Dennis Lillee summed up Ian's worth as a batsman and captain when he said, 'If I had to choose a cricketer to bat for my life, I would have no hesitation in choosing Ian.' Chappell played in seventy-five Tests, scored 5,345 runs at an average of 42.42.

Ian was an aggressive captain with a blunt verbal manner that often led to confrontations with opposition players and cricket administrators. He was the driving force behind the professionalism of Australian cricket in the 1970s. His grandfather and brother also captained Australia.

Chappell's trademark shot was the hook. He often said, 'Three bouncers an over should be worth twelve runs to me.' A specialist slip fielder, he was the fourth player to take one hundred Test catches.

Since his retirement in 1980, he has pursued a high-profile career as a sports journalist and cricket commentator. He remains a major figure in Australian cricket: in 2006, Shane Warne called Chappell the biggest influence on his career.

On 9 July 2009, Ian Chappell was inducted into the ICC Cricket Hall of Fame.

INTERVIEWED IN AUSTRALIA, 23 FEBRUARY 1983

GREG CHAPPELL

Greg Chappell's career straddled two eras as the game moved towards a greater level of professionalism after the World Series cricket split. He captained Australia between 1975 and 1977 and then joined World Series cricket, before taking over the captaincy of Australia once more from 1979 to1983. He held that position until he retired in 1983. Greg scored twenty-four hundreds in a total of 7,110 runs at an average of 53.86. If Chappell's batting average in Kerry Packer's 'Supertests' (the hardest cricket Chappell says he ever played) were added to his Test record, his overall average would be 54.30.

Chappell has the distinction of starting and finishing his Test career by scoring a century on each occasion.

The second of three brothers to play Test cricket, Greg Chappell was one of Australia's best and most elegant batsmen. His major strength was his enormous ability to concentrate particularly in tough situations. An exceptional all-round player who bowled medium pace and, at his retirement, held the world record for the most catches in Test cricket.

Since his retirement as a player in 1984, Chappell has pursued various business and media interests as well as maintaining connections to professional cricket; he has been an Australian selector, a member of the Australian Cricket Board, and coach of the India National Team from 2005 to 2007.

Chappell was a selector of the Australian national side from 29 October 2010 to August 2011. Greg is now National Talent Manager for Cricket Australia.

INTERVIEWED IN AUSTRALIA, 23 FEBRUARY 1983

GREG NORMAN

Greg Norman is one of Australia's greatest golfers. He was ranked as the number one golfer in the world for 331 weeks in the 1980s and 1990s. Nicknamed the *Great White Shark*, he is now a very successful businessman whose personal wealth is estimated to be in hundreds of millions of US dollars.

Norman will always be remembered for his style of play. He had one of the best swings in the game. He hit an incredibly high ball that allowed him to carry the ball very long distances. He demonstrated the best technique around the greens and was strong in all aspects.

Norman has won three Arnold Palmer Awards as the Tour's leading money winner in 1986, '89 and '95. He was also the first person in Tour history to surpass $10 million in career earnings. He has thirty top ten finishes in Majors, or more than 38 per cent of those he entered.

He won the Open championship twice and should have won a third Open championship, the Masters, the US Open and the PGA championship.

Norman won the PGA Tour of Australia Order of Merit six times: 1978, 1980, 1983, 1984, 1986 and 1988. He won the European Tour's Order of Merit in 1982, and topped the PGA Tour's Money List in 1986, 1990 and 1995. He won the Vardon Trophy for lowest scoring average on the PGA Tour three times: 1989, 1990 and 1994; and was inducted into the World Golf Hall of Fame in 2001. His dominance over his peers (despite his comparative lack of success in the Majors) was probably best expressed in the Official World Golf Rankings: Norman finished the season on top of the ranking list on seven occasions, in 1986, 1987, 1989, 1990, 1995, 1996 and 1997, and was second at the end of 1988, 1993 and 1994.

In 1986, Norman was awarded the BBC Sports Personality of the Year Overseas Personality Award, a feat he replicated in 1993 to join Muhammad Ali and Björn Borg as multiple winners. Roger Federer has since joined that distinguished list. Norman received the 2008 Old Tom Morris Award from the Golf Course Superintendents Association of America, GCSAA's highest honour, at the 2008 Golf Industry Show in Orlando. Norman is a member of The Environmental Institute for Golf's board of trustees and also chairs the institute's advisory council. He was also the the recipient of the Golf Writers Association of America's 2008 Charlie Bartlett Award.

INTERVIEWED IN AUSTRALIA, 20 FEBRUARY 1983

PETER THOMSON

Peter Thomson and Greg Norman were Australia's two best golfers. Peter won the British Open Championship five times, a record that was equalled by Tom Watson the American golfer, and second only to Harry Vardon's six wins. Peter was the only player to win the Open three times in a row in the twentieth Century – 1954, 1955 and 1956.

Thomson was a prolific tournament champion around the world, winning the national championships of ten countries, including the New Zealand Open nine times and the Australian Open three times.

Thomson never played much golf on the PGA Tour in America but in 1956, playing in just eight events, he won the rich Texas International, and achieved his best finish in one of the three Majors staged in the United States, fourth at the US Open.

Thomson enjoyed a successful senior career. In 1985 he won nine times on the Senior PGA Tour in the United States, and finished top of the money list. His last tournament victory came at the 1988 British PGA Seniors championship.

Thomson was president of the Australian PGA from 1962 to 1994. He was a victorious non-playing captain of the international team in the 1998 Presidents Cup.

He was inducted into the World Golf Hall of Fame in 1988.

Thomson was a guest at the presentation ceremony of the 135th Open Championship, which was won by Tiger Woods. The event marked the fiftieth anniversary of Thomson's third Open victory.

Thomson has designed several golf courses in Australia.

INTERVIEWED IN AUSTRALIA, 23 MARCH 1983

PETER BROCK

Peter Brock otherwise known as 'Peter Perfect', 'The King of the Mountain' or simply as 'Brocky' was one of Australia's best-known and most successful motor racing drivers. He won the Bathurst 1000 endurance race nine times, the Sandown 500 Touring Car Race nine times, the Australian Touring Car Championship three times and was inducted into the V8 Supercar Hall of Fame in 2001.

INTERVIEWED IN AUSTRALIA, 20 OCTOBER 1983

CHAPTER 1

PERFORMANCE

Part 1: Be A Better Player

Strength does not come from physical capacity. It comes from an indomitable will.

— *Mahatma Gandhi*

The mental part of the game helps you to transform your talent or potential into performance and that is what is ultimately required — performance.

— *V.V.S. Laxman*

If I had a free hand in coaching I would initially spend most of my time teaching the basics of the game. Thereafter, I would devote an equal amount of time teaching the players how to identify and deal with the many different situations they will face during the game. I feel that this combination gives the player the best preparation and the best chance to do well.

— *Sir Garfield Sobers*

THE SECRET OF SUCCESS ALREADY LIES WITHIN

Today, success in top-class sport is no longer possible with just talent and ability. Success must first be created in the mind, then planned and pursued diligently over time. It does not happen all at once or in a straight line. It is a journey that takes time and energy, patience and persistence, and is usually punctuated by ups and downs, successes and failures. Enjoyment of that journey is a key to good performance.

Too often we believe that we are not good enough; something is not working and needs to be fixed; something is missing; and something special needs to be added to make us worthwhile. These limiting beliefs often hide the wealth within.

Don't waste your time looking for a secret to success. This secret already lies within you. Work instead to develop your own system of success. You change your path and trajectory in sport and in life when you alter the way you talk to yourself and change the things you believe, value and picture in your mind. The thoughts, values and pictures that you imprint in your mind today determine what you become tomorrow.

A young man had a clay statue that was in his family for generations and he always wished that it were gold instead. When he earned some money he had the statue covered with gold and it looked just the way he wanted it. But after a while the gold plating started to flake off in spots so he had it gold-plated again. As time went by he spent his resources maintaining the gold façade of the statue.

One day when his grandfather visited him he showed the old man the statue but he was embarrassed because clay was showing through in some places.

The old man, who knew the statue well, took a moist cloth and started to rub it. After removing some of the clay he said, 'Many years ago the statue must have fallen on the ground and was covered in mud. You wouldn't have known that. But look here.'

As he continued to remove the clay a bright yellow colour shone through. 'Underneath the clay your statue has been solid gold from the beginning. You didn't have to put more gold on it. From now on all you have to do to show the gold is remove any clay or dirt that settles on the statue.'

Like the clay on the gold statue, poor vision, limiting beliefs, negative thoughts, self doubts, poor excuses and bad habits hide the wealth within and undermine our desire and ability to play well and achieve success. These obstacles are like an anchor in the bottom of the sea, slowing every move we make. Removing them sets our inner resources free. Playing better is often more about unlearning or removing bad habits, fears, hurts and outmoded traditions than learning or adding new ones.

Skill, desire, willpower, wisdom and good judgement are necessary for good performance. So too are opportunity, preparation, patience and mental control. Preparation and desire can at times make up for a lack of skill, but skill alone cannot compensate for a lack of willpower, preparation or mental control.

Your body depends on your brain for instructions and direction before every action that it takes. And yet, many players place mental conditioning way down in their list of priorities. To them it is just an unimportant add-on to that list. For example, it is not unusual for players who miss appointments with me to say, 'Doc, we wanted to come and see you but we had to go to the gym or to the pool with the fitness instructor.'

Ask yourself Three Important Questions

In sport and in business there are three very important questions you should think through very carefully and answer as honestly as you can.

First, what do you want to achieve and become, and why – your vision, preferred future and goals? If you know what you want and why you want it you will invariably find a way to get it. But if you don't have a vision or clear goals your performance will lack purpose and direction. Vision is a future that beckons.

Second, what do you stand for and believe in – your values, priorities, and principles? You achieve what you believe. What do you believe about yourself, your ability and your game? Your beliefs and values provide the energy and discipline that drive you towards your goals. Beliefs and values are to athletes what roots are to trees. Without roots, trees fall when they are shaken by strong winds. Without beliefs and values players' performance falls apart when it is hit by the powerful winds of competition and pressure.

And third, what is your action plan? How do you organize and execute to make your vision a reality?

The answers to these questions could be the platform on which you build your performance.

You increase your chances of playing well when you plan and prepare carefully, when you execute your tasks well, and when you respond sensibly and positively to results.

Good preparation requires clarity, simplicity, and attention to detail and superior execution calls for mastery of self, mastery of the basics, clear thinking, good concentration and calmness of mind. Debriefing performance at the end of the game is a powerful weapon that is too often neglected. It allows you to monitor standards, correct mistakes, make better plans, and play better next time.

ADVICE TO PROMISING PLAYERS

When I asked Peter Brock, one of Australia's best racing car drivers, what advice he would give to a promising player who is trying to reach the top of his sport he said he would stress five things. They are:

1. *A strong desire to succeed*: There is no substitute for this and if you don't possess it, don't even bother trying because it is very difficult to be among the best players. No matter how much talent and ability you have, you will never make it to the top unless you are hungry for success.

2. *Honesty with self*: In order to become a good player you must be painfully honest with yourself. Mastery of self is the key but you only achieve it when you are totally honest with yourself. On the way up it is difficult to assess how good you are and how good you can become. It is sometimes hard to answer these questions and you must get some kind of yardstick to use as a measuring device.

   In motor racing one of the best ways to do this is to put a very good driver in your car and ask him to drive it flat out. If he is two seconds per lap faster than you are, make that your target and don't stop until you achieve it. It is always tempting to make up the difference by fiddling with the tyres and the car. You must resist this impulse. If you use artificial aids to make up time you will be fooling yourself.

3. *Preparation, practice, hard work and grit*: There is no substitute for good preparation, persistent practice and hard work. It is impossible to succeed at the highest level unless you work hard and practise sensibly. Grit or mental toughness gives rise to stamina and persistence and takes the champions most of the way.

4. *Mastery of the basics*: This gives you an advantage over your opponent and increases your chances of playing well. Good execution of the basics of your game is a key to your success. Players who win usually execute the basics better than their opponents.

5. *Observe and study the best players*: You will learn a lot from observing and listening to good players. You must try to find out the secret of their success and work out what you should do to improve your game.

When you observe and study someone else playing, the same nerves in the brain that would fire up if you were actually playing become active. That's the brain's way of correlating what you do with what you see others doing. Learning by observing, listening and studying is very important. But too often it is not given the attention it deserves. Some players and coaches are so full of themselves and their opinions that they close their minds to anything new or different, and just stop learning. Once you do that, you stop completely! When I meet these players I tell them the following story: A student went to a Zen master to learn about Zen but instead of asking questions and listening to the master he proceeded to show him how much he knew by giving him a lecture. The master listened attentively and after a while offered the student a cup of tea. When the beverage arrived the master started to pour it into the student's cup. He kept on pouring until it started overflowing – first on to the table and then on to the floor.

The student could not contain himself and screamed, 'Stop! Stop pouring. The cup is full – no more will go in. The master stopped and replied, 'Just like this cup, your mind is full of your own ideas and preconceptions. How can you learn unless you first empty your cup?'

LOVE AND ENJOY YOUR GAME

When asked the same question about advice to young players, Indian cricket captain M.S. Dhoni said the following:

- First and foremost, you must love and enjoy your sport. Otherwise you will not learn to play the game as well as you ought to;
- Second, not only must you enjoy your performance on the field, you must also derive pleasure from sharing your experiences with other players and creating an atmosphere that will help them to play better; and
- Third, keep things simple, stay in the moment, focus on the process and be patient and persistent.

Dhoni's advice is important because the first step to success is to do what you love to do and become aware of doing it. Bill Russell the American basketball player once said that he always rated how well he played by how much better he made his teammates play.

REMEMBER

1. Internal obstacles like lack of vision, limiting beliefs, negative thinking, self-doubts and low self-confidence limit your performance. So do old habits, poor excuses and low motivation.
2. Clear away these self-imposed obstacles that are sabotaging your performance. Playing better is often more about unlearning or removing old habits than learning or adding new ones.

3. Performance depends on skill, willpower and judgement. It also depends on opportunity, mental control and preparation.

4. Preparation and will can at times make up for a lack of skill but skill alone cannot make up for a lack of will or preparation.

5. Know what you want and why. Articulate your values and beliefs, arrange them in order of priority, and write out an action plan. You achieve what you believe.

6. To play well you must plan and prepare properly, execute correctly, and respond and debrief sensibly to results.

7. Hunger for success, honesty with self, preparation, practice, hard work, mental toughness, mastery of the basics, good concentration, and love and enjoyment of the game are the ingredients required to build good performance.

8. The first step to success is to do what you love to do and become aware of doing it.

9. You should get pleasure from helping teammates play better.

THERE IS MORE TO PERFORMANCE THAN ABILITY AND SKILL

When we look at talent in cricket we often see it as the ability to hit a ball or bowl a ball. Most so-called talented players are deficient in the mental side of the game and hardly ever do well or make it to the top. They don't understand how the mind works and don't work hard enough to get to know and understand themselves.

– Rahul Dravid

Improvement is a continuous process and until you play your last game in professional sport, you should always be trying to improve all aspects of your game, not just your skill and preparation but also your mind and temperament. You should always think about becoming a better player.

– V.V.S. Laxman

God gives natural gifts to all of us. We need to realize that
and work to strengthen them and improve in those areas where
our weaknesses lie.

— M.S. Dhoni

In 1975-76, when the West Indies cricket team toured Australia, Viv
Richards was a very talented but relatively unknown player. People who
knew him had high expectations of him but he played poorly in the
first few Tests and was almost dropped from the team. No matter how
hard he tried, he could not understand why he was playing so badly. At
his request I intervened and tried to help him with his game.

Viv was a nervous player in those days and during that particular
slump his nervousness turned into performance anxiety, a killer in
sport. This type of anxiety creates poor and inefficient movements –
stiffens the body, disrupts motor skills, particularly the fine motor skills
and hand–eye coordination – and it messes up thinking, judgement,
self-confidence and concentration.

Viv was shown how to relax, calm his mind, simplify his thinking,
and keep his concentration in the present, following which he was
given ego-boosting suggestions to build self-confidence and self-
belief.

At the same time, he broke down his goals and challenges into small
segments and focused attention on the basics of batting – following
the ball out of the bowler's hand, picking up its angle, line and length
quickly, allowing his body to move freely and naturally into position
to receive the ball and stroking it or sending it to the gaps in the field.
Early in his innings he was asked to concentrate on stroking the ball.
in the 'V' between mid-off and mid-on to stop himself from playing
across the line and giving his wicket away. My aim was to get rid of
his tension, improve his confidence and concentration, and boost the
efficiency of his movements. You may notice that I did not tell him
to hit the ball to his targets. Instead, I asked him to stroke it or send
it there because the intent to stroke the ball results in smoother and
better-coordinated movements. Trying to hit the ball often causes
muscle tension, poor timing and inefficient movement.

Viv used visualization and mental rehearsal techniques to practise and imprint those skills in his mind. In the remaining games he played extremely well and soon after became the best batsman in the world.

It is very important to know precisely where your target is but you shouldn't be transfixed on it or be mesmerized by it. In golf, I ask golfers to take up their stance, shut their eyes and point to their target with their top hand. It is surprising to see how many times they are off target. I use the same exercise in cricket with batsmen to increase their awareness of the gaps in the field. I ask them to take up their stance, shut their eyes and point to various positions in the field. They too are sometimes off target. When they improve their accuracy I get them to imprint those positions in their mind and mentally rehearse stroking the ball to the gaps between the fielders.

Too strong a focus on the target can give rise to tension and result in partial body functioning. Many years ago, psychotherapist Milton Erickson was asked to help prepare the US Army rifle team for its contest against the Russians whom they had never beaten before. Renowned psychotherapist Ernest L. Rossi said that in teaching the rifle team Erickson first got them to relax their feet, knees, hips and entire body. He asked them to allow their hands to be comfortably placed and the rifle butt to rest against the shoulder just right. Then he asked them to slowly lean their cheeks against the butt until it felt comfortable and let the gun sight wander up and down, back and forth across the target, and at the right moment to gently press the trigger.

Erickson did not ask them to fix their eyes on the target. He explained that doing so would interfere with the micro-movements of their body and put them under some strain and tension. He wanted them to keep their body in natural movement with a sense of comfort and relaxation. Instead of selecting just one part of the total picture – the target – he took the entire picture of the total body functioning. That year, the Army rifle team beat the Russians for the first time.

Many sportsmen over the years have had an excessive natural ability, but there have been some who haven't quite been able to make the best possible use of it because of unruly and untrained mental activities and inadequate strategies.

Sir Garfield Sobers, the world's greatest cricketer, often said that the main difference between great players and good players is not natural talent or physical technique but rather (1) The capacity to identify the most important demands and challenges in the situations they face or are about to face; (2) The ability to think simply, clearly, sensibly and creatively about those situations; and (3) The competence to quickly tailor their skills, resources and strategies to 'fit' those demands. He added, 'As situations change so do their thinking and strategy. Great players think about and manage game situations much better than other players.'

Richie Benaud, a former Australian cricket captain was also on the mark when he said: 'There is never any shortage of talented sportsmen either in this age or past eras, some have even been potentially great but have never quite managed to take that little last step. It is in fact a giant stride! That advance is the difference between the good and the great player. The successful sportsman is the one who knows how best to handle the pressures of the day and the situations about to land upon him, the one who is able to gauge when the pressures are being applied to him and when they must be applied to others.'

Both ability and motivation are needed for good performance. One without the other is of no use.

Ability is an indicator of potential and only shows what a player is capable of doing. It does not guarantee that he will do it nor does it assure good performance.

Motivation on the other hand reveals why a player might do something and how likely he is to do it. It is a powerful force that drives performance and is usually a better predictor of future performance than ability. The depth of your motivation and self-discipline determines the level of your performance.

Improving performance should start with realistic goal setting and an honest evaluation of the most important mental and physical skills. Then, the gap between where you are and where you want to be, and between where your skills are and where they ought to be should be assessed. The next step is to narrow those gaps with good preparation and constant practice and to remove bad habits and other obstacles such as self-doubt, impatience, poor self-image and poor concentration that sabotage performance. Progress takes time, patience and hard work but there isn't anything that is not improved or made easier by good training and practice.

As I said before, improvement does not happen all at once, nor does it occur in a straight line. Players who think so get impatient and frustrated when things don't turn out the way they expect them to. Coaches should point out the dangers of unrealistic expectations to their players and emphasize that development takes time and is a process or journey that is punctuated by ups and downs, successes and failures.

When practice of a physical skill is reinforced by visualization and mental rehearsal, the skill is learned more quickly, executed better and imprinted more powerfully in the mind. That is why these techniques are so effective. As positive practices are strengthened by preparation, training, repetition and mental rehearsal, the negative ones gradually weaken.

REMEMBER

1. Ability and motivation are both necessary for good performance.

2. Ability indicates what you can do; motivation indicates why and how likely you are to do it.

3. The depth of your motivation and self-discipline determine the level of your performance.

4. To play well you must identify the most important challenges before you, think simply and clearly about them, and tailor your skills and concentration to meet them.

5. Visualization or mental rehearsal is important in learning skills and in performance.

6. Improvement takes time. It does not happen all at once or in a straight line. Patience and persistence are needed.

7. There isn't anything that cannot be improved or made easier by constant training and practice.

BUILD YOUR GAME ON FOUR PILLARS

Most top athletes have good technique, sound strategies and a reasonable level of fitness, but in competition their performance is controlled by the mind – their ability to get into the right frame of mind consistently and regularly, day in and day out. Your state of mind determines how well you combine and use your fitness, technical skills and game strategies.

– *Rahul Dravid*

There is more to cricket than physical fitness and technique. Good players know how to think, concentrate and play when they face challenging situations.

– *Sir Garfield Sobers*

Success in sport is built on four interconnected pillars: fitness, physical skill (technique), tactics and strategy (preparation and planning), and mental skills (control of the mind). If any one of these pillars is weak or neglected, performance will suffer. During the last fifteen years this has been a problem with the West Indies cricket team. Although the players have been fit, athletic and talented they still performed poorly because of inadequate strategies and a weak mental pillar.

Many athletes and coaches pay lip service to the mental skills but spend less time on them than they do on the other pillars. Fitness and technique are extremely important and are vital for success but they should be the servants not the master. Excellence in physical skills does not guarantee that the right skills will be chosen or executed, or that common sense will prevail. Your mental skills determine how well you use your fitness and technical skills because in every action you take your body depends on your brain for direction.

During his successful war campaigns, Napoleon Bonaparte, the great French general, highlighted the importance of the mind and strategy in the performance of his army. He said that in his campaigns, psychological strategy and mental control were to action what two is to one.

Basil D'Oliveira, the great South African 'coloured' cricketer, escaped the apartheid system, went to England and played League cricket for Middleton, then county cricket for Worcester, and finally Test cricket for England. When he was picked in the England team to tour South Africa, the government there banned the England side because it included a non-white player. The consequences of that decision went far beyond cricket because it sparked a twenty-year isolation of South Africa and contributed to the eventual breakdown of the apartheid system.

In his early days in England, Basil had to make enormous adjustments on and off the field. Not only was the social and political climate very different from that of South Africa, but also the cricket conditions, so he had to make major technical, strategic and mental changes.

As a boy he was a very attacking batsman and tried to hit every ball into the road from very early in his innings. But in England he had to work out a batting strategy to curb his early aggression and develop an effective method of building his innings. He said that the first hour belonged to the bowler and the second hour belonged to him. In the first hour his strategy was to be cautious, to keep his wicket intact and to get used to the pitch and other playing conditions. In the second hour, caution gave way to a free and natural style during which he took control and put pressure on the bowlers. Although he started his innings slowly he calculated that he would score a hundred runs in three-and-a-half hours. That change in batting strategy worked very well for him because he had great success as a county and England player.

Sir Garfield Sobers who played in the same Lancashire League as D'Oliveira often said that there are two things that he pays particular attention to when he is assessing a batsman. The first is the way the batsman starts and builds his innings and the second is the way he approaches and takes control of the situations that he faces. He feels that in general players do not pay enough attention to the strategic and the mental parts of the game.

M.S. Dhoni, the captain of the successful Indian cricket team stressed that in cricket you should concentrate on the physical part of your game – your fitness and technique – as well as the mental part – strategy and the mental skills – and that you should try to be good in all of them. But he claims that at the top level, the mental and strategic components are most important. He feels that these four sets of skills are interconnected and that if you draw circles around them they would overlap each other.

REMEMBER

1. Build up the four pillars – fitness, technique, tactics and strategy and mental skills – and make sure that each one is strong.
2. If you ignore any one of them your performance will suffer.
3. Napoleon Bonaparte said that in his campaigns, psychological strategy and mental control were to action what two is to one.
4. Don't ignore the mental pillar. The state of your mind will determine how well you combine and use your fitness, technical skills and strategies.

MASTER THE BASICS AND YOU WILL MASTER YOUR GAME

A building with a weak foundation could collapse at any time. If the basics of your game are weak your performance will fall apart under pressure.

– *V.V.S. Laxman*

When a skyscraper is being built a lot of time and money are spent on constructing the foundation under the ground. In sport, investment in the foundation is also extremely important.

– *M.S. Dhoni*

The basics form the foundation on which your game is built. Repeatedly practising and honing your basic skills until they

become part of who you are and what you are a key to good
performance and success.

— *Rahul Dravid*

Look after the ones, the twos and the fours and the sixes will
take care of themselves.

— *A cricketer*

Recently, there has been a tendency among sports people to play down the importance of the basics. This is a bad error on their part because the basics form the fabric of performance. If the fabric is feeble, it will weaken performance. The stronger the impulse to ignore the basics the greater is the need to stick to them. Pressure, poor concentration, negative thinking and low self-confidence can weaken that fabric.

Many years ago, Greg Chappell the great Australian batsman had a horrendous run of failures that left him so depressed that he wanted to quit the game. He made quite a few ducks against the West Indies team and on one occasion when he was walking off the field after having made yet another one, someone in the Melbourne crowd released a live Mallard duck on the field to accompany him back to the pavilion. Everyone watched with great amusement as it waddled its way slowly across the cricket field.

At that stage Greg did not know why he was playing so poorly. When I told him that I thought he was ignoring the most important fundamental in batting – watching the ball out of the bowler's hand – the penny dropped and he went into the nets to see if that was in fact the case. He immediately rectified his problem and soon after played some magnificent innings for Australia against New Zealand. In baseball a pitcher is often defined by the way the ball leaves his hand. In cricket the bowler can also be defined by the way the ball leaves his hand. The batsman, on the other hand, is defined by how clearly he sees the ball as it leaves the bowler's hand and how quickly he allows his body to get into position to receive it.

When I asked Greg what lessons he had learned from his failures and what advice he would give to players who were trying to improve their performance, he said he would tell them:

- To identify the basics of their game.
- Learn them well and practise them regularly and attentively under the same physical and mental conditions that they will face in the game.
- Learn how to calm the mind and relax the body.
- Use common sense to choose and execute the basics properly.
- Stick to the basics at all costs. Never ignore them or move too far away from them because the moment they do so their performance will suffer. The only way they will put it back together is to return to the same basics they had neglected in the first place.

Sir Garfield Sobers agrees with this advice but highlights an additional component. He said if he had a free hand in coaching he would initially spend most of his time teaching the basics of the game. Thereafter, he would devote an equal amount of time teaching his players how to identify and deal with the many different situations they will face during the game. He feels that this combination gives the player the best preparation and the best chance to do well.

Mastery of the basic skills takes your game to a new level and gives you a definite advantage over your opponents. The team that executes the basics best usually wins most of the contests.

It requires at least 10,000 hours of disciplined effort and normal and deliberate practice to master the rudiments of the game and to acquire the expertise of a top player. That works out to three hours of practice every day for ten years. Even then you must practise regularly to maintain that expertise. Success in sport is often about familiarity, discipline and good judgement.

Deliberate practice is not the same as normal practice. If you have trouble returning serves to the forehand in tennis, you may in the course of a set receive about fifteen or twenty of those serves. But with deliberate practice you would have a coach giving you hundreds of these serves with appropriate technical feedback during a day's practice session.

After thousands of hours of practice and disciplined effort, execution of the basics usually occurs naturally and freely. Mastery only happens when your movements are free and automatic and when you don't have to think about what your hands and feet should be doing; you just do it. This occurs when your intellect gets out of the way and your instincts take over. Your body will then follow commands that precede thinking. If your intellect tries to control your movements, it will mess them up.

Nowhere is this better illustrated than in the story about the centipede and the toad. The centipede was running along quite happily when a toad in fun asked, 'Pray, which leg comes after which?' This set his mind in such a pitch he lay distracted in the ditch thinking how to run.

Psychologist H.A. Dorfman says, a good baseball pitcher does not judge his performance by how the batters hit his pitches but instead by whether he threw the pitch he wanted to. After a game, Dorfman once asked former Major League pitcher Greg Maddux how he pitched. Maddux told him fifty out of seventy-three, that is he had thrown seventy-three pitches and executed fifty. Nothing is more basic than that. Instead of judging performance entirely on traditional bowling averages bowlers in cricket could adopt Maddux's outlook and judge their performance by how often they bowled the ball the way they wanted to.

Today, the analysis of players' movements and techniques has been taken to new heights because of the amazing technologies in the game. Still, coaches should use these new tools wisely and not create the 'centipede or paralysis by analysis syndrome' where they pay more attention to analysis and diagnosis of technique than to strategy and execution. Getting information is very important, but using it effectively to produce the desired results is equally so. The skills of acquiring information and knowledge – **literacy and numeracy** – and the skills of doing or execution – **operacy** – are separate and different things. We need them both and we must not allow knowledge and speed of thought to replace wisdom and good judgement.

Many coaches feel that physical skills are the ultimate component of performance and look at performance of their players through spectacles that focus predominantly on technique and technical faults. These coaches can learn a lot from the old African saying: 'When someone falls don't look at where he falls, look at where he slips.' So when examining a technical fault they should find out what went wrong just before the fault occurred. In most cases the trigger will be found in the mind, not body.

The explosion of information and digital technology has already made casualties of creative, innovative and strategic thinking – the very things needed for growth and good performance in today's complex and rapidly changing world. Digital addiction is bound to become a serious problem if we do not maintain and improve our capacity to think clearly, strategically and imaginatively. Logic and analysis can organize, but it is imagination that can create the future. Albert Einstein recognized this when he said, 'Your imagination is your preview of life's upcoming attractions.'

I became acutely aware of the importance and the power of the basics during my medical training at the University of Edinburgh in Scotland when I was trying to combine medical studies with my game of cricket for Scotland and professional cricket for the County of Warwickshire in England. It was a very difficult task and at times I found myself questioning the wisdom of attempting to do so.

After the games and practice I was usually too tired to read and study and neglected my work at times. Some of my colleagues thought I was crazy to jeopardize my university career and after a while I started to feel that way too. But necessity is the mother of invention and I soon came up with a creative plan.

Early in the mornings I would go on to the wards and ask the medical and surgical registrars to take me to patients with common illnesses and to go over the fundamentals in detail. During each visit I would see at least three or four cases.

I didn't have the time or energy to read up the cases in the books so I had to find another method to imprint information and knowledge in my brain. I used visualization and mental rehearsal techniques and soon understood how powerful they are. I visualized every patient that I saw and in my images I included such things as sex, age, looks, ward, the position of the bed in the ward, the history and symptoms, the physical examination, the findings, the tests prescribed, the differential diagnosis and the treatment. Several times during the day I would replay those images in my mind. Over a period of time those cases added up and I had lots of movies of my patients to replay. But I still wasn't confident about my work because like most students I rated my preparation on the amount of reading I had done.

Those techniques helped me considerably and enabled me to achieve the challenging goal of passing my examinations while playing professional cricket. Immediately after I passed my final examinations I celebrated by taking seven wickets for six runs for Warwickshire against Yorkshire in the first innings and finished with twelve wickets for fifty-eight runs in the game.

During that time the importance of the basics and the power of visualization and mental rehearsal in learning and performance were strongly imprinted in my mind. I subsequently used them to great advantage in my postgraduate studies and specialist examinations, and in the teaching of doctors and medical students.

Sometimes you can have the right strategy and plans and be focused on doing the basic things well on or off the playing field and, yet, in a moment of weakness or distraction, lose your common sense and do the most stupid things. This was the case when I went over to England from Montreal, Canada, to sit my specialist examination in Diagnostic Radiology, the FFR, the pass rate of which was less than 20 per cent. In Canada, I was working at an excellent hospital at the University of McGill and during that time I acquired a lot of knowledge and practice answering examination questions. By the time I got to England, a few days before the examination, I was very well prepared and confident I would pass the examination on the first try. But before I could settle down, some fellow students dented my confidence by telling me that one couldn't pass such a difficult exam by just popping into Britain a few days prior to it. They said one had to live there for some time to learn and understand the system. I thought, 'Surely, success in this exam does not depend on residential factors.'

I took the written examinations and felt that I had done well enough to pass. Only the orals remained. I did well in the radiology oral and just had to get over the orals in surgery and medicine. The evening before these orals my friend and mentor from New Zealand, John Heslop, a professor of surgery at Otago University in Dunedin, was in London. Professor Heslop got in touch with me and asked me to join him for dinner that evening. When I told him I had two exams the following day and would not be able to accept his offer he said he would go through some surgery questions with me over dinner. I relented and we went to dinner at the Cricketers' Club in London. It was a terrible mistake because I met with a few former cricketers with whom and against whom I had played. As we talked about old times the drinks kept coming. We left the club at 4 in the morning completely intoxicated.

When I got back to my room my head was spinning. I threw up a few times and as I lay in my bed I thought, 'How stupid could I be? How could I have gotten drunk on the eve of one of my most important exams? There is no way I will be in any condition to answer questions at the 9.30 oral in medicine.'

I got out of my bed early that morning and took a taxi to the examination venue to try to speak to the professor of medicine before he started his examination of the doctors. It was a long shot but he agreed to see me and as soon as I walked into the room he said, 'Dr. Webster, you don't look too good.' I told him that I was feeling awful and would like to get his permission to appear for the exam later in the day. I also told him that I had only been in Britain for a few days and that the English food and water were playing havoc with my system. I don't think he believed me but he agreed to see me at the end of his list. I thanked him and went back to my hotel and slept for about four hours.

Later during the day I had a good oral in surgery and at about 5 in the evening I went to see the professor of medicine for my oral. When I walked into the examination room he said, 'Dr Webster, how are you feeling? You look a lot better now.' I told him my tummy had settled down and I felt a lot better. I was sure that he had seen through my story. After a brief pause he looked at me and asked, 'How tall are you?' 'Six foot five,' I replied. 'OK, talk to me about dwarfism,' he said.

I couldn't believe my luck: a year earlier I had worked at a children's hospital in Melbourne, Australia, which was a world leader in dwarfism research. I spoke for about ten minutes and when I finished he asked, 'Where did you learn all this stuff?' I told him about the work we had been doing in Melbourne. He stared at me for a moment and then said, 'You may go now. That is the end of the innings.'

The next day I learnt that I was one of the few doctors to have passed the exam.

A few days later I called up Professor Heslop in New Zealand and chided him for leading me astray and also for putting my career at risk. He responded by saying he had great confidence in me and knew I would pass. He said our outing to the Cricketers' Club had helped clear my mind and get rid of examination jitters. At this point I laughed because I remembered Sir Garfield Sobers telling me that he used late nights and late-night drinking to relax, clear his mind and improve his performance during a game scheduled for the following day. Sir Garfield could go out and have a good time every night until the wee hours of the morning and still manage to play well the next day, but I was not in that league. My examination success under those circumstances was a once-in-a-lifetime achievement. I got plain lucky.

GET YOUR PRIORITIES RIGHT

Information overload and excessive pressure often play tricks with our minds and our perception. They distort our sense of priorities and make the line between what is really important and what is not blurry. We then give trivial things importance they don't deserve and often make mountains out of molehills. Concentrating on first-important priorities is a key to good performance.

In every game situation, players see things differently and identify different priorities, but no matter what the situation, mastery of self and mastery of the basic skills should be top priorities.

The story below about big and small apples illustrates the effects of high and low priorities on concentration and performance.

An apple farmer once asked his two sons to sort out a stack of apples into a pile of big and small apples. His sons worked hard all day and when they finished the job they called their father to show him their work. The father congratulated them on their effort and asked them to mix both piles of apples again. The sons were furious and thought they had wasted their time. The father then asked them about a small pile of apples lying nearby. They told him that the third pile was that of bad apples they had discarded. The farmer said, 'If I had asked you to toss out the bad apples you would have missed some of them, but because you had to look at each apple carefully to see if it was big or small, you didn't miss any bad apples.'

I often put players through that exercise, I ask them to identify as many aspects of their game as they can, examine each one (aspect) carefully and then place it into one of two groups – a very important group and an important group. I then get them to number the things in the very important group in order of priority. High-priority items are the ones that determine action. Low-priority items, however, should not be ignored; they must be taken into account. This exercise usually clears up the players' minds and helps them to concentrate and play better.

Years ago, an Australian Test batsman asked me to help him break a slump that he had been in for some time. During our interaction I asked, 'Do you enjoy batting?'

'Of course I do.'

'What do you enjoy about your batting?'

'I love to attack the bowling. I enjoy hitting boundaries and playing attractive shots, and I like to make half-centuries and centuries. I love to hear the applause of the crowd and I like to impress them.'

'That is terrific,' I said. 'Do you enjoy staying in the moment and playing one ball at a time? Do you enjoy playing simple defensive strokes? Do you enjoy taking quick singles and occasionally turning ones into twos? Do you enjoy frustrating the bowler? Do you enjoy leaving the ball alone outside the off stump when you don't have to play it?'

'I do those things but I don't really enjoy them. They are not very interesting.'

'Is that so? What percentage of your game is taken up with hitting fours, sixes and playing spectacular shots.'

'About 30 per cent,' he replied.

'So you are telling me that you don't enjoy 70 per cent of your game because you find it uninteresting and boring? You are neglecting the major part of your game, aren't you?'

'Gosh. I never thought of it like that.'

'What are your priorities at the start of your innings? What sectors of the field do you target? What are your priorities for building your innings? What are your priorities when you take control and start to dominate the bowling? What are your priorities for surviving tough crisis periods that are only temporary but might cause you to lose your wicket?'

I told him to go home and reflect on what we had just discussed and carry out a simple but important assignment. First, write down every aspect of batting that he could think about. Second, put them under two headings, *the very important* and *the important*. I knew that he would have to examine each aspect of batting carefully before he could put it in either column. And third, once he had finished the two columns, look at the list in the very important column and number the items in order of priority.

In the following weeks he reversed his form and performed very well. He later told me that after the exercise he started to pay more attention to parts of his batting that he was ignoring and neglecting and was now getting greater pleasure not just from his batting but also from other aspects of the game. He claimed that the exercise cleared his mind, changed his thinking and attitude, established a new set of priorities, improved his concentration and tossed out the 'bad apples' – self-doubts and lack of confidence – that were spoiling his performance.

Whenever we encounter a challenging situation we should ask ourselves four questions, 'What are the first priorities in the situation? What is their order of importance? How can we design our strategy to fit those priorities? What are the possible advantages and disadvantages in the situations?' Priorities should be constantly monitored and assessed because as attitudes, emotions and circumstances change, so can priorities.

REMEMBER

1. Mastery of self and mastery of the basics should be top priorities. Skillful execution of the basics is a key to good performance. If you ignore them or execute them poorly your performance will suffer.

2. Identify the basics of your game; learn them well and practise them constantly; and stick to them, particularly when you are under pressure. Learning how to approach and deal with different game situations is equally important.

3. The basics are the foundation and strength of your game. They form the fabric of your performance and if that fabric is weak your performance will be weak.

4. It takes at least 10,000 hours of practice to master the basics and acquire the skills of an expert – three hours of practice every day for ten years. You then have to practise them constantly to maintain that expertise.

5. Mastery of the basics only happens when your movements are automatic and when you don't have to think about what your hands and feet should be doing; you just do it. Remember the centipede and the toad.

6. A batsman's success is influenced by how clearly he sees the ball when it leaves the bowler's hand and how quickly he gets into position to receive it.

7. Learning how to approach and deal with different game situations is just as important.

8. The skills of doing – operacy – are different from the skills of literacy.

9. The basics are the foundation and strength of your game. They form the fabric of your performance and if that fabric is weak your performance will be weak.

10. Identifying priorities clears up thinking and improves concentration.

11. Align your strategy to your vision and first-important priorities.

FAILURE IS AN ESSENTIAL PART OF SUCCESS

Successful people, including sportsmen, experience several failures and setbacks and have to overcome many barriers and obstacles along the way. I would encourage young sportsmen to read books about successful people like Nelson Mandela and Mahatma Gandhi. They will see that success was not a cakewalk for them.

– V.V.S. Laxman

The main difference between great players and the others is the interval between mistakes. Good players make mistakes, learn from them and repeat them less frequently than other players.

– M.S. Dhoni

Victory often arises out of failure because the pain of failure sometimes breaks the shell that stifles talent.

– Anonymous

How a player rebounds after a failure or setback usually speaks volumes about his character. Good players see failure as a stepping stone not a stumbling block.

Olympic decathlon champion Rafer Johnson once said: 'The most enjoyment I had was not always winning, [although I hated losing]. But what gave me the biggest thrill was the way I reacted when I was beaten – what I thought about when I was beaten and how I came back from defeat. To my mind, the great champions are the ones who react to defeat in a positive way. I'd much rather climb into the head of someone who has lost, and see what made that person come back to be a victor, than to climb into the head of a winner. You can probably learn more from failures.'

Success is not permanent and failure is not fatal. Failure is an essential part of success. In fact, victory often arises out of failure because the pain of failure sometimes breaks the shell that stifles talent.

However well you prepare and plan for the game, something will always go wrong and mistakes will always happen. Despite that you can still play well and be successful. In sport you constantly have to correct, adapt and adjust to changing conditions. Part of playing well is about expecting things to go wrong and adjusting to cope with them. You must expect the unexpected and be prepared to deal with it.

But no matter how well you prepare for the unexpected there are times when it will catch you off guard. The key to maintaining good performance under these circumstances is to immediately redirect concentration to the task at hand, focus on executing the basics well, and staying as calm as possible.

A case in point was an unexpected incident in a finals game of Australian Rules football in Melbourne that shocked everyone watching it. I had been associated with the football club that had won the championship in 1979, and in 1980 I took up the challenge of working with a team that had finished near the bottom of the ladder. In those days, club loyalty was extremely important and my move did not please the members of my former club. The coach of that team, Peter Jones, was one of my best friends in Australia and we had shared many pleasant experiences together.

During the first quarter of the game my new team roughed up their opponents badly and pounded them mentally and physically. At the quarter-time break, Peter was furious about what had taken place and as he walked towards his players he saw me smiling and talking to some of the players in our huddle. This made him angrier. He suddenly changed direction, walked towards me and started to accuse me of being a turncoat. As he got closer his language became more colourful. My coach, Tony Jewell, was at first surprised by Peter's actions but it didn't take him long to react. The two coaches moved towards each other and within a few seconds started to throw punches. I couldn't believe what was happening. Eventually they were pulled apart and after a while they calmed down. It was a sensational incident witnessed by about 80,000 spectators at the game and millions of TV viewers across Australia.

Peter's team never recovered from that initial and unexpected onslaught. In the beginning of the second quarter our players remained calm, refocused their concentration on the challenges at hand and directed their aggression to winning and controlling the ball. We beat his team easily and went on to win the grand final and the championship two weeks later.

After the game a few mischievous members of the press tried to play up the incident as a racial one. Several politicians got involved and some of them even wanted a full inquiry. On a TV sports programme the following day, the two coaches were asked to give an explanation but they couldn't come up with a satisfactory one. The TV presenter then called me to the set and asked me what really happened. I said, 'I don't know, but this is the first time that I have had two white men fighting over me.' That comment seemed to put an end to any racist interpretations of the incident. A few weeks later, Peter gave me a photograph of the fight with a note that said, 'All over you, Rudi.'

It is better to build on the foundation of your game, the basics, and keep correcting mistakes as you move towards your goals than it is to discard everything and start afresh each time you have a failure or setback.

Success is not only about winning. If your goal in a race is to improve your best time and you do so but finish last, it would be called a success because you achieved your goal. One the other hand, if your goal is to win the race and you run your best time but finish last it would be a failure. Success and failure are usually tied to goals and targets.

When winning is your sole objective there is no room for failure. This attitude can create enormous pressure for athletes and set them up for disappointment and frustration. While winning is the desired outcome, being placed second among a mass of opponents is still a great achievement.

Wanting to win and not wanting to lose are not the same things. After a loss, some players enter the next game – 'wanting to win' while others go in 'not wanting to lose again'. These two attitudes produce different styles of play, aggression and positive play in one case and conservative and defensive play in another.

REMEMBER

1. Success in top-class sport is no longer possible with just talent and ability. Success must be created in the mind, planned and pursued diligently.
2. Failure is an essential part of success.
3. You often learn more from failure than you do from success.
4. Victory often arises out of failure because the pain of failure sometimes breaks the shell that stifles talent.
5. Good players use failures and mistakes to motivate themselves to play better and to fine-tune their strategies.
6. Some things will always go wrong during the game so you must be prepared to deal with them.
7. M.S. Dhoni once said that the main difference between great players and the others is the interval between mistakes. Good players repeat mistakes less frequently than other players.
8. Wanting to win and not wanting to lose are different things.

BE DISCIPLINED AND PERSISTENT

> Self-discipline creates the energy that takes you nearer to your goals.
> The depth of your discipline and motivation determine the level of your success.
>
> *— Jim Clemmer, Pathways to Performance*

At the start of the Kerry Packer World Series in Australia, Clive Lloyd and I felt that two things were holding back the West Indies team. The first was lack of a clear vision and the second was lack of self-discipline. Early in the series we put a few simple initiatives in place to correct those deficiencies and soon after we saw a turnaround in the discipline of the team. One night the team had to go to a party in Sydney. I went ahead of the team and spoke with Richie Benaud, the former Australian captain, for about half an hour before Richie asked, 'Where are your guys?' I looked at my watch and told him that they would arrive in five minutes, at 8.15. He smiled and said, 'You're joking. Your guys are never on time.' At 8.15 the team walked into the room. Richie's jaw fell open and he said, 'If your players show this kind of discipline on the cricket field nobody will beat you.' 'We are working on it Richie,' I responded. As the team became more and more disciplined, it trained and played better, eventually winning the series. That victory was the first step along the path that led to the team's dominance of world cricket for fifteen consecutive years.

It is easy to be disciplined and persistent when things are simple and are going according to plan. It becomes more difficult when things get tough. Tony Rafferty, an ultra-marathon runner who once ran 4,000 miles across Australia, says: 'Discipline and persistence can be learned and developed at training and practice but it requires strength of mind and hard work. To develop true persistence you must learn to push yourself mentally and physically to do the hard and painful things at training especially when you don't feel like doing them. If you do this more often it will become a habit and you will develop reserves that will help you deal with all of the challenges you might face during the game. When you push yourself to do these hard things at training, you strengthen your attitude, toughen up your mind and improve self-discipline.'

Tony adds, 'I believe that the most successful people are those who do the things that other people dislike doing or refuse to do. If you do these hard things often enough, you start to enjoy them and they become important to you because you know they will give you an advantage over your opponents and bring you success.'

The depth of your discipline and motivation determine the level of your success, but self-discipline is often a missing ingredient in the quest for success and good performance. It is a mental skill that is vital for good performance. Self-discipline creates the energy that takes you nearer to your vision, and vision provides the force that drives discipline. Without discipline, a vision is simply a dream and without vision, discipline is just a chore.

Discipline separates the doer from the talker. Talkers can always tell a good story about what they are going to do but without the discipline to follow through they can never do it. Some experts now claim that the correlation between self-discipline and success is twice as large as the correlation between ability and success.

GOOD LUCK OR BAD LUCK?

Many players blame circumstances and bad luck for losses and poor performance but the good players seldom use that excuse.

George Bernard Shaw the Irish playwright once said of circumstances and bad luck, 'People are always blaming their circumstances for what they are. I don't believe in circumstances. The people who get on in this world are the people who get up and look for the circumstances they want, and, if they can't find them, make them.'

A very old Chinese story about luck tells of a farmer living in a small village. His only possessions were a small house, in which he lived with his son, and a horse. One day his horse ran away. All his neighbours said, 'This is terrible. What bad luck!' The farmer simply replied, 'Maybe. Who knows what's good and what's bad?'

A few days later the horse returned with two wild horses. The neighbours all rejoiced and said, 'What good luck! This is the best thing that could have happened.' The farmer shrugged his shoulders and said, 'Maybe. Who knows what's good and what's bad?'

The next day the farmer's son tried to ride one of the wild horses and the horse threw him and broke his leg. The neighbours said, 'What bad luck! This is the worst thing that could have happened.' The farmer again shrugged his shoulders and said, 'Maybe. Who knows what's good and what's bad?'

Two days later the king's army came through the countryside

taking all able-bodied men off to battle where they were sure to die. But they rejected the farmer's son because of his broken leg. When the neighbours told him how lucky he was, the farmer replied, 'Maybe. Who knows what's good and what's bad?'

The meaning of any event depends on the way you look at it. When you change your perspective of a situation you change its meaning and when that happens your thinking and actions also change. Having two wild horses is a good thing until it is seen in the context of the son's broken leg. The broken leg seems to be bad in the context of life on the farm; but in the context of being conscripted to go to war, it suddenly becomes good.

How much does success really depend on luck? Someone once said that the harder he worked the luckier he got. Luck can affect performance positively or negatively. It depends on how you look at it. When you have good breaks, capitalize on them, and when you have bad breaks, accept them, reorganize your strategy and efforts and move on.

Pressure: Friend or Foe?

In his recent book, *Fierce Focus*, Greg Chappell, a former captain of Australia and a former coach of India, expressed his surprise at what he described as the mental fragility of Sachin Tendulkar in 2006 when he was having a lean time with the physical and mental aspects of his game. Brian Lara had similar problems on more than one occasion during his illustrious career and Tiger Woods, the great golfer, has recently been struggling with the same difficulty.

The enormous demands and the high expectations of millions of people around the world create pressures on superstars like Brian Lara, Sachin Tendulkar and Tiger Woods that can sometimes get the better of them and lead to mental fatigue or fragility. But after adequate rest and recreation these great players soon clear their minds, recharge their psychological batteries, regain their mental toughness and play like champions again.

Other players who are exposed to high levels of continuous

pressure also fall victim to chronic and unrelenting pressure and suffer from a type of mental or combat fatigue that result in negative thinking, self-doubts, a loss of confidence, poor concentration and judgement, impaired motor skills, and poor performance.

Pressure can be a friend or a foe. In the right proportions it can lift performance to new heights but if it gets out of hand it can mess it up and create health problems. The ability to cope with pressure usually separates the great players from the others but even the great players can fall victim to chronic pressure. Every player has a breaking point.

Research during World War II showed the effects of constant pressure on soldiers exposed to continuous combat. Sir Charles Symonds found that prolonged and unremitting pressure resulted in 'combat fatigue' and a breakdown in performance. Combat fatigue became visible between fifteen and forty-five days in most soldiers. Every soldier had a breaking point. After four weeks, soldiers concentrated poorly, performed badly and became mentally fatigued and mentally fragile. That fragility was usually followed by apathy, dullness, slowness, and even depression.

Sports administrators and selectors should be aware of the dangers of work overload and chronic stress and should ensure that players stay fresh and alert by getting quality rest and recreation during the season. Today's military protects its soldiers from 'combat fatigue' and the pressures of continuous combat by doing just that.

REMEMBER

1. Self-discipline creates the energy that takes you nearer to your goals.
2. The depth of your discipline and motivation determine the level of your success.
3. Some experts now claim that the correlation between self-discipline and success is twice as large as the correlation between ability and success.
4. But self-discipline is often a missing ingredient in the quest for success and good performance.

5.   Discipline and persistence can be learned and developed at training and practice but it requires strength of mind and hard work.

6.   The most successful people are disciplined. They do the things that other people dislike doing or refuse to do and enjoy doing them because they give them an advantage over their opponents and bring them success.

7.   Discipline separates the doer from the talker.

8.   When you have good luck capitalize on it, and when you have bad luck, accept it, reorganize your strategy and efforts and move on.

9.   The harder and smarter you work the luckier you become. The people who get on in life make their own luck.

10. Pressure can be a friend or a foe. It can lift performance to new heights or can literally destroy it.

11. Work overload and continuous and unrelenting pressure can cause mental fatigue or combat fatigue, an enemy of good performance. Every player has a breaking point.

Part 2: The Mind and the Inner Game

INNER AND OUTER GAMES

In sport, and in life, we constantly play two different but interrelated games – a public or outer game and a private or inner game. The outer game is played against our opponents and is the game that everyone is able to see. The inner game is played in the mind with or against ourselves. It is an unseen game in which there is constant interaction between our thoughts and feelings, our goals and fears. Many of us are unaware of this game and yet we play it all the time. Formal instructions and coaching do not usually address the inner game even though it is very difficult to play a good outer game without first mastering the inner game. Champion athletes play both games well.

DON'T BE AN ACADEMIC: USE YOUR SPORTS INTELLIGENCE

> Academic intelligence, sports intelligence and survival intelligence are not the same things.
>
> — *Rudi Webster*

> God made man before God made books.
>
> — *Anonymous*

Too many of today's coaches and sports specialists mistakenly believe that if they enhance the logical and analytical thinking skills of their players, their performance will automatically improve. The fact that so few academics and scholars excel at sport should be a wake-up call for these coaches. Logic and reason can analyse and organize but only the imagination can create and craft the future you want.

Rather than awakening the imagination and enhancing the gifts of curiosity, creativity and innovation in our young people, today's education system too often inhibits and limits them.

We must prevent the same thing from happening in sport. We must ensure that the negative effects of over-coaching and super-specialization in sport do not suppress or damage the imaginative, creative and instinctive functions of the brain that are so necessary for good performance.

In the human brain, the dominant left hemisphere is the seat of logic, language and analytical thinking. It functions best in academics, scholars, scientists and mathematicians.

The right hemisphere is concerned with imagination, intuition, creativity, body language and awareness of movements and body positions. It functions best in sports people, artists, dancers and musicians.

The thinking and intelligence needed to pass examinations in schools and universities are different from those required for success in any sport and business. According to Dr Edward de Bono, an expert in thinking, education today is essentially about the past, that is knowledge that is already in existence. It is a matter of learning, sorting, reviewing, combining and describing existing knowledge and information. Most university graduates wrongly assume that once they have knowledge, action would be easy and automatic.

In sport, knowledge and experience are important but performance demands much more. It requires creative and innovative ideas, and thinking about goals, strategies, tactics, motivation, priorities, consequences, team building, teamwork, leadership, failures and setbacks, physical and psychological battles with opponents, and psychological battles with the self.

I always remember the comments of a colleague, a brilliant and highly intelligent medical doctor, who struggled on the golf course. He said: 'I am a very good doctor and a reasonably intelligent person but the moment I walk on to a golf course things change. Even though I know the game very well and can discuss it sensibly with anyone, as soon as I start to play you would think that I am a stupid person. The sporting side of my brain doesn't work very well on the golf course.'

Clive Lloyd recently said to me, 'What people don't understand is that you don't have to be bright academically to be a good captain [or a good player]. Captaincy is about vision, good judgement and common sense and about motivating, managing and leading players. An old friend, Fred Wills, once said to me, 'Don't worry about this university stuff. If you have a modicum of intelligence you could become a lawyer like me, or whatever you want to be. But I can get all of the best coaches in the world to teach me how to play cricket but I would never be able to bat like you or Gary Sobers.'

Clive added, 'To be a good cricketer you must be able to think, particularly when you are under pressure. Successful players outthink, outplan and outperform their opponents. Just because someone might use a few green verbs or might not be well versed in grammar does not mean that he is not a good thinker. My players won the first two World Cups and should have won the third and they were world champions for fifteen consecutive years. Not many of them went to university or any great schools. Nevertheless, they could think and play like champions and that is what is important in sport.'

Many years ago, standard IQ tests were given to some aboriginal children who were doing poorly in school. Compared with the white students their test scores were quite low and they were said to be intellectually inferior.

When those aboriginal kids and white kids were given a different test, the results were reversed. The children were shown a rectangle that was divided into small squares with a different object in each square and they were told to view the squares and their contents for a couple of minutes. The objects were then removed and the kids were asked to reassemble the objects in the correct squares. The aboriginal kids did better than the white ones. This is not surprising since visual signals are very important to the aborigines. Finding their way in the vast and, to us, featureless desert in which they lived depended on their visual memory and visual intelligence. Their lives and survival depended on that intelligence.

In our schools, students take examinations to test their knowledge about subjects that they study in their classes. Those who score well are labelled bright kids, those who do moderately well are known as average, and those who score poorly are labelled as inferior students.

But examinations only measure what the students have learned, not what they can learn; what they have been, not what they can become. Students who base their self-worth solely on those examination results and accept them as the truth about themselves will behave like the students they believe themselves to be. The bright students will continue to be bright and the inferior students will continue to be inferior.

As long as the inferior students hold on to those negative self-beliefs, they will remain trapped in a negative performance spiral where they fail, expect to fail and fail again. To break free they would have to change self-beliefs, stop thinking about what they have been, and start thinking about what they can become. The same applies to sportsmen and sportswomen.

Before You Assess Intelligence Look at the Culture

In 1971, four researchers gave an intelligence sorting test to a group of Liberians. The purpose of the text was to arrange twenty objects into four different categories – food, food containers, clothing and instruments. Instead of sorting the objects the way the researchers expected they used functional pairings, sorting the potato, one of the food items with the knife claiming that the knife is used to cut the potato and that is the way anyone with common sense would arrange the two objects. Repeated attempts produced the same results.

The researchers then asked them to arrange the objects the way a foolish man would and they automatically did so the way the researchers wanted. The researchers' criterion for intelligent behaviour was the Liberians' criterion for foolish behaviour and the Liberians' criterion for wise behaviour was the researchers' criterion for foolish behaviour.

REMEMBER

1. To play a good outer game you must first master your inner one.

2. Scholars and academics do not usually excel in sport.

3. The intelligence needed to pass examinations is different from the intelligence needed to excel in sport.

4. Examination results tell you what you have learnt not what you can learn, what you have been not what you can become.

5. To improve your performance stop thinking about what you have been and start thinking about what you can become.

6. If you get your intellect out of the way during performance your body will do what it needs to do, automatically and freely.

How Hard do You Work and How Tough are You Mentally?

Nobody has got a right to be proud of natural ability. You got it from your father and mother. You did nothing to earn it. It is only what you do with the four-letter word work that is a legitimate cause for pride.

— Ron Barassi, Australian Rules football coach

The only place where success comes before work is in the dictionary.

— Vince Lombardi, American football coach

When Clive Lloyd showed me his vision for the West Indies team at the end of that disappointing Test series against Australia in 1975-76 and explained his strategy for achieving that vision, he told me that he would search the Caribbean for players with the 'right stuff' and would mould them into a tough and disciplined unit. He wanted players who were hardworking, enthusiastic and mentally tough.

Grit or mental toughness is just as important to performance as are talent and ability. Players who are mentally tough are usually disciplined and persistent and are motivated to pursue their goals despite failures and setbacks. It keeps them going when others lose interest or quit.

It is not always the player with the best genetic gift or talent that succeeds. It is often the player who is smart, persistent, mentally tough and hardworking. Hard work is necessary for good performance but it does not guarantee it. It is not a substitute for common sense and good strategy.

Some players get success without appearing to work hard and are often accused of being lazy. But they play well because they use efficient execution strategies that require less effort and time.

Hard work is not the same thing as stamina. Stamina is about staying power and perseverance and is the strength of all good players. It is the ability to maintain effort, concentration and motivation throughout the contest or throughout the journey towards their goals.

REMEMBER

1. It is not always the player with the best genetic gift or talent that succeeds.

2. Your talent comes from your father and mother. It is only what you do with the four-letter word work that is a legitimate cause for pride.

3. The only place where success comes before work is in the dictionary.

4. There is no substitute for hard work and persistent practice.

5. Grit or mental toughness is just as important as talent and ability.

6. Grit is the father of stamina and persistence.

7. To develop true persistence you must learn to push yourself mentally and physically to do the hard and painful things at training, especially when you don't feel like doing them.

8. The meaning of any event depends on the way you look at it. Change your perception and you will change its meaning.

CONTROL YOUR MIND: CONTROL YOUR GAME

Empty your mind of its trash and stay in the moment and you will be surprised to see what you can do. Being in the moment calms your mind, stops you from thinking about too many things, and helps you to play one ball at a time.

— M.S. Dhoni

In international cricket the stronger you are in the mind the better you will play. The contest is often a battle between yourself and your mind, not yourself and the bowler.

— V.V.S. Laxman

At the start of my career I would have said that performance
was 70 per cent physical and 30 per cent mental. But I would
now say that the reverse is true. You see the mind controls the
body. If you are fit and your body doesn't do what it ought to
do, you will often find the cause in the mind, not the body.

– *Dennis Lillee*

Years ago, a student of Buddhism went to his master and said, 'My
mind is very difficult to control. When I want some thoughts to go
they stay and when I want others to stay, they go. How can I control
my mind?'

The master told him, 'The mind is like a high-spirited horse. If
you try to control it by locking it up, it will become agitated and
restless. And if you try to force it to be still, it will kick and fight
even more.

'Look at control in a different way. Let the wild horse of your mind
run freely. With nothing to resist or fight against, it will eventually
settle down on its own. When it has settled you can tame it; when
it is tame, you can train it. Then you can ride it and it will take you
wherever you want to go.'

This is excellent advice but it needs training and practice.

Sir Garfield Sobers the world's greatest all-round cricketer has
always pointed out the importance of the mind in performance.
He says: 'The proper use of the mind is the one thing that separates
champions from merely good players. You won't cope with your
challenges in the game if you don't think properly. I have come across
lots of players who have had more natural skill than some of the great
players but they never made it because they couldn't think clearly and
sensibly. No matter how good a player you think you are you won't
reach the top unless you develop the mind. The top players know how
to think, how to concentrate and what to do in tough situations.'

Just before the 1980 Olympics, Russian coaches and scientists
conducted a series of tests to compare the effects of mental and
physical training on the performance of their elite athletes. The
training regimens included:

- Group 1: 100 per cent physical training;
- Group 2: 75 per cent physical with 25 per cent mental training;
- Group 3: 50 per cent physical with 50 per cent mental training; and
- Group 4: 25 per cent physical with 75 per cent mental training.

They found that athletes in Group 4 who spent 75 per cent of their time on mental training and 25 per cent on physical training showed the greatest improvement in performance, followed by Group 3, then Group 2 and finally Group 1. As mental training increased, performance increased and as mental training decreased, performance decreased. Some sceptics might challenge the accuracy of these findings but they cannot deny the fact that athletes perform best when they combine physical training with visualization and mental training.

Despite what many players and some coaches might think, training is not just about physical fitness or building bulk to overpower your opponent. It is also about teaching your brain, nerves and muscle fibres to work in harmony to improve the efficiency of your movements and execution of your skills. Remember that your body relies on your brain for instructions and direction.

Mental training and mental conditioning in sport have been around for thousands of years. Richie Benaud reminded me of this more than twenty years ago when he said: 'It is only in recent years that applied sports psychology has become a public part of sport though it would be untrue to say that it has not been going on privately for some time. The successful captains, the leaders in sport, have not missed a trick in that regard because had they done so they would have finished up nothing more than a disastrous statistic. So too the opening batsmen who have had to face Wes Hall, Frank Tyson, Ray Lindwall and modern-day fast bowlers like Michael Holding, Andy Roberts, Joel Garner and the other splendid bowlers in the West Indian attack. The successful ones have done it on their own, using their private methods.'

Playing better usually requires inner change. This is easier when the mind is quiet, calm and relaxed. A calm mind creates positive imagery and positive thinking and diverts attention from problems to solutions.

Training the mind is possible because of the structure and function of the brain. We are born with brains that are hard wired to help us think and act in specific ways, but this wiring is not fixed. If it were, we would be prisoners of our heredity. Changing the way we think and look at things can modify that wiring and build new nerve connections and action programmes. In fact, the brain is always changing, constantly rearranging its wiring and establishing a great number of new nerve connections to accommodate new thoughts, experiences and learning.

Rahul Dravid, the outstanding Indian Test batsman, claims, 'Your state of mind determines how well you combine and use your fitness, technical skills and game strategies. Talented players who are deficient in the mental side of the game hardly ever get the best out of themselves or make it to the top. These players don't understand how the mind works and don't work hard enough to get to know and understand themselves. When they move up to higher levels of sport, and competition becomes tougher, they get caught and perform below expectations.'

What is the 'X' factor that separates the great players from the good players or the great fighter pilots from the good ones? No single factor stands out but current research has shown that apart from good technical skills great players have excellent mental skills that enable them to read game situations more quickly and accurately and make better decisions in order to deal with them. They outshine their colleagues in these areas and execute their skills in a more efficient and timely manner. Research has also shown that they are able to stimulate specific and finely tuned neural networks in the brain that are relevant to the task at hand while suppressing other networks that distract, and sabotage performance.

Some scientists now claim that champion sportsmen and fighter pilots actually sense the immediate future, seeing or feeling what is going to happen just before it happens. As a result they are better prepared to deal with it. They trust their instincts and allow them to act freely and naturally. Their bodies then follow commands that precede thinking. Most of this occurs at an unconscious level and the players are not usually aware of it and hence cannot explain it in a logical or rational way.

I remember seeing Sir Garfield Sobers fielding at short leg to Lance Gibbs' bowling, and at certain times before the ball was bowled he would move a couple of feet to his left or right and the very next ball or the ball after would come straight to him. I have seen him take many sharp catches like that. Rahul Dravid often talks about the importance of priming your instincts to act quickly and efficiently.

REMEMBER

1. The stronger your mind, the better you will play.
2. You play better when your mind is quiet, calm and relaxed.
3. A calm mind encourages positive thinking and success imagery and diverts attention from problems to solutions.
4. You can train your mind just like you train your body.
5. There are players who have more natural ability than some of the best players but they never make it because they don't think clearly and sensibly.
6. The top players know how to think, how to concentrate and what to do in tough situations.
7. A combination of mental and physical training gets the best out of athletes.
8. Empty your mind of its trash and see what you will be able to do.
9. The great players seem to sense, see or anticipate things before they actually happen and their bodies appear to follow commands that sometimes precede thinking.

HOW GOOD ARE YOUR MENTAL SKILLS?

> The greatest discovery of our time is that man by changing the
> inner aspect of his mind can alter the outer aspect of his life.
> — William James, psychologist

> I think the mind is the most important factor because the
> thoughts in your mind control your attitude, movements and
> body language. I believe that once your thought processes
> are positive and you believe in yourself, you give yourself
> the best chance of playing to your potential. It all comes from
> the mind.
>
> — V.V.S. Laxman

Greg Chappell once admitted that after a run of poor performances
against a Rest of the World team early in his career, he sat down and
analysed his game and made a commitment to take it to the highest
level. The first things he looked at were fitness and technique. They were
quite sound and he couldn't see any dramatic improvements taking
place there, so he turned his attention to the mind. He immediately
recognized that his thinking, concentration and confidence were
not as good as they ought to be and he made a strong commitment
to improve his mental game. He felt that if he achieved that goal he
would become one of the best batsmen in the world. It didn't take
him long to get there.

Before the start of today's cricket games players go through an
intense session of physical training and a variety of fielding and
knocking-up exercises that can sometimes go on for well over an
hour. Relatively little attention is paid to mental preparation, and
back in the dressing room after their workout the players often have
self-doubts and many negative thoughts and emotions prior to the
start of the game.

A great part of the game is played in the mind before you set foot
on the field, so in that period you should ensure that you put the right
images and thoughts in your mind. Players would be better served
if they spend some of their preparation time sitting quietly in the

dressing room calming their minds, discussing key priorities, thinking about their strategy and plan of action, and mentally rehearsing their mission and basic skills. Visualization helps a player to concentrate and programmes the mind for action. It then becomes a natural progression from thinking to doing. It is vital to prepare your body for the game but it is equally important to prepare your mind. Winning the inner game is the key to winning the outer game.

Once you have learned a technical skill you don't suddenly lose it during the game. Your ability to bat, bowl, or catch a ball does not just disappear. However, if you make mental errors that result in low self-confidence or overconfidence, negative thinking, carelessness, poor concentration, or an inability to cope with pressure you will execute those technical skills poorly.

Players and coaches all agree that mental skills are extremely important in performance. Yet, they admit that they spend far less time on them than they do on the physical ones. Instead of improving them some coaches, by their words, attitude and actions, actually make them worse.

But there are some captains and coaches who truly understand the importance of the mental skills and work hard to improve them. Mike Gatting was one such captain.

At a press conference in Australia just after England won the Ashes in 1987, Gatting, England's cricket captain, revealed how England won the series against Australia. And he forecast that his secret for success would help him win the Benson and Hedges World International One Day Challenge Series against Australia and the West Indies. His forecast was spot on and England completed a clean sweep, down under.

Gatting said he found the secret in a book *Winning Ways: In Search of Your Best Performance* by Dr Rudi Webster that highlighted the importance of the mind in performance. He said that the book provided him with a formula for success particularly in the areas of self-confidence and motivation. Gatting claimed that he copied out some of the sections in the book that became his bible. He added that the motivation section should be compulsory reading for the entire team to beat the West Indians and become the world's best. He said that the contents in the book gave him a new philosophy and showed him the importance of mental conditioning and mental control in winning and becoming the best in the world.

Like Napoleon Bonaparte many years earlier, Bob Hawke the prime minister of Australia fully understood the importance and power of psychological strategy and mental conditioning in battle. After reading *Winning Ways* he wrote me a letter in which he said, 'I was delighted to read your book and I am very interested in the psychological methods you describe. I only ask you not to share your wisdom in this area with our opponents.'

Many coaches give inspirational talks to their players about the power of the mind but do not know how to teach the mental skills. They instruct their players to: 'Control your mind and concentrate, get your mind into gear, put your head down, be persistent, be mentally tough and learn to handle the pressure.' It sounds like good advice but is it really so? How do you do these things? How do you learn them? How do you manage them?

Mental skills are interdependent. When one changes the others usually follow. For example, if your confidence falls, your thinking, concentration, and ability to cope with pressure will also change.

The foundation for these skills is laid down in the early years of development when children are exposed to competitive games and unstructured play and are allowed to use their imagination and creative thinking to design their own strategies and find their own solutions to challenges. They build on that base later on.

Improving and controlling these mental skills may be your key to good performance. Don't ignore them. You can learn and improve them at training, at practice, and during the many matches that you play, and you can imprint them in your mind with visualization and mental rehearsal techniques.

Most good players have well-developed mental skills and techniques but sometimes they get distracted and don't use them as well as they ought to, particularly when they are overconfident or when they are under pressure or are in a slump.

This was the case with golfer Greg Norman early in his career when he was in a bad performance slump on the European circuit. Greg went on to be rated as the world's number one golfer for 331 weeks, to be outdone only by Tiger Woods who has held that position for 623 weeks so far.

In a mood of desperation Greg telephoned me in Australia during that slump seeking my help to restore his confidence and improve his game. I listened to him carefully for about half an hour when he talked about his plight, his negative thinking, his fears, his lack of confidence and his crumbling game. He told me that at first he thought his problems were technical and started to fiddle with his technique, but that made matters worse.

When he finished I started to boost his confidence and to reassure him that his golf skills had not deserted him – he was still a great player. But, I told him that he was sabotaging himself and his game by the way he was thinking, and talking to himself, and stressed that in professional golf the mind controls performance. I told him some slumps are initiated by technical faults but in the end poor mental functioning is the culprit that intensifies and magnifies the slump. I explained the importance of keeping his mind calm and in the present, and I reminded him of something he had said to me earlier: 'The game of golf starts from where the last ball finishes.' I then asked him to reflect on what we had discussed and I urged him to play his natural game, lower his expectations, enjoy the challenge, play one shot at a time and concentrate on hitting the ball to position.

In the days that followed he worked very hard at practice on the golf course striking hundreds of golf balls. He also repeatedly visualized hitting the ball to position, controlling its flight and distance in the process. A few days later at Chepstow, Greg won the Dunlop Masters Tournament with a score of seventeen under par, the biggest winning margin in British golf for seventeen years.

In his book *My Story*, Greg said that the win restored all of his old confidence, and convinced him that the money he had spent calling me in Melbourne was probably the best investment he ever made. He added that sometimes he looks back on that week at the beautiful

St Pierre layout at Chepstow and points to it in his mind as a real landmark in his career.

Greg later explained that his talk with me had not only jolted his mental processes towards a more positive direction but it had also made him aware that he had lost his aggression on the golf course. His negative thinking had made him play safe, which was not his style. He thrived on aggression.

REMEMBER

1. Concentration, self-confidence, clear thinking, positive self-talk, self-discipline, self-motivation and the ability to cope with pressure are mental skills that are vital for good performance.
2. The mental skills receive lots of lip service from coaches and players but the words of the coaches do not usually match their actions. These skills are often neglected.
3. Mistakes in the execution of the technical skills are often caused by mental errors.
4. You ignore the mental skills at your peril.
5. During preparation for the game you should organize both your mind and your body, not just your body.
6. Success in sport is not just about winning the battles with your opponents but also about winning the mental battles with yourself.

PERFORMANCE REVOLVES AROUND YOUR SELF-IMAGE, SELF-BELIEF AND SELF-TALK

Players who don't know themselves, believe in themselves, or understand how the mind works often do not fulfil their potential and seldom have the right coping skills to deal with players who are equally talented. They often have not figured out in their minds how to respond to pressure and challenging situations.

— *Rahul Dravid*

A lot of attention needs to be given to what thoughts are entering your mind. The more positive thoughts you have about yourself and your game the better you will play and feel about yourself.

— *V.V.S. Laxman*

The mind is like a sophisticated mirror; it reflects what it sees, so be careful what you show it.

— *Sujata, Buddhist monk and author*

For more than ten years the West Indies cricket team has been trapped in a failure spiral in which they fail, expect to fail and fail again. Once the world champion cricket team and one of the best sports team in the history of sport, they have been languishing at the bottom of the Test and One Day rankings for some time, not for lack of fitness or talent but poor self-image, low self-belief and negative self-talk. As soon as they improve upon these things they will get back on to the success spiral.

Your self-beliefs, self-image and self-talk cause you to behave and perform like the player you imagine yourself to be. Once you get your basics right your performance will revolve around these three things rather than your potential.

See yourself and you will become what you see. Your self-image is the subconscious picture you have of yourself. It is an image of who and what you think you are – how good you are, how athletic you are, what type of player or person you are, and how successful you are.

That picture is reflected in the way you talk to yourself, for example: 'I am a good player or I am a mediocre player, I handle pressure well or I handle pressure badly; I am a good batsman or I am a mediocre batsman; I am shy or I am outgoing.'

Seeing yourself as a winner, or thinking like a winner, does not guarantee that you will be a winner; you must have the necessary skills and strategies. But, thinking so increases your chances of being a winner.

Every athlete has a baseline self-image in his subconscious mind that determines how well he plays. It acts like a sensor or thermostat that regulates performance. Adjusting the level of that sensor changes the quality of his performance. If he raises it his performance is likely to improve and if he lowers it, his performance is likely suffer.

When you have a good game and exceed your normal standard your confidence increases and your expectations of playing well in the next game go up. But your subconscious sensor will recognize a deviation from the normal and will self-correct. Your mind might then say, 'What do you think you are doing? That's not like you. You know you are not that good. Correct yourself and get back to where you belong.' The brain will then take your performance back to its normal level.

Teams and players who are used to losing occasionally get into winning positions and then blow their chances. In those situations their internal sensor detects that something is wrong and their brain then self-corrects downward and causes them to play poorly and lose the game in a senseless manner. When asked why they lost they usually cannot give a good reason and often confess that they cannot make any sense of what happened. Consciously, it doesn't make any sense to them, but subconsciously it makes perfectly good sense because their poor play maintains the limiting self-image in their mind.

In 2011, West Indies lost the first Test match against India after being in a strong position to win the game. The same thing happened in the third Test where they had an even better chance of winning but could only manage a lucky draw. In a Cricinfo article a few days after the first Test, Harsha Bhogle, an Indian journalist, wrote:

> West Indies played the role of the challenger quite well but you always knew it was a question of when, rather than if, they would fall away. West Indies need someone on the field to show them how to win, for at the moment they give the impression it is out of bounds. Sometimes when you fear [or expect] the inevitable, you invite it. There is much promise in this side but it is on a long downward spiral, and the new

talent coming in will take the shape of the mould it is cast into. It is the mould, the air they breathe, the acceptance of defeat that needs to be demolished.

When the team is playing below its normal standard and is in a hopeless position, and the players think they can't possibly win, they might say to themselves, 'C'mon, We are better than this.' Their brain might then self-correct upward, lift their performance, put on a creditable challenge and leave everyone thinking, 'Why can't they play like this more often?' The West Indies batting in the Test match in April 2012 against Australia in Dominica where they had to score 370 runs in the last innings to win the match is a case in point. They didn't win the game but they lifted their performance and played very competitively.

So far, the West Indies team has been unable to break that confining mould because their 'thermostat' or 'sensor' is aligned to a losing self-image. But the moment they improve their self-belief and baseline self-image and readjust their sensor they will get better results.

Few things disrupt performance more than negative thinking or negative self-talk. Thoughts are not always connected with reality, so you should be aware of them before you are influenced or controlled by them.

An old Cherokee chief who was once teaching his grandson about life said to him: 'A fight is going on inside me. It is a terrible fight and it is between two wolves. One is evil – he is anger, negative thoughts, limiting beliefs, fear, self-doubt, greed, self-pity, inferiority, false pride, and arrogance. The other is good – he is peace, joy, love, positive thoughts, hope, kindness, truth, compassion and faith. The same fight is going on inside you – and inside every person too.'

The grandson thought about it for a minute or so and then asked the grandfather, 'Which wolf will win?'

The old chief simply replied, 'The one you feed.'

The subconscious mind is very sensitive to negative thoughts. It seems to be primed to accept them. This is not surprising since it receives more negative than positive thoughts and comments in a ratio that is greater than five to one. But if you replace those negative thoughts with smart and sensible self-talk you will soon notice a difference in your performance.

YOU SEE THINGS NOT AS THEY ARE BUT AS YOU ARE

Reality is in your mind, not in the world around you. Your perception is your reality. If you change your perception you will change your reality. What you see in a situation is not only influenced by your position and the direction in which you look, but also by your beliefs, expectations, memories, needs, goals and priorities. How you talk to yourself and question yourself about the situation also determine what you see. It is the brain that sees not the eyes. The eyes collect information and then relay it to the brain for interpretation and action.

Let's imagine an Indian and a West Indies cricket supporter sitting next to each other watching Brian Lara bat against an Indian fast bowler. Suppose Brian plays at a ball and the fielders appeal for a catch behind the wicket. Let's also suppose that the umpire gives him out. The Indian supporter will be pleased and might claim that he saw the deflection of the ball as it hit the bat. The West Indies supporter might dispute that claim and say that the ball missed the bat by at least six inches and that the umpire is of no good. Although the two spectators are watching the game from the same position, they see different things because they have different expectations and priorities and want different outcomes. This happens to TV commentators too. During live matches, commentators, who sometimes have their own little prejudices, often see different things and it is only after they watch slow-motion replays that they see the same thing.

We all live under the same sky but we don't see the same horizon. If reality were objective we would all have a uniform view, but because it is subjective we see different things and think and behave differently.

Sir Garfield Sobers was an outstanding champion who played under the same sky as other cricketers but saw different horizons and opportunities. He once scored a century in a Test match against

England in Jamaica on a horrible wicket that, by the fourth day, had cracks so wide that a finger could pass through. For the first few days of the game the wicket played reasonably well and England scored 376 runs in the first innings and then bowled out West Indies for 143. West Indies followed on 233 runs behind and were 204 for five, still twenty-nine runs behind, when the game was interrupted by a bottle-throwing incident. Sobers was seven not out at the time and it seemed that England would certainly win the match. But Sobers had other ideas. He batted magnificently for the next six hours to score 113 not out and he declared the innings closed at 391 for nine. England had to make 159 to win the game but at close of play they were sixty-eight for eight and drew the match by the skin of their teeth. Sobers took three of the eight wickets for thirty-three runs.

Sir Garfield told me that most of the batsmen were psyched out by the wicket and did not believe they could play well on it. He felt that they got out mentally before they went in to bat. He had a different view. He believed he could bat on the wicket and saw it as a great challenge and an opportunity to show everyone how good he was.

He said: 'I have always enjoyed difficult and challenging situations. They motivate me to do well and that is when I concentrate and play best. In these situations I always say, "Now, this is the test. These are the conditions that sort out the players and differentiate the greats from the merely good ones."'

Sir Garfield explains that if you have a negative view of yourself or your challenges you automatically reduce your chances of success. He said, 'I believe that if you face up to challenging situations with a negative self-image and negative thoughts, and worry about the things that may or may not happen, you won't play well.'

Someone once said that the true measure of a person's wisdom is his capacity to see and understand things from different perspectives and his ability to respond appropriately. This is true of champion athletes. They see and understand the game and its challenges from different perspectives and know how to tailor their thinking, strategies and actions to meet those challenges. Where champions see challenge and success others often see difficulty and failure.

Some coaches and players are so limited and rigid in their thinking and perception that they find it difficult to adapt to the pressures of rapidly changing situations. When they are uprooted from their comfort zone by new challenges and demands, they instinctively revert to the safety of their old ways of thinking and behaving. Their entrapment reminds me of an old Sufi parable:

An old man was walking home one dark night when he saw a young friend on his hands and knees searching for something under a streetlight. 'What are you doing?' he asked his friend. 'I dropped the key to my house.' 'I'll help you look,' said the old man. After a few minutes of frustrated searching, the old man asked, 'Where exactly were you when you dropped the key?' His friend pointed toward the darkness, 'Over there.' 'Then why are you looking for it here?' 'Because this is where the light is,' the young man replied.

Those coaches and players are like that young man. They search for the keys to success in the illuminated area – in their comfort zone – because that is where their thinking, knowledge and experience lie. But, the keys to good performance often lie outside the confines of their comfort zone– in the dark, not in the light of their thinking, knowledge and experience.

REMEMBER

1. Once you get your basics right your performance usually revolves around your self-image and self-belief rather than your potential.

2. Change your self-image and self-beliefs and you will change your performance.

3. Every person has a baseline self-image that regulates his level of performance. It behaves like a thermostat. If he plays above his normal level, it will regulate his performance downward and if he plays below his normal standard it will regulate it upward.

4. The baseline self-image can be improved.

5. The way you talk to yourself and look at any situation is a reflection of your self-belief. So if you change your self-talk and perception you will change your performance.

6. Your self-talk causes you to behave and perform like the player you believe yourself to be, so be careful of what you say to yourself.

7. Your reality is not in the world around you. It is in your mind. Your perception is your reality.

8. Your thoughts are not always connected with reality so you should be aware of them before you are influenced or controlled by them. *Fear* is false evidence about reality.

9. Remember the wise words of the Cherokee chief who said that every person has two wolves inside of him constantly fighting each other for supremacy and control. One is good and the other is evil. Who wins? The one that you feed.

10. You might sometimes have to look outside the limits of your thinking and the light of your knowledge and experience to find the answers to your problems.

CHANGE YOUR BELIEFS AND PERCEPTION AND YOU WILL CHANGE YOUR PERFORMANCE

If you believe you can or if you believe you can't, you are right.

— *Henry Ford*

Roger Bannister the English athlete created history by breaking the four-minute barrier for the mile. Until then everyone believed that it was impossible to run the mile in less than four minutes. Once Bannister smashed that limiting belief, the task became easier because everyone knew it could be done. Within a year, the race was run under four minutes at least forty times and within ten years, 296 times! What is the lesson here? If you want to improve your performance, change the limiting beliefs that are holding you back and the negative self-talk that is sabotaging your performance.

Your beliefs determine the limits of what you can achieve. What you achieve is largely a matter of what you believe.

Until recently scientists felt that genes controlled behaviour. If this were true all our programmes for behaviour would be present at birth and we would not be able to do anything about them. We would be prisoners of heredity. When the nucleus that contains the genes is removed from a cell the cell behaves normally and lives for about four to six weeks. But when the cell membrane is damaged the cell dies immediately. The cell's survival depends on the integrity of the cell membrane and its behaviour is determined by the way the cell membrane perceives its environment. The cell membrane might very well be the brain of the cell.

Some scientists now believe that it is the signals that the cell membrane receives from its environment and the messages that it sends to the genes and DNA that control behaviour. They claim that genes and DNA do not control our biology, but instead DNA is controlled by signals from outside the cell, including messages from our brains – our thoughts, self-talk, pictures and feelings. If this is true we should be able to change our bodies and behaviour by retraining our thinking and changing our beliefs and attitudes.

We know now that beliefs, perception and self-talk control our emotions and behaviour. If you change your beliefs, you will change your perception; if you change your perception, you will change your thinking or self-talk; and if you change your thinking and self-talk, you will change your feelings, actions and performance.

If a plant is grown in a bottle it will take on the shape of the bottle and would be confined to it even though it has the potential to become a large and beautiful tree. To get that plant to fulfil its potential you would have to set it free by breaking the bottle. The plant would then grow, mature, bear fruit and propagate. Like the bottle, limiting beliefs inhibit growth and achievement in sport.

Just before the great West Indies fast bowler Malcolm Marshall died, Desmond Haynes and I played a game of golf with him in England. At that time he was extremely ill, was very weak and was in excruciating pain each time he swung the golf club. His cancer and the chemotherapy he was undergoing were destroying his body. As expected he played very poorly, became terribly dejected and felt that he was making a fool of himself.

On the fourteenth tee Desmond started to tease him about his game and told him not to make excuses because he was never any good at golf anyway. Those remarks irritated Malcolm and his attitude and demeanour suddenly changed. He then threw out a challenge to both of us and told us that he was going to win the five remaining holes. Desmond who is very competitive on the golf course laughed at him. He also asked Malcolm to stop dreaming and to control his imagination. Instantly, Malcolm's swing improved and he started to play really well, so well that he proceeded to win the next four holes. Only a lucky chip-in by Desmond on the last green prevented him from winning that hole.

I was dumbfounded. I had seen some amazing things in sport but nothing to match what I had just witnessed. 'How the hell did you do that?' I asked. 'It was simple,' said Malcolm. 'You see I believe in myself and in my game and I knew I could beat the two of you. I never even considered losing to you. In my mind I saw myself winning those holes. Once I saw those images I knew you were gone. All I had to do then was talk to myself positively, relax and let it happen.'

Desmond and I walked off the course trying to come to terms with what we had just seen. We soon realized that Malcolm, who was then at the lowest point in his life – he died two months later – turned his game around because of his powerful belief in himself and in his golf game. No wonder he was such an outstanding champion in cricket.

In December 2006, soon after I returned to the Caribbean from India where I had just finished a short stint with the Indian Cricket team, I fell seriously ill. The illness involved my spinal cord and left me paralysed from my waist down. I couldn't walk, stand or even sit up straight because I had lost power, sensation and balance in my trunk and lower limbs.

I went to Barbados for treatment and in January 2007 I told my doctors that by June, I would go to the USA to play golf at my favourite golf courses. The doctors ticked me off for being unrealistic and told me that as a doctor I should know better. They added that my recovery would be slow and that I would be like a baby once more and would have to learn how to crawl, stand and walk again.

After that interesting conversation with my doctors, I became more committed to my goal. I started to use several mental techniques on myself that I had applied successfully on sportsmen over the years to see if they would help me to heal, and return to the golf course in record time.

I had a very positive attitude and strong self-belief at that stage. I wanted to get better but I thought, 'If I don't get over this, I will just have to change my lifestyle. I will still have my most valuable asset, my brain, and I will make sure that I use it efficiently and creatively to do things that I couldn't do in the past.' But I had a strong belief that I would get better so I didn't think very much of that fallback position.

Visualization and mental rehearsal were the techniques I used the most. In my mind's eye I would see myself as a healthy person. Several times a day and night I would imagine myself running and getting really fit. But most of my time was spent visualizing myself on the golf course playing every shot possible, over and over again. During my recovery I must have played hundreds of golf games and thousands of golf shots in my mind.

My recovery was steady and I am confident that the mental techniques that I used during that period speeded up the healing process. I learned to crawl, sit, stand and eventually walk. I welcomed and celebrated every small success that I had during my recovery because I knew that when small successes are repeated they often give rise to quantum leaps in self-confidence. At least, that is what I stressed constantly to my players.

By the end of June, I went to the USA on my own and played golf with my friends. In my first game my legs were still weak and my balance wavered but I played very well and executed most of my shots the way I had visualized them during my illness. My golf partners who knew of my illness were surprised by the way I played.

Throughout my illness I always knew that I would get well. I believed strongly in myself, in the healing powers of my body, in the competence and care of my doctors and physiotherapists, and in the effectiveness of my mental techniques.

I went through a similar but life-threatening episode in 2012 when I fell ill immediately after my team's victory in the IPL Final against the Chennai Super Kings. I underwent surgery in Bangalore and soon after became terribly ill and had to be rushed to a hospital in Atlanta, Georgia, in the US where I spent four months lying on my back fighting for my life. During that time I was admitted to the intensive care unit on three separate occasions. The expert treatment of the doctors and nurses and the medical and surgical procedures that they performed kept me alive. But I believe that my healing and eventual recovery was largely driven by the state of my mind. Throughout my illness I remembered the advice that I often gave to my patients: 'You have the resources and power within you to heal yourself and to bring about beneficial changes in your lives, so use your mind to tap into these resources and bring about the changes you desire.' And that is what I tried to do.

Changing the way you look at things affects your thinking and performance. What seems impossible or difficult from one perspective might become possible and easy from another. The story below is a case in point.

Three men each with a piece of wood in his hand let go of the piece at the same time. In one case the wood fell, in the other it went upwards and in the third it stayed at the same height. You might say it was impossible because like most people you assume that all three men were standing on the ground. But if I told you that one man was standing on the ground, the second was under water and the third was in space you would automatically come to a different conclusion and recognize that what you thought impossible is in fact possible.

Years ago in Australia, an Australian Rules football coach asked me to see one of his players who was having a horrible run on the field. During the session I played a question-and-answer game with him about football. I asked him to finish the sentence. 'It is important that....' He thought for a while and then said: '...I impress the selectors.' 'Why did you say that?' I asked. 'Something must have happened to you in the past to create that belief.'

After thinking for a while he told me that when he was a teenager he was on the verge of being selected for the Tasmanian Junior State team. The selectors had informed him that he and three other players were competing for the last two places in the team.

He gave an account of the events leading up to selection. 'We played a trial game soon after and I thought that I would really have to impress the selectors in order to be selected. I did many spectacular things during the game and I thought I had played very well. However, I wasn't selected and I concluded that the selectors rejected me because I hadn't impressed them enough. Since then I believe that I must impress the selectors to make the team and stay in it.'

I told him that was one way of looking at the selectors' decision but it wasn't the only one. I speculated that the selectors might have been disappointed with him because he played as an individual and not as a team player and that he might have executed the fundamentals below their expectations.

He admitted that he had never looked at it like that. I then asked him to think about what we had just done. I also assured him that within a day or two he would find the answers to his performance problems.

In the next three games he played exceptionally well and was one of the best players on the field. Thereafter, he became one of the team's finest and most dependable players.

He told me later that he played better because he started to believe in himself and changed the way he looked at the game and thought about it. Moreover, he relisted his priorities. Preparing well, mastering the basics, executing the game plan, fulfilling his role, staying in the moment and enjoying the process were now his first-important priorities. Impressing the selectors was no longer important.

REMEMBER

1. Believe = achieve.
2. Your beliefs, perception and self-talk control your behaviour and performance, not your genes.
3. If you want to improve your performance, change the limiting beliefs that are holding you back and the negative self-talk that is sabotaging your game.
4. You change your path and trajectory in life when you change what you believe, value and picture in your mind.
5. What seems impossible from one perspective might be possible from another – three pieces of wood.
6. Visualization and mental rehearsal techniques are powerful procedures for bringing about change and improving performance.
7. V.V.S. Laxman: 'I improved dramatically as a player when I started to use visualization and mental rehearsal techniques. But how many players actually use these techniques to practise their skills and prepare for the game?'

Part 3: Motivation and Goal Setting

MOTIVATION: PLAY WITH PASSION, PURPOSE AND COMMITMENT

I believe that the love and passion for the game and playing for your country should be the players' main motivating forces but at the same time players need to have a good livelihood or income.

— M.S. Dhoni

There are two types of motivation — external and internal, but the most powerful and lasting motives come from within.

— *V.V.S. Laxman*

Motivation depends more on the needs and aspirations of the people who are to be motivated than on the needs of those who are doing the motivating. It is about goals, energy, information feedback and rewards.

— *Anonymous*

There is an old Chinese proverb that says, 'Man who waits for roast duck to fly into his mouth must wait for a very long time.' Motivation is an action programme in the brain that creates drive, direction and purpose. The depth of your motivation and self-discipline determine the level of your performance.

In motivation, you expend energy, effort, and time to achieve a goal in exchange for a particular result or reward. If you think that the reward is worth your time and effort you will commit yourself to go for it. But if you don't think so you will probably ignore it, unless you are forced or pressurized to go for it.

After beating Australia in 1980, the West Indies cricket team headed across the Tasman Sea to play a Test series against New Zealand. Motivation levels were very high in Australia but dropped to a dramatic low as soon as the series ended. None of the players wanted to go to New Zealand. They all wanted to go back to the Caribbean.

Knowing that their team was superior in every aspect of the game, the West Indies players thought they would beat New Zealand without too much effort. But they underestimated the enormity of the challenge and didn't know how motivated the Kiwis were and how eagerly they were looking forward to the contest. The motivational gap between the two teams was huge. The New Zealand players lacked the skill of their opponents but they made up for it with their motivation. Helped by poor umpiring decisions, the underdogs defeated the champion team in a controversial series.

In selecting players for their team and assessing future performance, coaches give more importance to the players' skill level than to the things that motivate them – their motivational profiles. As I said earlier, skill indicates what a player is capable of doing while motivation indicates why the player might do it, and how likely he is to do it. Many experts claim that motivational profiles are better predictors of future performance than ability and skill sets.

THERE IS MORE TO MOTIVATION THAN THE CARROT AND STICK

Motivating a player requires more than yelling, abusing, threatening, punishing or instilling fear – the stick; and more than encouragement, praise, pats on the back, trophies and money – the carrot. To motivate a player effectively you must learn about his personality, interests, needs and concerns. You must also know his game or sport, recognize the situations in which he is operating, and identify the negative and positive stimulants governing those situations. And you must understand the way in which the player and the situations are likely to interact – how the situations will affect him, the demands and pressures they will put on him, and the way he is likely to behave in them. The best way to motivate a player is to enter his world or environment, get into his head, heart and belly and motivate him from there.

Most people see motivation in sport as psyching up athletes to play better. They mistakenly think that the more the athlete is psyched up the better he will play. Some people use fear, criticism, abuse, threats, and punishment to motivate while others prefer praise, trophies, money, encouragement and inspirational pep talk.

Psyching up (arousing) players is a good way to motivate in some circumstances but in other situations it can psyche them out (over-arouse) and ruin their performance. In fact, in most games the players need to be calmed down to achieve their best level of arousal. The trick for both players and coaches is to know when and how to psyche up and when and how to psyche down. That is not as simple as it sounds because the optimum level of arousal varies from one player to the other and from one situation to the next.

There is much more to motivation than psyching up or psyching down players. Goals, desire, love, enjoyment, hunger for success, needs, passion, enthusiasm, fear, novelty, curiosity, learning, strategy, information feedback and rewards are other important ingredients.

Some players set challenging goals and are motivated to take the first steps. They put in the initial preparation and effort to move towards their goal only to lose enthusiasm and interest further along the way. So in most cases there is the motivation to get going in the beginning.

There is also the motivation to keep going. Many players quit halfway. What are the negative stimulants and obstacles that hold them back and what are the missing positive stimulants?

There is also the motivation to finish a job. Some players do well in the first two stages but ease up in the last part of the journey. As result, they finish the job poorly or not at all.

Motivation can be broken down into the following components: a goal or purpose; the generation of energy and the direction of that energy towards the goal in the form of a plan or strategy; the feedback of information that lets you know where you are and how you are doing; and the type and value of the rewards you will get while you are pursuing your goal and after you achieve it.

Some rewards like money, trophies, material possessions, praise, criticism and punishment come from the outside and others like pride, enjoyment, love for the game, and a sense of achievement, a feeling of importance and belonging, and personal satisfaction come from the inside.

Professor John Hunt of the London Business School says that throughout history, parents have used external rewards to entice or threaten their children into behaving in certain ways. In schools, teachers use grades, promotions and punishment for the same purpose. By the time these children become adults they have been conditioned to behave in predictable ways to external rewards.

The problem with external rewards is that the more you give the more you will be expected to give next time to produce the same effort and result.

The most powerful and lasting motives seem to come from within – pride, satisfaction, love, enjoyment, happiness, and a sense of achievement. Novelty, curiosity, challenge and learning are also strong internal motivators. In the group, internal motivation comes from a sense of identity, a feeling of importance, a feeling of belonging, and a sense of responsibility towards the team.

M.S. Dhoni feels that although love and passion for the game and playing for the country are, for him, the most important motivating factors, they must be supplemented with external rewards like encouragement, praise and money. He said, 'In today's competitive and fast-changing world we cannot ignore the importance of money in the life of a cricketer.'

Peter Thomson, one of Australia's greatest golfers, made these comments about motivation:

> High achievers in sport are sometimes very desperate people crying out for love, recognition and public acclamation. It is sometimes very sad to watch someone who is desperate to succeed doing anything and everything.
>
> However, there are other motives such as winning or trying to make a living. I suppose the purest motive is to win for yourself and experience that quiet inner feeling of satisfaction, and a sense of achievement. That is the noble end.
>
> This motive seems to be the most powerful and it keeps you going longer. However, when you become a champion and you have achieved success over a long period of time even this loses its power. You then become disinterested, you eventually give up your sport and you turn to other things for stimulation and motivation.

Yet, some champion athletes who have met with great success over the years can still maintain a high level of motivation and performance towards the end of their careers. Rahul Dravid and V.V.S. Laxman, two of India's greatest batsmen, fall in that category. They claim that their passion, love and enjoyment of the game and their strong desire to help the Indian team maintain a top position in world cricket are still powerful motivators.

Sir Garfield Sobers had a rather unique way of motivating himself. He said there were two main things that motivated him – wanting to do well for the team, and going out late at nights to have a good time. People laugh when he talks to them about his late-night motivation. But having to stay in his hotel in the evenings used to drive him crazy and he insists that the late nights stimulated him to play better. He enjoyed drinking, dancing and having a good time. But if he was spotted out at 2 or 3 in the morning and didn't do well the following day people would criticize him severely for what they would see as his wayward ways. In order to avoid that sort of criticism he made sure that he played well the next day, because he wanted to go out again the following night!

Sir Garfield stressed that every player is different and he must work out what is best for him. He added, 'Some players like to spend their evenings in their room watching television, some enjoy a quiet dinner, and others like to spend their time at the bar. I enjoyed going out at nights to dance and have a good time. Getting away from the cricketing environment relieved me of a lot of the pressure and helped me to relax. I could then go out on the field well motivated the following day with a relaxed body and a fresh and alert mind.'

In business, management regards motivation of staff as vital, but motivation depends more on the needs and aspirations of those who are to be motivated than the needs and goals of management. The same applies to coaches. Too often they place their needs and goals above those of their players.

This is true of change as well. Coaches who are suggesting the change are convinced of its importance and benefits, but the players who have to implement the change might not see its value because it might not meet their needs or address their concerns. Even when the need for change is accepted there might be arguments and disagreements about the method and the pace of change.

Approaching and Avoidance Motivation

Sir Garfield Sobers said that he was very optimistic and always set positive goals. For example, if he had to bowl on a good batting wicket he would say to himself, 'This is the test that will show how good I am and will separate me from the other bowlers. I'm going to take five wickets today. I will concentrate on the basics, pressure the batsmen by bowling a good line and length and make the batsmen earn every run.'

In contrast, Dennis Lillee said that negative thinking helped him to play better. If he had to bowl on the same wicket he might say, 'This is a perfect batting pitch. How do they expect me to get wickets on this track? I could easily finish the day with no wickets for a hundred runs and make a fool of myself. People will then criticize me and even laugh at me. So to avoid that from happening, I will concentrate on the basics, pressure the batsmen by bowling a good line and length and make the batsmen earn every run.'

Sir Garfield and Lillee had different perceptions of the same situation and motivated themselves differently – one by moving towards his goal (approaching behaviour) and the other by moving away from failure and humiliation (avoidance behaviour), but they both chose the same action plan.

REMEMBER

1. Ability and skill indicate what you are capable of doing but they do not guarantee that you will actually do it.

2. Motivation on the other hand indicates why and how likely you are to do it.

3. Skill without motivation is just as ineffective as motivation without skill. Motivation gives drive, direction and purpose.

4. Motivation is usually a better predictor of future performance than skill.

5. In motivation you expend energy, effort and time to achieve a goal in exchange for a particular result or reward.

6. There is motivation to take the first steps towards your

goal; there is also the motivation to keep going; and there is motivation to finish the job.

7.   In general motivation has these components: a goal or mission, the generation of energy and the direction of that energy towards the goal, information feedback and rewards.

8.   The best way to motivate a player is to enter his world or environment, get into his head, heart and belly and motivate him from there.

9.   The carrot and the stick are two common tools that coaches use to motivate their players.

10. There are two types of motivation – internal and external – of which the former is more important. But a combination of external and internal motivation is often needed.

11. The problem with external motivation is that the more external rewards you give the more you will be expected to give next time to produce the same effort and result.

12. In sport, motivation depends more on the needs, concerns and goals of those who are to be motivated – the players – than on the needs and goals of those who are doing the motivating – the coaches.

13. According to Vince Lombardi, 'Coaches who can outline plays on a blackboard are a dime a dozen. The ones who win get inside their players and motivate.'

DESTRUCTIVE CRITICISM: OTIS GIBSON AND CHRIS GAYLE

Coaches sometimes use destructive criticism to motivate their players after a loss or poor performance. This type of criticism rarely improves performance; it usually harms it.

Destructive criticism is cruel and personal and usually results in anger, resentment, loss of confidence and poor teamwork. Psychologist

Baron claims that the best way to repair that damage is with an apology particularly when the apology contains a credible explanation and an assurance that the accuser did not mean to be cruel or personal. If he does not apologize, the accused might retaliate by venting their feelings to a third party – the press or team mates – thereby intensifying anger and hostility.

What can we learn from Baron's research? If a coach uses destructive criticism he should try to repair the damage by apologizing to the player as soon as possible, telling him that he did not intend to demean or humiliate him, even if it looked that way. The longer the apology is delayed the worse things become and the player might then use that time to launch his own destructive criticism of the coach. Hostility and other destructive emotions will then escalate until or unless both parties apologize to each other.

In the 2011 Cricket World Cup the West Indies team played poorly and the disappointed coach, Otis Gibson, publicly castigated the senior players for the team's failure. He hardened his stance in the following days, weeks and months with the support of the CEO of the West Indies Cricket Board. Gayle and the other players retaliated with their own destructive criticism of the coach. The coach then demanded an apology from Gayle and the other senior players. When Gayle did not apologize he was dropped from the team. At the time Gayle was the most feared batsman in the game and arguably the best player in the team. His omission created a lot of fear, confusion and bad feelings among the players in the team who performed well below their potential.

About a year later, the prime minister of Jamaica intervened and urged the Board to reinstate Gayle to the team only to be greeted with an arrogant and insulting response from the Board. Angered by this response the Caribbean prime ministers closed ranks, became involved in the stand off and eventually persuaded the two warring parties to bury their differences and accommodate each other for the good of West Indies cricket.

Gayle was later recalled to the team and the team's performance immediately improved. The team beat New Zealand in a Test and

One Day series and then went on to win the 2012 T20 World Cup in Sri Lanka.

One of the most important jobs of a coach is to create an environment in which the players can learn, grow and play to the best of their ability. Otis Gibson is potentially a good coach but he failed badly in that area. Autocratic coaches who abuse their power and rely solely on the power of their position to get things done often fall short of their objectives because of an inherent power gap that can only be bridged by cultivating honest, trusting, respectful and cooperative relationships with the players. Clearly Otis did not understand the limitations of his power and the importance of building and maintaining those types of relationships. During the crisis there was a conflict of values and change in the first-important priorities; power and control took centrestage and trumped common sense, team selection, team performance and the welfare of West Indies cricket. When the stick is used to motivate the players it should be done sensibly, wisely and sparingly.

Goals: Where are you Going and What do You Want?

> Setting goals is important but enjoying the journey that takes you to them is equally important. If you stay in the moment and enjoy the process and the day-to-day activities of batting, bowling and fielding you would find the game more rewarding, learn faster, perform better and reach your goals quicker.
>
> – *Rahul Dravid*

Goal setting gives purpose and direction and should be at the heart of every improvement programme. All good performance starts with clear goals. But it is not enough just look at the steps and talk about them; you must actually climb up the stairs.

V.V.S. Laxman said the major goal of the Indian team was

becoming the number one Test playing nation. 'We broke that goal down into smaller goals. We had goals for every Test series, every Test match, and every session during the Test match. There is a board in our dressing room on which we write down sessions one, two and three for every day of the Test match. At the end of each session we assess our performance to see if we won the session or lost it. That feedback then influences our commitment and performance in the next session. The goal is to win each session.'

Good players think about and visualize their goals as if they have already achieved them. They see the future now. For instance, instead of saying, 'I want to be the best player in the team,' they say, 'I am the best player in the team.'

Once you know what you want and why, you will find a way to get it. Not only does your brain create your goals but it also subordinates its activities towards achieving them.

Goal setting starts with your imagination. It is about changing the beliefs, pictures and thoughts in your mind. If you are not satisfied with the type of player you are, imagine yourself as the player you want to become. If you are unhappy about where you are going, imagine yourself going down a different path to a new destination. Wherever you want to go or whatever you want to improve, repeatedly visualize your new future and familiarize yourself with it.

Your goals will only get momentum and power when you add emotion to them – joy, passion and pride. For instance, you might know exactly what you want to achieve but if you do not pursue it with pride, passion and enthusiasm you will not attain it.

On the way to your major goal there is usually a chain of smaller goals or sub-goals, each one following on from the previous one. They are like places on the map through which you must pass to get to your final destination. They give feedback about progress and allow you to assess the situation at regular intervals and alter strategy when necessary.

Tony Rafferty, an ultra-marathon runner, highlighted the importance of sub-goals when he said: 'On my run across Australia, from Perth to Sydney, I learned how vital sub-goals really are. After struggling to complete the first 1,700 miles, I realized that I still had another 2,300 miles ahead of me. At that stage I was tired, hurting all over, depressed, and feeling sorry for myself. The task looked impossible and I was thinking about quitting but I didn't want to let down all the people who had given up their time to help me. I then changed my thinking. Instead of worrying about the 2,300 miles ahead of me, I decided to focus on running 60 miles every day and to concentrate on repeating it to see how far I would go. As soon as I made that decision my depression vanished and I started to feel enthusiastic again, because I was confident that I could run 60 miles every day. Taking my mind away from the result (2,300 miles) and focusing it on my daily assignment gave me a new lease of energy. Because of this I was able to complete the run. Had I not changed my thinking, I would not have reached Sydney.'

To create stimulating and effective goals you should:

1. *Be specific about your aims and objectives*: The more specific the goal, the greater is the chance of reaching it. The goal of becoming a better cricketer is too general. What exactly would make you a better cricketer – greater fitness, better technique, more efficient practice, smarter tactics, better strategy or better mental skills? Don't just articulate your goals; write them down.

2. *Set positive goals*: Say exactly what you want to achieve and what you want to happen rather than what you want to avoid. Make your goals challenging but achievable. Setting goals that are too high can create anxiety, fear and self-doubts. But, if they are too easy they might produce apathy and boredom. In both cases you are unlikely to put out optimum effort.

3. *Break down your goals into sub-goals*: For example if you want to make a hundred runs in cricket you could break the task down into units of tens.

4. *State your goal in the present tense as if you have already achieved it*: When you say, 'I intend to be' or 'I can be' you might then think, 'Yes, but right now I am not.' If you say, 'In the next five

months, I intend to improve the way I deal with pressure,' you might unconsciously think, 'But right now I can't.' You could change that future statement into the present by saying, 'During the game, I am calm and relaxed and I use pressure to lift my game,' or 'Pressure brings out the best in me. It improves my concentration.' Putting goals in the present tense may seem strange and hollow and you may not at first believe what you say. But the present tense seems to engage the brain more actively and creatively, especially if you can picture yourself behaving like the person you say you are.

5. *Create a vision board*: Making a vision board is simple: Cut out images and words that match your goals and glue or tape them to a poster board. Then hang it in a place where you can see it several times a day. Each time you look at it imagine that you have already achieved those goals, and feel happy about it.

When I was living in Melbourne, Australia, Sri Lanka's high commissioner to Australia telephoned me and asked me to speak to the visiting Sri Lankan cricket team. I agreed to do so and the meeting was arranged at a private residence in one of the suburbs. I thought I would meet the players privately but when I arrived to talk to them I walked into a lively party that was attended by about a hundred Sri Lankans who were living in Melbourne. So much for my private meeting; I had to speak to players in front of their supporters. As my original plan went through the window, I thought, 'What on earth can I say to the players in this setting?' Immediately the answer came to me. 'Be as simple as possible. Take their minds away from the result of the game and the perceived supremacy of the Australian team and focus them on one or two simple process goals.'

I told them that the upcoming game would be a contest between themselves and the cricket ball not between themselves and the Australians. While batting, their goal is to see the ball the moment it leaves the bowler's hand and to move into position to receive it; while fielding, their goal is to pick up the ball the moment it leaves the bat and move quickly to catch, chase it or stop it and return it smartly to the wicketkeeper; and while bowling, their goal is to put the ball in the right areas. I asked them to think about and visualize those contests with the ball before they went to bed that night and before going out on to the field two days later. There was nothing in the instructions about the result nor was there anything to tempt them to compare themselves with the Australians. The goal and focus were very simple – concentrate on the cricket ball and win your contest with it.

In the game, the team performed exceedingly well, outplayed the Australians and won their first ever One Day match against Australia down under.

REMEMBER

1. Goal setting should be at the heart of every performance improvement programme.
2. If you forget your goals you will lose purpose and direction.
3. Once you know exactly what you want to achieve and why you want it, you will find a way to get it.
4. Your goals should be clear and specific.
5. State your goal in the present tense as if you have already achieved it. Instead of saying, 'I will be or I intend to be one of the best players,' say 'I am one of the best players.'
6. Goal setting starts with your imagination. It is about changing the beliefs, pictures and words inside your mind – the type of player you are, the things you want to achieve, where you want to go and what you want to become.
7. Setting goals should not just be an intellectual exercise. Your goals will only get legs when you add emotion to them.
8. On the way to your major goal there is usually a chain of smaller goals or sub-goals, each one following on from the previous one.

9.   Sub-goals give feedback about your progress and help you to persist and persevere when things get tough.

10. Set positive goals. Be specific about your aims and objectives; break down your goals into sub-goals; state your goals in the present tense as if you have already achieved them.

11. Believe in your goals.

Part 4: Execution and Visualization

EXECUTION CYCLE: HOW DO YOU ORGANIZE AND EXECUTE?

> Plans and strategies amount to nothing if they are not executed well.
>
> — *Anonymous*

When I lived in Melbourne, I attended an Australian Rules Football Grand Final and had the pleasure of visiting the dressing rooms of both teams while the coaches and players were preparing themselves for the game. The teams had different but excellent strategies and game plans and at the time I thought how could either side lose with such good strategies? But then I remembered that strategic plans amount to nothing if they are not implemented well and I said to myself, 'The team that executes better today will win the game.' And that is exactly what happened.

Coaches are always looking for ways to get their players to play better. Sound execution of the basic skills is one of the most vital challenges facing the individual and the team. The better each player executes, the better the team will perform.

But excellence in physical skills does not guarantee that the right skills will be chosen and executed or that common sense or good judgement will prevail. Knowing what to do does not mean that you will do it. There is a common belief that once you have knowledge, action will be easy and automatic. But that is not true. The skills of doing are extremely important and are very different from the skills of acquiring knowledge.

Unlike professionals in other fields, athletes often have to push themselves close to their mental and physical limits to beat their opponents and win the game. To succeed at all, they must execute their skills under great pressure in a disciplined, competent and consistent manner.

How do you execute better? Is there a process you can learn to improve the execution of your skills? The US Air Force has developed an execution model or execution cycle that can help in this respect.

Once you have created a clear and detailed vision of what you want to achieve, and have formulated a simple but intelligent strategy to achieve it, you can use the execution cycle to put your strategy into action. You should use this cycle for every mission, assignment or task you have to perform.

The cycle consists of five parts: preparation, planning and organizing; briefing; execution; debriefing; and planning for the next game.

Planning and Organizing

The purpose of organizing is to prevent confusion. If you know what needs to be done, what is being done at the moment and what is to be done next you are probably organized. Whatever your mission, you should always ask, 'How do I organize this?' That question invariably leads to a plan.

Planning is thinking ahead to see how you are going to do something: play, behave, deal with the challenges and mistakes in the game or beat your opponents. It requires thorough physical and mental preparation and full consideration of all the important factors in the game. You should ask yourself three simple questions: 'What are the requirements in the situation? What is their order of importance? How can I tailor my skills and resources to fit those requirements?' You should know exactly what you want to achieve and why, and what you must do to achieve it. Importantly, you should have alternative or back-up plans ready in case circumstances change or in case something goes wrong with the original plan. And something always goes wrong. Finally, you should keep your plan as simple and as clear as possible.

Remember that your opponent is out there planning for you too. So you should take your plan apart and ask yourself, 'How can I beat myself? How can I undermine my plan? What are the faults and weaknesses in my plan? How can I remove them? Are there other ways of looking at this situation?' By dismantling your plan and trying to defeat it you will discover its weaknesses and correct them before your opponents find them and exploit them.

Briefing

Just before you go into the game you should have a short briefing session to remind yourself of the plan. You should simplify it and clarify it further, focus on the process rather than the result, identify your first-important priorities and concentrate on the key things you must do to implement your plan. Visualization and mental rehearsal are very effective and important at this stage.

Execution

On the field your aim is to execute well using your mind and common sense to master the basics of the game. Alertness, clear simple thinking, confidence, patience, persistence and good concentration are necessary in this stage.

Here is a routine that Greg Chappell used successfully to control his concentration and to enhance his batting skills. He said: 'I have always prided myself on my ability to concentrate for long periods. I found it important to develop a mental routine that helped me to relax, conserve my mental and emotional energy and switch in and out of different levels of concentration. Early in my innings my intent is to play in the "V" between mid-off and mid-on. This helps me to play with a straight bat and stops me from hitting across the line and giving my wicket away. While building my innings I keep my concentration in the present by playing one ball at a time and by focusing on scoring runs in units of ten. When I get to what some people describe as the nervous nineties I remain calm and in control and focus on the next unit of ten, not on the hundred.'

Between overs and even between balls Greg was aware of the things going on around him but when the bowler reached the top of his mark he would narrow his concentration and focus on the bowler's face. Then at the point of delivery he would lock in his concentration on the ball as it was leaving the bowler's hand, pick up its line and length and allow his body to move smoothly into position to play the ball. Once that play was over he would switch back to the crowd momentarily to give his mind a rest. To shift his concentration back to the next ball he would count the fielders and then refocus on the bowler's face at the top of his mark.

Greg went through this routine for every ball that he faced and any time he broke that routine distractions crept in and disrupted his batting skills.

Debriefing

The fourth factor in the cycle is debriefing. This is one of the most powerful weapons in performance. At the end of every performance the individual or the team should sit down and debrief. In this session standards of execution are closely examined, the good things are recognized, mistakes are identified, their root causes are revealed, lessons are learned, and a better way to play, raise standards and reduce mistakes is then channelled back into the next planning and preparation cycle. Ideally the debriefing should be done as soon as possible after the performance.

M.S. Dhoni understands this process and always stresses the importance of not repeating mistakes. He feels that the main difference between good players and average players is the interval between mistakes. Good players repeat mistakes less frequently than mediocre ones. Dhoni also feels that no matter how disappointed you are after a failure or a bad day you should always learn something from your experience. He stresses that soon after a contest you should examine the positives and the negatives of your game, and recognize the things you have learned from the game. You should then incorporate those lessons into your planning and preparation to improve performance in the next game.

In the old days, debriefing was done routinely in the dressing room after a day's play but today this hardly happens in cricket. Team members always seem to be in a hurry to leave the ground. I don't think that coaches and players fully appreciate the tremendous importance of early debriefing sessions.

Planning for the next game

This should start as soon as possible after the debriefing session.

Tactics and strategy are not the same things. Strategy is the overall intention and way of playing. Within the strategy there are moment-to-moment moves that have to be made. These are tactics.

If you have a good strategy you can succeed with mediocre tactics. But, if you have good tactics and a poor strategy you might still lose. For instance, in his book, *Flawless Execution*, James D. Murphy said that in the Vietnam War, the US Army won 90 per cent of the battles because of superior tactics and equipment but strategically they were humbled and humiliated and in the end had to withdraw from Vietnam.

He added that the North Vietnamese had a simple strategy: 'Foreigners will not occupy our country. We will wear the Americans down and be happy as long as we are moving towards Saigon.' It didn't matter how many battles they lost. As long as they were moving towards Saigon they were happy.

AIM FOR HIGH STANDARDS

Clive Lloyd once reprimanded one of his best batsmen after he made a superb century in Australia because he turned blindly while going for a second run during his innings. We thought he was rather harsh but he explained that high standards must be maintained and monitored carefully at all times. He added that if you get blasé about them they could deteriorate right before your eyes, and when that happens performance automatically suffers.

Good training and high standards are two of the pillars on which the execution cycle is built. Great teams are better than other teams because their team members are trained to a higher standard.

But training is not only about physical fitness or building bulk to overpower your opponent but also about teaching your brain, nerves and muscle fibres to work in harmony to improve the efficiency of your movements and the execution of your skills.

The challenges, standards and training for Test cricket are very different from those in the shorter versions of the game. So preparation, exposure and concentration must be different.

Most young cricketers today are captivated by the Twenty 20 game and do not put in the necessary time, practice and mental effort, or get the right exposure to develop the skills, patience and concentration that are so vitally important in the longer version of the game. That is probably why so many of them play poorly in Test cricket and have difficulties handling its challenges and pressures. Good Test players who master the basics of the game make the transition to Twenty 20 cricket more easily than the good Twenty 20 players do to Test cricket.

As I said before there isn't anything that cannot be improved or made easier by constant training and practice. But the practice must be of the right kind. If you want to do well in Test cricket you must train and practise in Test match conditions.

Rahul Dravid, one of India's greatest Test players, understands this problem and recently told me, 'In India there are many exciting young batsmen coming through our cricket. They have talent, desire and hunger and have done well in Twenty 20 cricket and One Day cricket but they will face a tough road in Test cricket. It will be a challenging journey for them and they won't get away with lots of things that they do in Twenty 20 and One Day cricket. When you look at the players who do well in Twenty 20 cricket, apart from the odd exception, they are usually good Test players who have the base that allows them to be innovative and creative.'

You can improve your training by going through a four-part process. First, know exactly what you want to learn, practise or achieve, and why. Other people can help you, but you must take responsibility for your own learning.

Second, learn about the task, watch experts doing it and then copy them. Try to get accurate feedback about how you are doing and repeat the process over and over until you can master the task. It is useful to write down, in your own words, what you have to do and why and visualize yourself doing it. Teachers and coaches can tell you how to do something, and you can even study it, but you will not learn it until you actually do it. Training is a hands-on process.

Third, improve your self-discipline by maintaining the necessary effort, motivation, patience and persistence to learn and perform the task according to the required standard.

The fourth part is continuing training during which you strive to maintain and improve high standards. This is often a neglected factor in performance.

REMEMBER

1. Common sense is often a forgotten factor in performance.

2. Having the right skills does not mean that you will choose or use them correctly in the game.

3. Knowing what to do does not guarantee that you will do it.

4. Clear vision and good strategy are necessary for good performance. But they come to nothing if you don't execute well.

5. How do you execute better? Use the five-part execution cycle — prepare, plan and organize; brief; execute; debrief; and plan for the next mission or performance.

6. Before you implement your plan, mentally rehearse your strategy and the execution of your basic skills.

7.   Debriefing is one of the most potent but most neglected
      weapons in performance.

8.   Training, on-going training, and high standards are keys
      to good execution. You ignore training and standards at
      your own peril.

9.   You can upgrade training by deciding what you want to
      learn or improve; watching the experts copying them and
      getting accurate feedback; improving motivation and
      self-discipline; and practicing continuously.

VISUALIZATION: SEE AND FEEL WHAT YOU WANT TO ACHIEVE AND BECOME

> Imagery might be our highest form of mental energy. Reason
> can analyse and organize but only the imagination can create
> the future.
>
> — *Emile Coue, French chemist*

> Before the last World Cup I saw myself holding up the cup
> and I kept replaying those images in my mind over and over
> again.
>
> — *M.S. Dhoni*

> Visualization focuses concentration and programmes the mind
> for action.
>
> — *Anonymous*

Your imagination is a preview of life's upcoming events. You
construct your future in your mind before it even happens. If you
imagine a negative future or negative results your brain will do its best
to make that future a reality. The same applies to a positive future and
positive results. So you have a choice. How you talk to yourself about
the future or think about it controls the way you feel and perform.

The brain cannot differentiate between something that actually
happens and something that it vividly imagines. That is why

visualization and mental rehearsal are such powerful techniques in performance. By simply visualizing yourself running you stimulate the same neural circuits in the brain and the same nerves and muscles in the body you utilize when you are actually running. In addition, you use about 25 per cent of the calories you would burn in the real run.

In the third Test match between West Indies and Australia in Barbados in March 1999, West Indies had to make 308 runs to win the game on the last day. The day before, Lara and I had a short but important conversation about the challenge. My advice to him was to imagine the game as already won and to visualize and feel himself constructing that victory. I asked him to mentally rehearse seeing the ball the moment it leaves the bowler's hand and to feel his movements as he gets into position smoothly and quickly to stroke the ball into the gaps in the field. I also asked him to see and feel himself playing his natural game, facing one ball at a time, and enjoying the challenge.

In an epic battle on the following day, Lara played one of his greatest innings, 153 not out, and against the odds won the match for the West Indies. Later that evening he said to me, 'I was seeing the ball so clearly that I couldn't miss it. Everything worked out the way I imagined.'

Peter Brock the racing car driver says, 'Before the race, I like to take a few moments to visualize, feel or mentally rehearse what I want to do. It then becomes a natural progression from thinking about it to doing it. Visualization programmes my mind for action and when I get out there I am relaxed and confident and I concentrate better.'

V.V.S. Laxman said something similar in a recent interview. 'I improved dramatically as a player when I started to use visualization and mental rehearsal techniques. But how many players actually use these techniques to practise their skills and prepare for the game? I feel that every young player should learn how to develop and use these techniques because the rewards can be great. I believe they should make them an important part of their practice and preparation routine.'

It is worthwhile repeating the findings of the Russian scientists in 1980 when they compared the effects of mental training and physical training on the performance of elite athletes. The training regimens included:

- Group 1: 100 per cent physical training;
- Group 2: 75 per cent physical with 25 per cent mental training;
- Group 3: 50 per cent physical with 50 per cent mental training; and
- Group 4: 25 per cent physical with 75 per cent mental training.

They found that athletes in Group 4 who spent 75 per cent of their time on mental training and 25 per cent on physical training showed the greatest improvement in performance, and that athletes in Group 1 who did 100 per cent physical training showed the least improvement.

The ancient Okinawan karate masters and Indian yogi knew of these results many centuries ago. While teaching students Kata – detailed choreographed patterns of movements practised either solo or in pairs – the masters told their students that through visualization they should first picture themselves doing exceptional Kata before they physically perform it.

As I said before, the values and pictures that you imprint in your mind today determine what you become tomorrow. You change your path and trajectory in life when you change what you believe, value and picture in your mind. You construct your future in your mind before it ever occurs.

In sport and in business, the best performers have a highly developed capacity to create and imprint success images in their minds.

Visualization is the mental creation or mental rehearsal of an act. The imagination is more active, much clearer and more powerful when you are relaxed or in a meditative or hypnotic state. That is why it is so lively just before you go to sleep at nights and soon after you wake up in the mornings. You can use your imagination to:

- Improve performance;
- Improve and rehearse technical skills;
- Improve thinking and self-talk;

- Change self-image and self-beliefs;
- Improve self-confidence and concentration;
- Stay calm, relaxed and clear-minded during the game;
- Deal with pre-match and post-match tension;
- Prevent and manage pressure;
- Cope with fears and performance anxiety;
- Set goals and motivate yourself to achieve them;
- Practise coping with the many different game situations you will face; and
- Speed up the healing of physical and mental injuries.

The brain can often not differentiate between something that actually happens and something that it vividly imagines. That is why visualization and mental rehearsal are such powerful techniques. By simply visualizing yourself running you stimulate the same muscles that you use when you are actually running and you use about 25 per cent of the calories you would burn in the real run.

When you practise a physical skill and then follow it up with repeated mental rehearsals you automatically get better at it.

In a research study in 1980 on the impact of visualization on performance in basketball, John Lane asked twenty athletes to practise shooting free throws at the basket twenty minutes a day for two weeks. One group practised free throws only while the other group practised free throws and visualization of those throws. When the groups were tested, both improved but the one that had combined physical with mental practice was found to have improved more.

MANIPULATE YOUR PICTURES

One of the good things about visualization is that you can control and manipulate the images to change the power of your experience. For instance, when you make an already pleasant image bigger, brighter and zoom in, you create a more powerful and pleasant experience.

The same applies to images of negative experiences. When you make them bigger and brighter, and zoom in, the negative state and the bad feelings get worse. When you make those images, smaller, dimmer and zoom out they lose their power and intensity. You can get similar results by manipulating the sound in your images.

In Clive Lloyd's West Indies team there was one batsman who was particularly anxious and afraid when he was facing Jeff Thompson, at the time the fastest and most dangerous bowler in the world. To reduce his fear and anxiety, I first put him through a relaxation procedure, gave him some ego-boosting suggestions, and then stimulated his imagination with creative visualization.

I got him to slow down his psychological clock by imagining that everything was happening in ultra-slow motion. When he was batting he was relaxed and comfortable at the wicket and could see every movement of the bowler in his run-up and delivery. At the point of delivery he was able to see the bright red ball leaving Thompson's hand and could see the seam of the ball rotating as it came slowly towards him. He automatically assessed its line, angle and length and moved freely into position to play his shot. That imagery was repeated several times. With each repetition he became more relaxed and in control, and the ball got bigger, brighter and easier to track.

Bill Russell the basketball player claims that top players in any sport look at things differently from other people. He said that good baseball players often speak about seeing the ball in slow motion when they are batting well or when they take a great catch. Joe Morgan, a baseball player was once asked how he was able to handle hundred-mile-an-hour fast balls. He said when he was batting well he never saw hundred-miles-per-hour balls. He claimed that in his mind he could slow the ball down to about seventy miles per hour and was able to see the ball more clearly. In cricket good batsmen have made similar comments about handling fast bowling. They say when they are in good form the ball seems to come to them more slowly and it looks as big as a soccer ball. But, when they are tense and uptight the opposite happens – the ball looks smaller, travels faster and bounces higher. Peter Brock, the racing-car driver claims that in very fast races when he is driving well everything seems to move in slow motion.

After practising against Thompson in slow motion, I got the player to imagine that Thompson was bowling at his normal speed. Throughout this imagery he remained relaxed and in control. He saw the ball so early and judged its line and length so quickly that he had ample time to get into position to play his shots. Even at normal speed the ball looked bigger and brighter. After visualizing these images for a while he then went to the next stage.

This time he imagined that Thompson was bowling at twice his normal speed. The key was to stay calm and relaxed and allow his body to move freely and quickly into position. At that pace he could still see the ball the moment it left Thompson's hand, judge its line, angle and length, and get into position easily to play his shots. He repeated those images several times in the session. Before the session got over I gave him the suggestion that no matter how fast Thompson bowled he would be able to stay relaxed and in control and would be able to see and handle whatever ball he bowled.

The moment of truth soon arrived. In the next Test match he batted extremely well and made eighty runs in the first innings. He was hit by a demon of a ball that jumped from a good length but he never flinched. After he got out he said to me, 'I showed those bastards, didn't I! Everything happened the way we visualized them. I was alert but relaxed throughout my innings and at no stage did I lose control. And I saw the big bright red ball the moment it left the bowler's hand.'

I have done similar mental rehearsals and manipulations of images for spin bowling. In these rehearsals the batsman is relaxed, very light and quick on his feet, and is able to see from the bowler's body action and wrist movements how the ball will emerge from his hand. The moment the ball leaves the hand the batsman picks up its spin and its rotations, quickly judges its flight, direction and length, and automatically gets into position to play his shot. These pictures are run in slow motion, then at the normal speed, and finally at high speed. This practice has been effective in teaching batsmen how to play spin.

GIVE STRENGTH TO YOUR IMAGES

Visualization is most effective when you:

- Are clear about what you want to create and practise;
- Relax and go into a meditative or hypnotic state;
- Create images of both the process (performance) and the result;
- Use as many of your senses as you can – vision, sounds, touch, feelings, smell and taste. The more senses you use the more powerful is the imagery;
- Make your images as clear and as detailed as possible. The more detail you put in the more effective they become. 'I am on the beach and feeling relaxed,' is not as effective as, 'It's a nice sunny day in the Caribbean with a gentle breeze blowing… and I am walking along my favourite beach on the firm white sand near the edge of the water where young children are playing a game of beach cricket. Every now and then the water washes over my feet and up past my ankles. I can feel the breeze in my face and can taste the salt on my lips… and I can hear the loud cries of the seagulls and the noisy cricketers. I can see the fielders jumping into the water to retrieve the cricket ball and can also see my house on the hill overlooking the beach and the beautiful plants and flowers in the garden. And I am calm and relaxed;'
- Believe in your images to make them more powerful; and
- Mentally practise the correct actions. If you rehearse the wrong skills and techniques you will become good at doing the wrong things.

When you create images where you watch yourself or other people performing, you are using external or disassociated imagery. This is similar to watching videos of yourself or your team.

But, when you create images where you are actually in your own body looking out, you are using internal or associated imagery. Both types are effective but internal imagery is much more powerful and beneficial. In general, coaches are not aware of this and devote most of their time with players watching external imagery.

A three-step visualization method of learning skills uses both external and internal imagery. It is the way children learn from their parents and the people around them. The first step is to observe someone whose attitudes and actions you want to copy. The second step is to see yourself acting exactly like that person. And the third step is to feel yourself acting like the person. When you go through this process carefully and systematically, you automatically improve your chances of learning the skills you are trying to copy.

Someone once said that if you create an image of your future that is clear, sharp, and detailed and more powerful than your image of reality at present, you will automatically be drawn towards that future and overcome any obstacles or setbacks along the way. But if the image of your future is vague and unclear and is not much stronger than that of the current situation you are in, the moment you meet with a failure or setback you will be likely to revert to the status quo.

Years ago I was asked to join the Australian Rules football team, Essendon, to help the team win a Grand Final and a championship. In the previous year the team came close but lost the Grand Final to its bitter rival Hawthorn, with whom I had done some mental conditioning work a few days before the game. During the season both teams played well and faced each other once more in the Grand Final. Most people expected Hawthorn to repeat its victory because it had beaten Essendon in the three games that they played against each other during the regular season. The Essendon players, however, had other ideas. Throughout the season, particularly leading up to the Grand Final we did a lot of visualization work.

We all knew that the Grand Final would be a tough contest and that the team that was mentally tougher would win in the end. In the two weeks leading up to the game there was one particular situation that we repeatedly rehearsed in our minds. Why I focused the players on that situation I still don't know. Some people might call it precognition, premonition, intuition or even a self-fulfilling prophecy.

We imagined that we were four or five goals down at the start of the last quarter and then mentally rehearsed how we were going to get out of that losing position and turn the game around. We repeatedly visualized ourselves playing confidently and aggressively in that quarter, doing the basic things well, and outperforming the Hawthorn players.

The game was rough, tough and very physical, and Hawthorn dominated the first three quarters and was up by four goals at the end of the third quarter. Essendon looked as though it would lose again. In the break before the start of the last quarter the coach was blowing his top and was having a go at a few of the players. He could see defeat staring him in the face. A couple of players then interrupted him and said, 'Coach, we know what we have to do. We have rehearsed this situation with Rudi several times and we know how to deal with it.'

At the first bounce of the ball in the last quarter, one of our players gathered the ball and the drive started from there. We overwhelmed our opponents, kicked a record score for that quarter and won the championship. The Australian Grand Final is the equivalent of the English FA Cup Final or the American Super Bowl.

Meet Your 'Twin Self'

Over the years I have used a visualization technique that has helped many athletes to find their best performance. I put the athlete in a light hypnotic trance and take him into a magic garden where everything is possible. There he meets a twin version of himself who in the past made different decisions and took different actions that resulted in enormous success in all the areas that the athlete is weak. I then tell the athlete to talk to his 'twin version', ask him how and why he became so successful and what advice he would give him to overcome the inner and outer obstacles that are holding him back. How can he change course and follow in his footsteps? This interaction usually occurs at an unconscious level and I tell the athlete that after his conversation he will have a strong compulsion, every day, to visualize and follow the advice of his 'twin self'. This often enhances self-confidence and improves performance.

REMEMBER

1. You construct your future in your mind before it ever happens.

2. If you feed your brain with images of negative results or a negative future your brain will do its best to create those results and that future.

3. The values and pictures that you choose to imprint in your mind today determine what you become tomorrow.

4. You have a choice. You can continue to feed your brain with negative pictures or replace them with positive images of the future you want to experience.

5. The brain often cannot differentiate between something that actually happens and something that it vividly imagines. That is why visualization and mental rehearsal techniques are so powerful.

6. The best performers have a highly developed capacity to create and imprint success images in their minds.

7. When you practise a physical skill and then follow it up with repeated mental practise you automatically increase competence in that skill.

8. During visualization, use as many of your senses as you can – vision, sounds, touch, feelings, smell and taste. The more senses you use the more powerful the imagery becomes.

9. Make your images as clear and as detailed as possible. The more detail you put in, the more potent they become.

10. You can manipulate your images to make your experience or your preparation more powerful or less powerful.

11. Learn to talk to your 'twin self' and follow his advice.

Ego-Boosting Technique

Ego boosting is mentioned several times throughout this book. This technique, developed by psychiatrist John Hartland, is a routine that is used during relaxation and hypnosis to strengthen self-worth, self-esteem and self-belief. I have employed it extensively and successfully for many years to deal with the performance problems that athletes face. I used it with Viv Richards when he was going through a slump in Australia early in his career and the results were remarkable. It is a powerful technique that has a great impact on the way the athlete thinks, feels, controls his emotions and performs during the weeks and months following the session. Once the player is in a relaxed or hypnotic state I spend the next seven to eight minutes going through this routine. Only when I have finished it will I give specific suggestions to improve performance.

Here is a version of Hartland's technique.

You have now become so deeply relaxed, so deeply asleep, that your mind has become so sensitive, so receptive to what I say that everything that I put into your mind will sink so deeply into the unconscious part of your mind and will have a so deep and lasting impression there that nothing will eradicate it.

As a result, these things that I put into your mind will have a lasting and powerful impression on the way you think, on the way you feel, and on the way you play. All these things will happen for your own good exactly the way I tell you, more and more powerfully and completely with every treatment that I give you. And you will continue to experience these things just as strongly and just as powerfully every day at home or at the game when you are no longer with me,

As you become and as you remain more relaxed and less tense each day things that used to upset you and worry you will cease do so. They won't seem to matter so much any more. From now on you will see things as they really are – in their true perspective - without magnifying them or getting them out of proportion. Consequently, you will become much less easily upset, much less fearful and apprehensive, much less easily depressed.

You are a worthwhile and valuable person. You are worthwhile in yourself quite apart from your performance or your status. You are worthwhile because you are a valuable human being. Since you are human you will have weaknesses and make mistakes but you will use your setbacks and failures to motivate yourself to play better next time.

As you become and as you remain more relaxed and less tense each day you will become so deeply interested and involved in whatever you are doing and in whatever is going on around you that your mind will become completely distracted from yourself, your problems, your difficulties and your worries. Your nerves will become stronger and steadier and your mind calmer and clearer, more composed, more tranquil, more placid.

As you become and as you remain more relaxed and less tense each day you will feel stronger, fitter and more energetic in every way.

You will be able to think more clearly and concentrate more easily and you will give your whole undivided attention to whatever you are doing to the complete exclusion of everything else.

When you go to sleep at night your sleep will be calm, peaceful and profound marked only by pleasant dreams. And when you wake up in the morning you will feel alert and refreshed, eager to get on with your daily tasks, feeling that each day is the first day of the rest of your life, a life that will be better and better in all the ways you want it to be better.

As you become and as you remain more relaxed and less tense each day you will get more confidence in yourself and more confidence in your ability to do whatever you ought to be able to do without any self-doubts, apprehension, anxiety or fear of failure. You will be able to stand on your own feet, make up your own mind and rely more and more on your own judgement and opinions and less and less on those of other people.

As you become and as you remain more and more relaxed and less tense each day your confidence will continue to grow and words like 'It is too difficult; I cannot' will disappear from your vocabulary and their place will be taken by this phrase, 'It is easy and I can.'

Just because something once negatively affected you in the past doesn't mean that it will continue to do so in the future. You are a different person now from what you were in the past.

Every day you will feel a greater feeling of personal safety, a greater feeling of well being than you have felt for a long time. If at any time you feel stressed you can calm your mind, relax your body and clear up your thinking by taking five slow deep breaths.

At the end of the procedure, when the player is fully awake, I remind him of the four important things that the ego-strengthening routine will do for him.

1. *Relaxation*: You will become more relaxed and remain so each day.
2. *Calmness*: Relaxation will lead to a higher level of calmness. Everyday your mind will become calmer and clearer, more composed, more tranquil.
3. *Self-control*: Calmness will then lead to greater self-control. You will gain more and more control over the way you think, the way you feel, the way you play and the way you control your emotions.
4. *Self-confidence*: Greater self-control will build more self-confidence. Everyday you will become more confident in your ability to be able to do whatever you set out to without any self-doubts, apprehension, anxiety or fear of failure.

INTERVIEWS

DENNIS LILLEE

Dennis. At the start of my career I would have said that performance was 70 per cent physical and 30 per cent mental. But I would now say that the reverse holds true. You see the mind controls the body. When you get tired and you give in, it is your mind that gives up first. If you are fit and your body doesn't do what it ought to, you will often find the cause in the mind, not the body. The mind is very powerful and can help you to achieve anything that you are capable of achieving and much more sometimes.

Rudi. Your figures about performance are interesting because they reflect the research findings of Russian scientists and coaches. Just before the 1980 Olympics they conducted tests to compare the effects of mental and physical training on the performance of their elite athletes. The training regimens included:

- Group 1: 100 per cent physical training;
- Group 2: 75 per cent physical with 25 per cent mental training;
- Group 3: 50 per cent physical with 50 per cent mental training; and
- Group 4: 25 per cent physical with 75 per cent mental training.

They found that athletes in Group 4 who spent 75 per cent of their time on mental training and 25 per cent on physical training showed the greatest improvement in performance, followed by Group 3, then Group 2 and finally Group 1.

Do you know about these findings?

Dennis. No I don't but our figures are pretty close.

I have had some very bad back injuries during my career. The trouble with my back was a major problem. You know what I am talking about because you diagnosed the four fractures in my back and helped me to take the first few steps on the road to recovery. It was my mental toughness that got me through that crisis period and helped me to go on to realize all of my dreams.

Rudi. It was wonderful to see what you did after your injury. I know that you have enormous self-belief, so I wasn't surprised when you got fitter and became a much better bowler after eighteen months of rehabilitation. Some people see you as the greatest fast bowler of any era. I am sure that in the years to come that will not change.

Dennis. Self-belief is extremely important. Your performance and your achievements are strongly influenced by your beliefs. You achieve what you believe. If I didn't believe so strongly in myself I would not have overcome the serious back injuries and would probably have given up the game.

Rudi. Had you done so, think what we would have missed.

Advice to Young Players

Rudi. What advice would you give to a talented young athlete who wants to get to the top of his field?

Dennis. There are three areas I would discuss – training and physical fitness, skills training and mental training. The mind controls the first two.

Physical fitness is very important. I always set myself goals at training – so many laps, so many push-ups etc. Every time I went to training I tried to go past these goals. I would say to myself, 'One more, five more, ten yards more, twenty yards more etc. In theory what you are doing is pushing your body that is controlled by the mind through the barriers. You are training your mind and body to stretch themselves beyond their limits. It is amazing how much more you can get out of your body when you push yourself mentally. Your body often has reserves you are unaware of that you don't realize are there. Your mind gives in before your body when you stop trying. If you push your mind through the barriers at training you will push it through them during the game. There have been times when my feet were sore, my legs and back were aching, when I have had difficulty breathing and felt faint, but I was able to continue because I had pushed myself at training. If you are rooted physically, the mind can get you going again.

The second area is technical skills. I think you should practise the basic skills over and over until you get them right and then keep on practising to maintain them. You must practise them under the same conditions you will encounter in the game. Preparation and practice are very important. At practice you only have about two or three hours so make the best of them. Don't waste your time. A lot of people fail to develop their skills because of poor preparation, planning and organization at training, a poor attitude or because they spend insufficient time practising them.

Rudi. What about the mind?

Dennis. Well, your mind controls both your fitness and technical skills. As far as fitness is concerned, it is the mind that gives up first, not your body. And as far as the basic technical skills are concerned, if you don't use your mind to concentrate and practise properly, you won't improve your skills. In the game if you don't use your mind to think clearly and positively, to concentrate well, to maintain self-confidence and to handle the pressures of the game you won't use those skills properly. Your performance would then be substandard. So you see they are all tied up.

WASIM AKRAM

Mental Conditioning

Rudi. Most experts say that you, Malcolm Marshall and Dennis Lillee are the three greatest fast bowlers in the history of the game. How important was the mind in your performance?

Wasim. When I started playing cricket as a professional nobody told me how important the mind was in cricket. Then, I focused all of my energies on fitness, training everyday, and practice. But when I got married six or seven years later at the age of twenty-five my focus changed. My late wife Huma was a psychologist and psychotherapist and she taught me about the importance of the mind in sport. Being a typical guy from the Orient I didn't listen to her in the beginning but she showed me how vital positive thinking, visualization and reading of the opposition's body language were in performance. These things helped me a lot.

In golf, the good players visualize the shot before they actually play it.

The same should happen in cricket. In fact, I used to visualize most of the deliveries that I bowled. For example, if there were reverse swing I would bowl three away swingers and then the in-swinger. But before I bowled the in-swinger I would visualize it and would see the ball swinging from outside the off stump into the batsman's pads or the stumps. And that is what actually happened 70 per cent of the time.

The mind matters; it controls everything. It doesn't matter how quick you are as a bowler or how talented you are, you won't progress to the next level unless you use your mind to improve and control your skills. Positive thinking and visualization are powerful tools.

Rudi. Your wife must have been very observant and understanding.

Wasim. Yes. She was very perceptive and she knew me very well. If I had a big game she would say things like, 'You have an important game tomorrow, so get a good night's sleep tonight. Before you go to sleep, imagine yourself in a peaceful place, allow yourself to relax, think about what you want to do in the game and what you want to achieve and visualize yourself achieving them.' When I woke up next morning, I always felt relaxed and free of tension, looking forward to the game and the contest.

Your performance suffers when you are tense, because your mind is tense and you don't think clearly and sensibly. Your muscles also get tight and your body does not move freely or do what you ask it to do.

In the World Cup Final in 1992 Huma helped me with my pre-match preparation. She relaxed me and went through some visualization exercises with me the night before the game. I had a peaceful and restful sleep and when I woke up in the morning I felt refreshed, confident and eager to play the game. When I went to the ground my body felt so light that I thought I could fly. Pakistan won the game and World Cup and I won the Man of the Match Award.

When your mind is tense you think too much about the game and focus on problems – on what might or might not happen. But when your mind is calm you concentrate on what you want to happen and then let it happen or make it happen.

I don't think that a lot of today's cricketers understand the importance of these things. But if they do, they don't believe in them strongly enough.

Rudi. Some coaches and many players do not think very much of these mental exercises or mental conditioning – they are way down their list of important priorities. For instance, players who miss appointments with me often say, 'Doc, I wanted to come and see you but I had to go to the gym or to the pool with the fitness instructor.' They see mental conditioning as just an add-on that is less important than the other things.

Wasim. That is a bad mistake, I tell today's players. Since there is so much money in cricket they should try to be at the top of their game and do their best, not just for the next one or two, but the next ten or twelve years. To do that they would have to motivate themselves to work hard, keep themselves fit, and learn to develop and control their minds. I also advise them to get into the habit of reading books because reading increases knowledge and broadens their mind.

I tell them that if they don't know English they should start off by reading books in Hindi or Urdu, and that reading would increase their self-confidence and help them to deal with many of the pressures they will face on and off the field.

Rudi. What impact did your late wife have on your development and performance?

Wasim. She had an enormous impact. To give you a figure, I would say 80 per cent. I was diagnosed as a diabetic when I was twenty-nine and I became very depressed and thought that my life as a sportsman was over. She then said to me, 'Let's read about this disease together and deal with it. You will be fine.' So we read about it and learned about the importance of diet, exercise, proper rest, and about monitoring blood sugar levels during the course of a day. I had to change my lifestyle and many of my habits but after a while I was able to manage the disease successfully. In fact, I went on to get 250 wickets after I was diagnosed with the disease.

Huma was my mentor. I miss her everyday. She knew me very well. She said when anyone is not telling the truth you could spot it easily by their body language.

Rudi. Talking about body language, were you able to read the batsman's body language?

Wasim. I used to read the batsman's body language the moment he left the pavilion on his way to the wicket. Huma taught me how to do that and I was then able to detect whether the batsman was confident or worried and under pressure. I would then adjust my bowling strategy to take advantage of the batsman's mental weakness. If the batsman looked confident, I would plan carefully and be more patient. I wouldn't just attack with all guns blazing.

Coaching

Rudi. If you had a free hand in coaching fast bowling today what things would you stress?

Wasim. Coaching today has changed. For a start, many of the coaches were not good players themselves. That doesn't mean they can't be good coaches. But they don't fully understand the mental and physical challenges that fast bowlers face at the top level. Too often they overload their players with information and confuse them. Information overload is not a good thing for a young mind. The best thing they can do is to keep things clear and simple and teach the players one thing at a time and make sure that they understand fully what is being taught. This is crucial if the coach and player do not speak the same language. I believe that coaches should teach one new thing in a day and allow the bowler to practise it before they move on to something else. They should tell them simple things in their own language and make sure that the players understand what they are saying.

For overseas coaches it is important for them to learn and understand the culture of their players. Otherwise their communication and effectiveness will suffer. If I were coaching a West Indian player I would find out what West Indian culture is all about.

In Asia we have close family units that are sometimes quite large. The player has to often look after and financially support not just the immediate family but also cousins and other members of the family unit.

Our eating habits are different from those in the West. When I started playing I didn't know anything about good eating habits. I was told to work hard and eat whatever was on the plate. So I ate everything, most of which was unhealthy. Now I eat less, but healthy food. Good nutrition is beneficial to health, fitness and good performance.

Advice to Young Players

Rudi. What advice would you give to a young player who wants to get to the top of his game?

Wasim. I would stress the simple things and tell him that his fast bowling will only improve if he spends lots of time bowling fast. We used to go into the nets for three hours in a day. Now the bowlers are only allowed to bowl a few overs at each practice session. The fast bowling muscles from the top of your head to the soles of your feet are only used when you are bowling fast. They act in a coordinated and sequential manor. You don't use that combination of muscles when you are working out in the gym. Gym exercises help to strengthen isolated groups of muscles but they don't improve your bowling. You have to bowl two or three hours a day for that to happen. The more you bowl the stronger and better trained your fast bowling muscles become. That is how you get control over your bowling. Telling players about how to jump, swim and exercise is fine but these are just superficial things. There are lots of good things that add the fundamentals of bowling but they are not key factors.

Rudi. You said you used to bowl three hours a day at practice. Research has shown that in order to become an expert in your field you need to put in at least 10,000 hours of practice. That works out to three hours a day for ten years. And when you become an expert you have to continue practising to maintain your expertise. Do you think that today's bowlers are putting in enough hours at practice?

Wasim. No. I don't think so. Apart from Dayle Steyn who is a hard worker, I don't see any of today's bowlers going on to get 400 Test wickets. They will do OK in T20 and ODIs.

I didn't know about the figure of 10,000 hours but I know that if you work hard, enjoy your bowling and do the basic things well you will get wickets and enjoy success. And with that success money and other rewards will follow. But if you make money your priority, your performance will suffer, because you will have things the wrong way around. You cannot get to the top of your sport and stay there without hard work, stamina and mental toughness.

Bowling is More than Mechanics

Rudi. Today a great deal of emphasis is placed on the mechanics of bowling at the expense of other things.

Wasim. The mechanics of bowling are important but there is much more to bowling than biomechanics. There is no single ideal or correct action.

I had a very weird action. Nobody fixed it or changed it. Had they done so, I probably would not have been as successful as I was. I played for twenty years with great success in all forms of the game. Changing the mechanics of a bowler's action not only takes time, but too often it cuts down on his speed and the quality of his bowling.

Biomechanics has in the last few years become very fashionable and has created a lot of jobs for the boys.

Coaches need to spend more time teaching players how to read the batsmen and the different game situations. They must then show them how to alter their tactics and bowling strategies to deal with those situations and get the batsmen out. These things will only be possible when the coach motivates his players and teaches them how to think for themselves.

But to motivate a young player you must get to know him well and understand his family and social environment, his religion, his culture and the things that make him tick. Anybody can learn how to set up practice and coach the mechanics of bowling but successful coaches motivate their players to learn and to play well.

In Pakistan coaches and captains have to be firm with the players and not give them too many options. Otherwise they will take the easy way out.

Rudi. Is that why Imran was so successful?

Wasim. Imran was tough but he was fair and he led by example. I once saw him take five wickets in a game and at the end of the day's play he went out on the field and ran five laps.

Rudi. Dennis Lillee used to do similar things. After a hard practice with the team he would go to the nets to bowl four or five extra overs. He felt that he had to learn how to bowl well when he was tired because that is what he might be called upon to do in a game.

Wasim. Imran used to tell me that if I am bowling the last over of the day in a Test match, I should run in faster and put in extra effort.

In the last few years cricket has evolved considerably but the player's mindset has become softer. They are not as mentally tough as they should be.

Rudi. Who taught you to do all those amazing things with the ball?

Wasim. I learnt a lot from Imran. I also learnt from Waqar. We didn't like one another but on the field we helped each other and discussed how to bowl at different batsmen. For instance, we might decide to give a particular batsman an out-swinger, then an in-swinger followed by a bouncer and quite often that would get him out. Sometimes I would come around the wicket to change the angle and get reverse swing.

When a left arm bowler comes around the wicket it is very difficult for him to deliver from close to the stumps. But I learned how to do so. I used to run up to the wicket directly behind the umpire and the batsman could not see me until the very last moment before delivery. Running along that path allowed me to deliver the ball from close to the stumps. That is something that I developed myself.

Playing for Lancashire helped me a lot. There, you played everyday and you became more professional. As an overseas cricketer, you were always under pressure. But I enjoyed pressure because it brought the best out of me. For me pressure was a positive and not a negative factor. The bigger the game, the better I played.

Rudi. County cricket was the cricket academy for many overseas players. Did you set yourself goals?

Wasim. Not goals to get so many wickets in a game or in a season. I just wanted to be recognized as one of the best bowlers in the game. I wanted to be like Imran, on and off the field. He was my mentor and my role model.

Leadership and Self-belief

Rudi. How important is self-belief in performance?

Wasim. Self-belief is very important. At the top level of sport, self-belief accounts for about 80 per cent of your performance. If you work hard, prepare well and believe in yourself, you will give yourself the best chance of playing well.

Some people do not plan or prepare for their net sessions and as a result they practise without a purpose. It is not unusual for them to get out several times and each time they do so they lose a bit of confidence and self-belief.

Rudi. I tell people that at the highest level of sport performance revolves more around self-belief than it does around potential.

Wasim. That's right. If you don't believe in yourself you won't play well.

Rudi. What is self-confidence?

Wasim. Self-confidence is belief in yourself and in your ability to do whatever you have to. It comes from your preparation, your fitness, your practice and your experience. Practising with a plan and a purpose gives you confidence. Practising well in the nets gives you confidence that you can then take into the game. Even in county cricket where I played, everyday I went into the nets and practised with a purpose.

Rudi. You said that in your culture the leader has to be firm and strong and that Imran was very firm but fair. What else did he bring to the table as a captain?

Wasim. He was a great motivator. He understood his players and led from the front, by example, and he got his players to trust and follow him. He was a very hard worker. A captain can't sit on a chair and ask his team to run around for a whole day and then expect them to respect and follow him. He won't motivate them that way. Imran always led the way at training and at practice and he didn't ask us to do anything that he didn't do.

He was a great confidence builder. He would inspire us and encourage us to believe in ourselves and in our ability. He spoke to us before the Final of the 1992 World Cup and told us that if we think about and visualize the things we wanted to happen, play as a team, do the little things well and believe in ourselves, we would win the game. We all believed him and went on to win the World Cup.

Imran was also a good organizer and a strong disciplinarian because he knew that discipline would be necessary for his team's success. In a team each player and support staff is important. The team is like a necklace. If one bead falls off, others will follow.

Rudi. Apart from leading from the front and by example he was able to bring the players together to form a strong and cohesive unit.

Wasim. Yes. People were a bit scared of him as well. He was very street-smart and knew immediately when players were not genuine about what they were doing. He hated players who worked hard just to impress him. He used to make us watch cricket and would ask us questions about the game afterwards. He felt that the more you watched the game the more you learn about it.

Rudi. Did you know what his vision was for the team?

Wasim. Yes. I knew his vision, hopes, goals, moods, and the things that made him angry.

Rudi. Lloyd and Imran had a lot in common. Their styles were different but they led from the front, performed well and inspired their players to follow them.

Wasim. I believe that the captain should be the leader of the team, not the coach. The captain must be in charge. The coach's job is to stay behind the captain and support him and not say too much in the media.

Rudi. Some coaches try to dominate the relationship with the captain and take over many of his duties.

Wasim. That is wrong. Gary Kirsten is a very good coach. First of all he was a very good player. But he supported the captain and never projected himself in the media. When India won the World Cup, you hardly heard anything from him.

Rudi. What is this thing called concentration?

Wasim. Concentration is key. You have to be focused and play with a purpose if you want to be successful.

Rudi. What did you concentrate on when you were bowling?

Wasim. On getting the batsman out. When I was bowling at a batsman I would say to myself, 'How am I going to get him out?' I would bowl over the wicket and if nothing happened I would go round the wicket, and then go back over the wicket if I had to. I would also try bouncers and yorkers. I always had a plan and zeroed in on it. I knew that if I stuck to my plan I would always get a wicket.

The Best Batsmen and Bowlers

Rudi. You bowled to some of the best players in the world. Who are the greatest batsmen you have seen or played against?

Wasim. Viv Richards was the best. Then there were Brian Lara and Desmond Haynes from the West Indies and Sunil Gavaskar from India. From this era it would be Adam Gilchrist.

Rudi. Who were the great fast bowlers that you saw?

Wasim. Obviously Waqar Younis was one of them, but as far as I am concerned Malcolm Marshall was the greatest fast bowler ever. He used to get wickets everywhere including places like

Pakistan and India. Many of the other fast bowlers never did that well in the subcontinent. I rate a fast bowler highly when he gets wickets on every surface, particularly those in Pakistan and India, and for me that is why Malcolm Marshall was the best ever. He had everything.

JACQUES KALLIS

Rudi. Some experts say that performance in cricket is built on four pillars – fitness, technique, strategy and mental skills. How important is the mind in performance?

Jacques. It is right at the top. I think it is the most important part of the game. Everyone goes through bad patches where they lose form and confidence and if their mind is strong and they believe in themselves they soon get out of those patches. The four things you mentioned are all connected and each one plays an important role in performance. If you are fit, trust and believe in your technique and work hard at it, your confidence and other mental skills will improve.

Rudi. You just mentioned self-belief. How important is it?

Jacques. If you don't believe in yourself and trust your game you won't get the best out of yourself. When you are batting there are certain times when doubts creep into your mind. You must then be able to clear your mind in the fifteen seconds or so between balls or between overs. A calm and clear mind helps you to see the ball the moment it leaves the bowler's hand. If your mind is focused on your technique when the bowler is running in or is about to deliver the ball you will get into trouble. You bat best when your mind is clear, when you see the ball early and when you allow your instincts to take over. Your thoughts are usually negative and muddled when your mind is tense and you might then start to premeditate about the shot you are going to play. In One Day and Twenty 20 cricket you do premeditate but it should be calculated premeditation. You might say to yourself, 'If the ball pitches here I will hit it there but if it pitches somewhere else I will have the option of hitting it to another part of the field.' If you are going to premeditate you should always have options.

Rudi. In the old days we were told that the first foot movement in batting against fast bowlers should be back and across, and against spinners a little step forward. You bat like the old-time players.

Jacques. Yes. To fast bowlers I go back and across after a slight forward press. I don't think this technique has changed that much over the years. I am not a huge believer in foot movements. I think that weight transfer and balance are far more important. You can have good foot movements and still not hit the ball well because of poor weight transfer. And you can get into a bad position with poor foot movements but still hit the ball well if your weight transfer is good. Your foot movements take you to the line of the ball but your weight transfer takes you to the ball.

Graeme Pollock the great South African batsman had a wide stance and hardly moved his feet but when he rocked forward and back, his weight transfer and balance were so good that he was able to play just about every shot in the book.

You do need a bit of foot movement to transfer your weight but more emphasis should be placed on the actual transfer of weight from one foot to the other.

Rudi. That's interesting. You can step forward towards the ball and yet leave most of your weight on the back foot. In golf, one of the keys to a good swing is the proper transfer of weight from one foot to the other during the backswing and the downswing.

Going back and across, does it help you to play the short ball better?

Jacques. I think it gives me a bit more time to play the ball and it lines me up with the stumps. When I am playing in South Africa and Australia where the wickets are fast and bouncy, going back and across allows me to get into line and cover my off stump. On the slower and flatter pitches I probably won't go across as much.

Taking a small step forward to the spinner puts me in a good position. It allows me to rock back on to the back foot to hit the ball if it is short and to transfer most of my weight to the front foot if the ball is full or on a good length. It also helps me to stay low to deal with the spin and to better assess the bounce of the ball.

Rudi. Looking back at your own development what advice would you give to a young player who wants to get to the top of his sport?

Jacques. In Twenty 20 cricket today I see a lot of young players trying to hit each ball out of the park but that is not a good base on which to build your game. I would tell them to learn to get into good and strong positions when they are batting and to develop a sound defence because most of the attacking strokes are an extension of the defensive. I would also tell him that they must be keen on the game, be hungry for success and work and practise hard to develop his physical and mental skills.

Rudi. There are a lot of young players who don't appreciate the importance of the basic skills and get bored when they have to practise them in the nets or in the game. What are your feelings about the basics?

Jacques. Mastering the basics is extremely important. It is a key to success. For example, if you don't have a good defensive technique you will struggle to recover when you are not in form. When you are in form your instincts take over and you do the basic things well. You must put in the hours learning how to improve the basic skills and how to execute them better during the game.

Rudi. If you had a free hand in coaching today what would you stress to the players?

Jacques. In batting, I would tell them to:

- Work and practise hard;
- Clear their minds and watch the ball out of the bowler's hand;
- Learn how to turn on and turn off their concentration;
- Learn how to transfer their weight efficiently from one foot to the other and how to get into good strong positions;
- Know their own game;

- Identify their strengths and weaknesses – capitalize on their strengths and improve their weaknesses;
- Learn how to manipulate and work the ball;
- Play their own style of game;
- Value their wicket; and
- Learn to deal with different game situations.

Rudi. What would you change?

Jacques. In some ways, coaching today is like a dictatorship. By that I mean that players are too dependent on their coaches and that coaches don't encourage them to stand on their own feet, back their own judgement and make up their own minds. The player needs to be more self-reliant, learn all he can about his game, and take responsibility for improving and managing it.

When you are batting in the middle, the coach can't help you – you are on your own – and if you can't think for yourself, make proper decisions and deal with the different situations you are going to face, you won't do well. Today when something goes wrong, one of the first things the player does is to go to the coach to get his opinion about what is wrong and what he needs to do to correct his fault, instead of trying to figure it out for himself. The coach can be helpful in these cases but the player must take responsibility for finding the solutions to his own problems. Of course he will make mistakes and have failures but that is a normal part of the game and he will learn more from failure than from success.

Rudi: You and Sir Garfield Sobers are the two best all-rounders in the history of the game. Your statistics are indeed very similar. But when people talk about the best batsmen of this era, they mention Lara, Tendulkar and Ponting and when your name is mentioned they add you to the list almost as an afterthought. And yet your batting average in Tests is better than that of the other three players. Why does this happen?

Jacques. The way I play my cricket is probably the reason for that. I am not a flamboyant player. I always stay below the radar and just try to play to the best of my ability, enjoying the game and the things that I do during the game. I quietly get on with the job and try to do it well. I never play the game to get recognition or publicity. I just go out there to enjoy the challenge of competing against the best players. That's my approach to the game and it is probably the reason why I am not mentioned with the other three players.

Rudi: I think you are one of the best examples of the quiet achiever that I have seen. Do you set goals?

Jacques. My goal is always to play the situations in the game as well as I can. If the situation requires me to get a hundred runs or thirty runs in fifteen balls that would be my goal. My goals are always related to the situations I face. I am not particularly interested in statistics or in setting goals to reach those statistics. For me it was always about recognizing the situation and devising a strategy to handle it.

Rudi. Sobers once said that the greatest lesson he can give to young players is to teach them how to recognize and deal with the many different situations they are likely to face in the game. He said that the good players do this much better than the other ones.

Do you visualize yourself batting when you are preparing for the game?

Jacques. Yes, I do. When I am preparing for the game I would visualize myself batting against every bowler playing the way I want to play. I do it for a few minutes and then I switch off completely and relax. When I go out to bat, my mind is clear and primed for action and I just let things happen.

I am not always the greatest fan of net practice and sometimes I use visualization techniques as an alternative. The great thing about visualization is that I don't play any bad shots like I do in the nets.

Rudi. Who are the best bowlers you have seen?

Jacques. Wasim Akram is the best fast bowler. He could do all sorts of things with the old as well as the new ball and was always attacking the batsman. And he had a very good mind. Shane Warne is the best spinner.

Rudi. You would not have seen much of Malcolm Marshall but Wasim rated him as the best ever because unlike the other bowlers he got wickets on every surface, including those in the subcontinent. I suppose you can use that same criterion to rate your batsmen.

Jacques. I saw Malcolm near the end of his career and even then I could see why he was rated so highly.

Rudi. Who is your best batsman?

Jacques. Brian Lara. He was in a different league. I have seen a lot of good players from the subcontinent but they spend 80 per cent of their time batting on wickets in the subcontinent.

Rudi. You should have won the World Cup in England in 1999 but lost a close game with Australia in the semifinal. Did the pressure get to you there?

Jacques. I believe we put too much pressure on ourselves from the beginning and made some silly mistakes during the game. I believe that there were some individuals in the team who wanted to be the man of the day during the match, and when that happens the individual tries to play too aggressively or too conservatively. In these situations, instead of trusting and helping the man next to you and working together to play as a team, some of the players go after their personal goals. In that game, I don't think we had the balance between individual and team goals right. In the last few years we have been getting closer to that balance and hopefully by the next World Cup we will get it right.

V.V.S. LAXMAN

Rudi. We are told that performance is built on four interconnected pillars: fitness, technique, strategy and mental skills. And yet, players and coaches alike pay very little attention to the mental component. How important is the mind in performance?

Laxman. I think the mind is the most important factor because the thoughts in your mind control your attitude, movements and body language. Mental conditioners are very important in performance, especially for new players, but there are so few good ones around. Players with experience usually develop their mental skills over the years. They know and understand their game and know how to play in each and every situation. The newcomers often do not know these things and need to have an experienced mental conditioner to help them improve their thinking and concentration, and their ability to cope with different game situations.

Rudi. Sir Garfield Sobers often said that one of the best lessons in sport is to teach players how to deal with different situations – how to think, concentrate and approach them.

Laxman. He is absolutely correct. I believe that once your thought processes are positive you give yourself the best chance of playing to your potential. It all comes from the mind and self-belief. Over the years I realized that the stronger you are in the mind the better you will play. I also realized that in most instances your mind is your best friend or your worst enemy. The contest is usually a battle between yourself and your mind, not yourself and the bowler.

You need to pay close attention to the thoughts in your mind. The more positive thoughts you have about yourself and your game the better you will play and feel about yourself.

Rudi. Many coaches and players pay lip service to the mental skills. Why do they spend less than 10 per cent of their time developing them?

Laxman. You know, I improved dramatically as a player when I started to use visualization and mental rehearsal techniques. But how many players actually use these techniques to practise their skills and prepare for the game? I feel that every young player should learn how to develop and use these techniques because the rewards can be great. I believe they should make them an important part of their practice and preparation routine.

Rudi. Regarding your comments about improvement through

visualization, studies have shown that when players combine physical and mental practice they improve much more than they do with just physical practice.

Laxman. Young players must learn how to think, concentrate, build confidence, cope with pressure, set goals, motivate themselves and deal with success and failure.

Rudi. Exactly!

Laxman. They must also understand that successful people face many barriers and obstacles and have several failures and setbacks along the way.

I would encourage young sportsmen to read books about people who have excelled in their lives and professions, like Nelson Mandela and Mahatma Gandhi. They would then see that it was not a cakewalk for them. Every one of these people had to overcome several problems and crises along the way. Learning how they dealt with their failures and setbacks and how they beat the odds are lessons that the players should take from these books.

Rudi. I agree with you 100 per cent but a lot of the players don't like reading. Videos of these people's lives might be more appealing to the players.

Many players with lots of talent never play to their potential. Under the same circumstances less talented players do much better and get the best out of themselves. Why does this happen?

Laxman. If you get anything easily you tend to take it for granted and think that it will just happen for you. When you are very talented and can play some good shots you tend to become overconfident and feel that you already have the skills to do well in your matches. The less talented player on the other hand is usually less confident and works harder to improve his game. He is usually more patient and persistent.

The less talented player uses his mind better, works harder at his game, and creates better game plans. I don't want to generalize about this but I think he is usually stronger in the mind and more committed.

The best combination though would be a talented and well-motivated player who works hard, knows his game and knows himself. Once you know yourself and understand your game it becomes easier to transform your talent into performance.

Rudi. An Australian football coach with whom I worked in Australia once told his players, 'Nobody has got a right to be proud of natural ability. You did nothing to earn it. You got it from your father and mother. It is only what you do with the four-letter word, work, that is a legitimate cause for pride.'

Laxman. I totally agree with that. I think everyone is naturally talented, some more so than others. The important thing is to recognize your talent and decide how you are going to improve it. Improvement is a continuous process and until you play your last game in professional sport, you should always be trying to improve all aspects of your game, not just your skill and preparation but also your mind and temperament. You should always think about becoming a better player. Once you do that the results will usually follow.

Over the years my preparation has improved. If you prepare well for each and every match, when you are in the middle, your mind will be relaxed, not restless, and it will just react to the ball. In international cricket you often have to face very quick bowlers and when you are batting you must be able to react quickly and effectively. Having a calm and composed mind helps you to see the ball early and move into position easily.

Here is a lesson that my father taught me about the importance of good preparation. If you are preparing for an examination and you only study part of the book from which the examination is to be set, you would be worried about the examination and hope that the questions come from the part of the book that you have studied. So you will go into the examination room nervous and fearful. If the questions come from the part you have studied, you will feel good and count your lucky stars, but if they come from the other part of the book you would be in serious trouble.

But if you study the whole book and prepare well, you will go into the examination room with a healthy level of confidence and with a clear, calm and composed mind ready to answer any question that is thrown at you and the answers will just flow.

The Basics

Rudi. Some of today's players play down the importance of the basics and often say that they find them boring when they have to practise them regularly. How important do you think the basics are?

Laxman. The basics are the foundation and strength of your game. A building with a weak foundation could collapse any time even if it has the best marble flooring and other superb interiors. Your basic techniques are like that foundation, so you should make sure that they are right and that you stick to them. Then you can become creative with your game and develop new shots because the way the game is going today you have to be innovative and inventive. Otherwise, the bowlers will work you out. The information that they get from today's technology and the technical analyses and reviews that are available to them make it easier for them to do so. As a batsman, it is very important to be always one step ahead of the bowlers. And as a bowler you should be one step ahead of the batsmen.

If the basics of your game are weak it will be difficult to learn new shots. But worse than that, your performance will fall apart under pressure.

Motivation

Rudi. What motivated you when you were young?

Laxman. When I was young I wanted to be a doctor. Both of my parents are doctors and my father was my role model. Like any young kid in India I played cricket but I never thought that I would play it as a professional. I got a lot of opportunities after I turned sixteen and I capitalized on them.

Until I played for the Under-19 team against an Australian youth team in 1994, I never thought that I would actually get into the big league and be recognized for my talent and potential. The series against Australia was a turning point for me. My major motivation was to represent my country. In India where cricket is more like a religion than a sport, playing for your country is a dream that very few cricketers ever achieve.

Once I got my India cap I felt I could serve my country by doing well on the field. I learned about the importance of service to country from my father who throughout his career dedicated himself totally to the service of medicine. And he encouraged me to do the same thing with my cricket.

Rudi. Coaches pay more attention to ability and skills of players than they do to the players' motivational profiles, and yet motivation is considered to be a better predictor of future performance than ability. How important is motivation?

Laxman. Motivation is very important in today's game because of our packed schedules. It maintains the player's drive and purpose. There are two types of motivation, internal motivation and external motivation, of which internal motivation is the more important. The inner drive to achieve the best you can, or to play to your potential, is critical in performance. Coaches and support staff should constantly create exercises and challenges for the players in the team. Setting challenging goals can be a source of great inspiration and motivation. Older players should guide and motivate the younger ones by giving them support and helping them to set meaningful and realistic goals.

I get a lot of motivation from playing in tough situations. That is when I get the best out of myself and take my game to a higher level.

For me internal motivation is extremely important. Coaches can help you to set goals and devise game plans but in the end it will be your responsibility to go for those goals and implement those game plans. You are the one who will have to go out on the field and perform. When you are batting you are really on your own. You might get some support from the other batsman but you are the one that will have to face up to the bowler and take full responsibility for your performance. As long as you are clear about your goal and are committed to it, motivation will follow.

Rudi. Many players say that a lot of their motivation comes from their love and passion for the game. But after having success over a long period it is only natural to lose some of your motivation. How important are love and passion for the game?

Laxman. Yes. It is only natural for any player who has to perform constantly under pressure to lose his edge, or some of his drive and enjoyment. You should always remember why you started playing the game as a young person and when you dreamt of one day playing for your country. Then recall what it was like when you got that opportunity and started to live your dream. Those memories often restore some of your passion and enjoyment, especially when you realize how lucky you are to be playing this wonderful game for your country.

I feel that cricket is one of life's greatest teachers. Everyday, it conditions you to deal with success and failure. One day you might get 100 runs and the next day you might be dismissed for a duck and you have to deal with that emotionally. Cricket helps you to handle the challenging situations in your life in a more mature fashion.

Rudi. Talking about maturity, here you are thirty-six years of age, and you are as passionate and enthusiastic about the game as you have ever been and you are playing as well as ever. You are like red wine, getting better with age. Why are you still so passionate about the game?

Laxman. As I mentioned before we started the interview, the turning point was 2007 when I played county cricket for Lancashire. Since then my performance has gone to the next level because I am enjoying just about every aspect of the game.

The relaxed environment in the Indian team is also inspiring me. In the last four years, our team environment has been very good. Now, each player enjoys the success of the other players and we help and support each other in times of stress and adversity. This environment has been great for me now that I am getting near the end of my career. The bigger picture of doing well for the team and taking the team to a higher level is now much clearer in my mind and I am very proud to be part of this Indian team that is currently one of the best if not the best Test team in the world.

I am also very proud of the way we have been playing all over the world. When I started my career we played poorly overseas. That has changed and we are now expected to win when we go on overseas tours.

So the team environment and my zeal to continue performing and winning matches for my country are what drive me to keep going and get the best out of myself.

Teamwork

Laxman. Hunger to do well and pride in performance are very important. We are lucky to have a team of players who take a lot of pride in their performance. Once a player takes pride in his performance he will always put up his hand and perform no matter how difficult the situation is. In the last four years that is what we have been experiencing in our team and I believe that is also the reason why we are able to bounce back and win in tough situations.

Once you have pride in your performance, hunger automatically comes and once you have hunger you prepare well for each and every match, and you make sure that you play to your potential. One of the most important things is to know that you can win a match almost single handedly. So you do not depend on just one or two individuals to win the match. You know that in the squad you have fourteen or fifteen potential match winners. During the last four years each player has contributed significantly to the winning of Test matches. So each player knows what he is capable of and respects the ability of other team members. That is vital in team dynamics.

Having the respect of your colleagues is very important. Wishing and praying for them to be successful is also very important. When players care about each other they play like a close family and become a cohesive unit. We are a happy team with many match winners who respect and believe in each other.

The Indian team prepares itself well for every match and the atmosphere in the dressing room is calm and relaxed. If the coach or team members are panicking and the atmosphere in the dressing room is tense you will most likely take that tension with you when you go out to bat. Since 2007 the atmosphere in the Indian dressing rooms has been calm, positive and vibrant.

Rudi. What was the common goal for the team?

Laxman. The common goal was to become the number one Test playing nation. That was the big picture we were always striving to achieve. But we also had other goals – goals for every Test series, every Test match and every session during a Test match. There is a board in our dressing room on which we write down sessions one, two and three for every day of the five-day Test match. At the end of each session we assess our performance to see if we won the session or lost it. That feedback influences our motivation and performance in the very next session. The goal is to win each session.

Rudi. I often tell players that performance is like a jigsaw puzzle. If you have all the pieces to the puzzle and don't have a picture on the box it becomes difficult to put those pieces together. But if you have all the pieces and a picture on the box, the task of identifying the pieces and putting them together correctly becomes easier. The picture on the box is like the common goal, the pieces are like small goals and putting the pieces together is like the process.

Captaincy

Rudi. You never captained India? How important is captaincy?

Laxman. No, but I captained just about every other team that I played in. Captaincy is very important. I believe that the leader or the captain should be a visionary. Every captain is different and each one will probably have a different vision for his team.

The captain should know where he wants to take his team. He should then communicate that to the team simply and clearly to show team members what his major goal is and where he wants to take them. The team will then know that they will be going in a particular direction and that everyone will have to go down that route whether they like it or not. All team members will then be moving in the same direction. That is very important.

When the captain communicates his vision and major goal he should ensure that each player actually sees his vision and understands his goals because communicating the goal is one thing but getting the players to understand it is another thing. He should explain why his vision and goals are so important and show the players how they will benefit personally from achieving them.

Having done those things he should back each and every player and express his faith and confidence in them. Instilling confidence is very important because some young players might not know how good they really are and might have to be told so. Any lingering self-doubts will then be reduced or removed.

A good captain tries to lead by example. He has to show his zeal and passion to the team and keep himself motivated. He also has to spend a good deal of his time encouraging and motivating team members.

RAHUL DRAVID

Rudi. How important is the mind in performance?

Rahul. The mind is critically important. So are fitness, technique and strategy. They are all interconnected.

Most top athletes have a reasonable level of fitness, good technique and sound strategies, but in competition their performance is controlled mainly by the mind – their ability to get into the right frame of mind consistently and regularly, day in and day out. Their state of mind determines how well they combine and use their fitness, technical skills and strategies to produce the best performance.

When we look at talent in cricket we often see it as just the ability to hit a ball or bowl a ball. But, talent can only take you so far. Lots of other factors contribute to performance. Most of these so-called talented players who are deficient in the mental side of the game hardly ever do well or make it to the top. They don't understand how the mind works and don't work hard enough to get to know and understand themselves. When they move up to higher levels of sport and encounter tougher competition and greater pressures they get found out and perform poorly.

Basic Skills

Rudi. Today, some players downplay the importance of the basics and complain of boredom and a lack of interest when they have to practise them regularly. How important are the basic skills?

Rahul. The basics are extremely important and are the foundation on which your game is built. That foundation gives you the confidence to be creative in your stroke play and in your approach.

When you look at the players who do well in Twenty 20 cricket, apart from the odd exception, they are usually good Test players who have the base that allows them to be innovative and creative.

Repeatedly practising and honing your basic skills until they become part of who you are and what you are is a key to good performance and success. Even if you find them boring at practice, mentally they give you a certain amount of self-confidence that you can then take into the game. When you know that your foundation is strong you have the confidence to say, 'I have good basic skills, I've done this before and I can still do it.'

If certain parts of your game are not as good as they ought to be and you keep working at the basics, those deficiencies would eventually be corrected. If you ignore the basics you will put your performance at risk.

Advice to Young Players

Rudi. What advice would you give to a young player who is trying to develop his potential to get to the top of his game?

Rahul. I would tell him that learning and the quest for knowledge should be a top priority. I would encourage him to enjoy the process or the journey that will take him to his goal and tell him not to worry about the score or result or get caught up on where he wants to be. If he enjoys the process and the day-to-day activities of batting, bowling and fielding he would find the game more rewarding, learn faster and perform better.

In the long run he will realize that he will get to his goals more quickly and easily if he keeps his mind in the present and in the focus than if he gets too stressed about what might happen, where he wants to be in the future, and how far he is from where he is supposed to be.

Goals are very important. It is good to set goals and targets but it is also important to break them down into smaller goals. These sub-goals are like small steps along the way or places that you must pass through to get to your destination. That journey can be a process of self-discovery. If he enjoys the process and executes the basics well he will give himself the best chance of doing well.

I would also tell him that cricket is a great game that gives young international cricketers the opportunity to travel to all parts of the world and meet many interesting people.

If he enjoys all these things and doesn't worry about the runs on the board, the wickets he takes or the result of the game he will get close to fulfilling his potential.

These are things I wish I had paid more attention to when I was younger. So I would tell the young player to enjoy learning about the game and about himself, love and enjoy the process, and master the basics of his game.

Rudi. Some players are so preoccupied with the result that they forget the journey and place themselves under a lot of unnecessary stress.

Rahul. That is true. These players must learn to get pleasure from their practice sessions, even when there is no one watching. They must listen to the sound of bat on ball and enjoy the small improvements and small successes that they have in those practice sessions.

It is critical to enjoy the journey and take pleasure in the process of discovering who you are and what you are as a person and cricketer.

MOTIVATION

Rudi. What motivated you when you were young?

Rahul. I just loved the game. My oldest memories are about handling the ball and holding the cricket bat and asking my dad to throw balls to me. I can't explain why I did that or why I enjoyed it so much.

My motivation to play the game was my love of the game, the love of being outdoors and having fun.

Rudi. You are now in the September of your career and you are playing as well as you have ever played. You are like red wine. You get better as you age.

Rahul. I am in the November of my career, not September. Rudi, I still love the game. I still love the contest. I still love the journey and this process of self-discovery.

When I started playing for India, the team was not a major force in Test cricket. When we travelled abroad no one gave us much of a chance. But we have now reached a stage where we are expected to win. In the past, if we won one Test match abroad it was regarded as a success but now if we don't go home with a series win it is considered as a failure.

I have really been privileged to be part of that exciting journey with today's players and I am still enjoying it. I hope that India can continue to maintain the top position in Test cricket.

Being part of this successful team gives me an opportunity not only to play with young players but also to pass on some of my ideas and knowledge to speed up their development and make things easier for them. I don't know how much longer I have in cricket but for now I will just try to enjoy the game and enjoy playing in the team.

Rudi. What kind of relationship do the older players have with the young players in the team?

Rahul. We have a pretty good relationship with them. They are a highly motivated group. I hope we can carry their legacy forward. Some of the young players are a little shy. I was like that when I joined the team. I always tell them that they should seek out and listen to advice. In some cases, 99 per cent of the advice might be useless but the other 1 per cent might be important and might make a big difference to their game.

There are many exciting young batsmen coming through our cricket. They have talent, desire and hunger and have done well in Twenty 20 and One Day cricket but they will face a tough and hard road in Test cricket. It will be a challenging and tough journey for them and they won't get away with lots of things that they do in Twenty 20 and One Day cricket.

At 22–23 years of age, when people give you advice you often say, 'What on earth are they talking about?' But years later you might recognize the value of that advice. It takes time for things to register. It takes time to learn. Sometimes you are not ready to learn or to see what you are being shown. Some lessons must be learned from experience. You often need to go through your own discovery process. You need to do things for yourself and learn from your mistakes. That's life.

On Tendulkar

Rudi. What is it like playing with Tendulkar?

Rahul. For me Tendulkar is the best of all time. He is the greatest batsman I have ever seen. It is a great privilege to play with him. I've learned so much from him, particularly the way he conducts himself on the field and the way he plays different types of bowling. We all look up to him. He is our role model.

Sachin and I are the same age but when I started playing he was already in the team for seven years. Since he was my own age, I thought if he can do it, I too should be able to do it.

Sachin's love and enthusiasm for cricket is evident and the meticulous way in which he prepares for the game is truly amazing. That's what I mean when I talk about enjoying the process and loving the game. Sachin embodies all that.

The lofty standards that he demands of himself and the high expectations and enormous pressures that are placed on him by over a billion people seem to motivate him to play better and live up to those expectations. As you get older, it becomes more difficult to do those things and yet he seems to have found a way to accomplish them. I think that he is able to do so because of his love and respect for the game and his love of batting and just playing the game.

M.S. DHONI

Rudi. How important is the mind in performance.

Dhoni. It is very important. In cricket there are many players with talent and good technique who never get the success they deserve. Some players with good technical skills sometimes do well for a while but then fail to carry on or perform consistently. I believe the missing ingredient is mental control. The mind plays a very big part in performance.

Cricket has changed over the years and is now a very demanding game. Mental and physical preparation are critical today. For instance, you can't just turn up to training and decide not to dive at the ball during the practice session. At training you must consistently practise everything that you do in a match. You must do them every day and at every session to improve and maintain your skills. The mind then helps you to transfer the things you do at practice to the game.

The Four Pillars of Performance

Rudi. Players often say that at the top level of sport there isn't much difference between the teams in fitness and talent and that the mind is the thing that separates the teams.

Dhoni. At that level, the mind is the determining factor, but you still have to be fit and have good technique. If you rate fitness on a scale of one to ten you might feel you should get your level to seven or eight to perform well. You don't have to be at ten. But if you make circles around the pillars of fitness, technique, strategy and mental skills, the circles would overlap each other, so you have to be good at all of them.

When you prepare yourself for a game you can't just prepare your body, you must also prepare the mind to get 100 per cent out of yourself in the game. Both physical and the mental components are vital but the mind is the more important.

Rudi. What motivated you when you were a young player to make the exciting and successful journey that has taken you to the pinnacle of your game and profession?

Dhoni. I love sports, not just cricket. During my teenage years I used to play several different sports and although I was not good at all of them I was nevertheless very competitive. When I played I wanted to win and I was very determined to win. But I knew that if I was just playing a game and if I lost, it wasn't the end of the world or the end of my life.

I constantly tried to give 100 per cent to whatever I was doing. I also realized that my opponents might be more talented and better prepared than I was, so I never left any stone unturned if I thought it would help me to win. That will to win was strengthened by my love and passion for sports.

I love the challenge and the pressure. They have always pushed me to do well. People say a lot of negative things about pressure. Pressure to me is just added responsibility. That is how I look at it. It's not pressure when God gives you an opportunity to be a hero for your team and country.

Sometimes you get disappointed after a bad or a tough game. It is natural to feel let down after a bad performance but you should always learn something from your experience and your failure. You should identify the positives of your game and the lessons you learned and then use them to improve your planning, preparation and performance in the next game. You should also watch the other players to see the things they do well and spot the mistakes they make and the things that restrict them.

Every player should regard the journey to success as an exciting and challenging learning experience. Even for the very talented players performance is a learning process that takes time, effort and persistence. If you are motivated to learn you will learn something new every day.

Advice to Young Players

Rudi. What advice would you give to a young player who wants to improve his game?

Dhoni. First and foremost, I would tell him that he must love and enjoy his sport. If he does not enjoy it he would not learn to play the game as quickly or as well as he should.

Second, I would tell him to keep things simple. The more he complicates the process the harder it will be for him to improve his game. For example, when he tells himself to watch the ball and play it on its merits, he might have other thoughts like scoring runs or not getting out in his mind. Those thoughts can break his concentration and prevent him from watching the ball. If he knows that the bowler can bowl an out-swinger, an in-swinger and a good bouncer as well, he has three other things to think about. But the more he thinks about what the bowler might do the more complex and difficult batting becomes.

Third, I would tell him to capitalize on his strengths, improve his weaknesses and recognize his limitations.

A lot of people talk about the problems players face when they have to play in conditions that are foreign to them. For instance, when Indian batsmen who are brought up on slow flat wickets have to play on the fast and bouncy wickets in Australia and South Africa.

When I go to Australia or South Africa I try to be positive and see the visit as a challenge and an opportunity to explore, learn and improve my game. I try not to be negative or worry about the pace and bounce of the wickets or the things that could possibly go wrong.

Learning and improvement take time. When you leave nursery school you don't expect to go straight into a graduate school. In the following years you slowly improve as a student and when you reach a certain standard you graduate and afterwards go on to higher levels. The same thing happens in sport.

The player should therefore be patient and persistent and he should keep things simple and enjoy his sport. Not only should he enjoy his own performance on the field but he should also get pleasure from sharing his experiences with other players and from creating an atmosphere that helps the guy sitting next to him in the dressing room to perform better.

This is one area where the Indian team is very blessed. The senior players in our team have helped the younger players to learn, develop and perform better. Your individual performance is important but how much better you help your teammate to play better is equally important.

The Basic Skills and Motivation

Rudi. How important are the basic skills?

Dhoni. God gives natural gifts to all of us. We need to realize that and work to strengthen them and to improve in those areas where our weaknesses lie.

Mastering the basics is a key to good performance. When a skyscraper is being built a lot of time and money are spent on constructing the foundation under the ground. In sport, investment in the foundation is also extremely important. The basics are the foundation on which performance is built. If that foundation is weak, performance will fall apart under pressure and intense competition. A strong foundation improves confidence, concentration and performance.

Rudi. What motivates today's cricketers?

Dhoni. Playing for your country should be your main motivating force. But today you need to have a good income and livelihood. Only a few players have a professional education or academic qualifications. A good cricketer has seven to ten years to earn the money that will sustain him for life after cricket. So he must balance his love for the country with a good income and livelihood. Of course, love and passion for the game and the need for recognition are other powerful motivators. But, in today's competitive and fast-changing world we cannot ignore the importance of money in the life of a cricketer.

SIR GARFIELD SOBERS

Rudi. How important is the mind in performance?

Sir Garfield. The proper use of the mind is the one thing that separates champions from the merely good players. To handle the situations that you face during a game, you must think clearly and sensibly. You will then be able to apply your skills in the best possible way to overcome the difficulties and challenges you face. You won't get over these problems if you don't think properly. I have come across lots of players who have had more natural talent than some of the great players, but they never made it because they couldn't think clearly and sensibly. They didn't use their common sense. No matter how good a player you are, you won't reach the top unless you develop your mind. The top players know how to think, how to concentrate and what to do in tough situations.

Rudi. The way you think is important, is it?

Sir Garfield. Yes. Along with concentration it is the key to your game.

Having said that I must say that I don't think you can separate your thinking and concentration. If you think sensibly and positively, you will concentrate well, but if you think negatively, you won't.

I have always approached the game with a positive attitude and positive thoughts. The way you approach situations in the game is critical. You must assess the situation quickly and calmly, and choose the approach that you think is most appropriate to deal with it.

If your team is in a diabolical situation and you are faced with the job of changing it, you must decide what the most important demands and priorities are, what you want to do, how you are going to do it and then do it. You must devise some sort of plan and know what to concentrate on to carry it out. If you have practised dealing with difficult situations, the answers will come to you quickly, almost automatically at times.

I feel that one of the most important lessons you can teach anyone is how to approach and handle the many situations he is likely to face. He will then know what to do and how to do it when he encounters them.

You may think that the situation is too desperate to play defensively, so you choose the aggressive approach and attack the bowling. But you have to know how, when and where to attack. You don't throw the bat indiscriminately at everything. You play the percentages. A lot of people don't understand this.

At another time a similar situation may require a defensive approach. In some cases, your main concern is just to survive. If you do, and you get over the first hurdle, you can then go on to build your innings and take control of the situation.

If I had a free hand in coaching, I would first spend most of my time teaching the basics of the game but I would then spend an equal amount of time teaching players how to identify and cope with the many different situations they are likely to face during the game.

Rudi. Did you get negative thoughts when you were playing?

Sir Garfield. Not very often. If they came they didn't stay with me for very long because my strength was positive thinking. Negative thoughts stack the odds against you, make your job harder and defeat you before you start. If you approach the game with a sensible and positive attitude, the odds will immediately be placed in your favour, at least 70 per cent your way. They are great odds.

Rudi. Did you ever get very nervous during the game?

Sir Garfield. Tense, not nervous. People who get nervous become too keyed up and they don't think clearly. Sometimes they become too stiff and can't get into position to play their shots. They might even freeze up. I think that you must be a little tense. If you are too relaxed it is just as bad as being nervous, because you become careless and sloppy and make easy mistakes. The tension tells you that you are ready for action and for me it was a feeling of wanting to do well. When I am a bit tense I prepare myself by saying or thinking, 'I have got to do well today. I will apply my skills well. I will concentrate and get the team going.'

Motivation

Rudi. When you were young, what was your main motivating force?

Sir Garfield. I wanted to play cricket for the West Indies. I achieved that at a very young age, and my aim was then to retain my place. I thought the best way to do this was to play well for the team. I wanted to help the team in every department and I tried to develop every aspect of my skills. I practised very hard and I tried to improve my batting, my fielding and my bowling. After a while everything fell into place. The bowling department was quite exciting because I was able to bowl fast, medium pace and many varieties of slow bowling. Having a lot of strings to my bow allowed me to make major contributions to the team effort. These gave me tremendous enjoyment and satisfaction.

I was never particularly interested in my individual performances. My main concern was how my performance would help the team and my teammates. Personal achievements never turned me on, but my contribution to team achievements did. The team came first. Had I been a selfish player, my Test record would have been much more impressive.

Rudi. So one of your most powerful motivating factors was the team?

Sir Garfield. Yes. There are many ways of motivating yourself and they vary from one person to the other. There are two things that motivated me. The first was the team and wanting to do well for it. The second was my social activities, particularly going out at nights to enjoy myself. Most people laugh when I tell them that. But it is true.

Having to stay in my hotel room used to drive me crazy, so I had to get away. I liked to live and I enjoyed dancing, drinking and having a good time. There was more to life than cricket. But in order to enjoy my nocturnal activities I had to perform well during the game. My late nights stimulated me to play better.

If you have a late night and play poorly you expose yourself to severe criticism the next day. People around you are able to say, 'What do you expect? He was out until three o'clock this morning drinking and dancing. How can he play well? He is not serious about his game; otherwise he wouldn't do these crazy things.' I had to make sure that no one had an opportunity to criticize me in this manner, so there was pressure on me to play well, because I wanted to go out again on the following night. When you are playing well, your social activities go unnoticed, but as soon as you start to fail, people around you begin to pick on you.

Every player is different. Some players like to spend their evenings in their room watching television, some enjoy a quiet dinner, and others like to spend their time at the bar. I enjoyed going out at nights to dance and have a good time. Getting away from the cricketing environment relieved me of a lot of pressure and helped me to relax. I could then go out on the field well motivated on the following day with a relaxed body and a fresh and alert mind. You have got to work out what is best for you.

Rudi. How did you motivate yourself after you had achieved everything in the game?

Sir Garfield. I couldn't. That is the reason I gave it up. I couldn't do it because I was mentally fatigued and mentally stale. If you lose your mental alertness, you are finished. You know what you have to do and how to do it, but you just can't do it.

───────

GREG CHAPPELL

Rudi. How important is the mind in performance?

Greg. It is extremely important. You can't perform well unless you are able to control your mind. If you are mentally tired, as I have been at certain periods during the last two years, you won't play well. Mental tiredness creates physical tiredness.

When I was young, my father stressed the importance of the mind to me. He planted the seeds that later grew. Some of his advice sank in then, but the rest only did later on when I started to make my mark in cricket. Something would happen and I would say, 'Gosh, Dad told me about that years ago.' Early in my career he emphasized the value of positive thinking and a positive approach.

In 1971, I played a game for Australia against the Rest of the World team and performed badly. After the game I sat down and had a good look at my game and made a firm resolution to improve it. The first thing I looked at was my technique. It was quite sound and I couldn't see any dramatic improvements taking place there so I decided to look at other things and turned my attention to the mind. I suddenly realized that I had to learn to control it and improve my concentration. That was my goal. I knew that if I achieved it I would become one of the best players in the world.

Many people think that my batting technique is good. That may be so, but there are others whose techniques are equally good or better. Yet, they haven't been as successful. I think I use my mind better than most other players. I am able to concentrate well under pressure. Once these things started to work for me my confidence improved and I began to believe in myself. My confidence is such that no matter how tough things get, I know I will pull through. Failures and poor performances are temporary events.

Persistence

Rudi. What about persistence?

Greg. Most good players are persistent. They are very proud people and they don't like to be beaten. It may be an ego thing as well, I don't know.

When I was young, I was small and weak and I always played with boys who were older, stronger and bigger. I had to learn how to cope with losing and how to fight to survive. This was great training because it taught me how to overcome obstacles, and how to keep the struggle on when things didn't work out the way I wanted.

I have little respect for talented players who give in easily. Many of them have such great natural ability that most things come easily to them. However, when they get into a tight spot where they have to fight back, they can't because they never had to. They never learned how to handle failure and disappointment. To reach the top, you must learn to use your mistakes and failures in a positive way. All of the superstars have had failures and disappointments at some time or other. When things get tight, you can't depend on these types of players because they let you down. I was very hard on them and tried to pressure them into fighting back.

Imagination

Rudi. Do you use visualization techniques or mental imagery?

Greg. I use both quite a lot. I am not great at net practice. In fact, I don't spend a lot of time practising. But I spend a bit of my time mentally rehearsing what I want to do, and these techniques have been very useful to me. I try to visualize the things I want to achieve. I sometimes visualize the things I don't want to happen and notice the differences between my thinking, my attitude and my feelings.

I set myself a goal and see myself reaching it. I don't go through my innings, over by over, or ball by ball. Instead, I try to initiate the thought processes that will get me there. I see myself doing the important things. Sometimes, I just put my imagination in motion and it takes over.

When I have a bad trot, I often go to a quiet place and mentally replay some of my best innings to try to recapture my confidence and the correct thought processes.

Teaching Skills

Rudi. What advice would you give to a young player who is trying to make his mark in the game?

Greg. I would tell him to:

- Find out what the basics of your game are;
- Learn them well;
- Practise them attentively under conditions that physically and psychologically resemble those in the real game;
- Learn to apply them sensibly; and
- Never go too far away from them. If you do, your game will suffer. No matter what happens you always have to go back to the basics.

CHAPTER 2

LEADERSHIP AND TEAMWORK

I am not a lone wolf. I am a team man. I need to have people around me. If you give me the toughest assignment possible and I have people with me, I would definitely give it my best shot.

— M.S. Dhoni

Clive Lloyd brought together a diverse collection of talented individuals who lacked direction, focus, discipline and common purpose and transformed them into a highly professional and all-conquering unit that dominated world cricket for fifteen consecutive years, and became one of the most successful teams in the history of sport.

— Rudi Webster

Beliefs and values are to athletes what roots are to trees. Without strong roots trees fall easily in the wind; without beliefs and values players' performance falls in the winds of competition and pressure.

— Anonymous

Great teams are built around good individual performance; the better each member plays the better the team will perform. But when players work together with a common purpose they accomplish more than the sum of individual achievements. This usually happens when they prepare, plan and execute well, and when they aim for high standards, debrief their experiences, and use the feedback to plan and play better next time.

In any dynamic system there are forces that hold things together and opposing forces that take them apart. In the team there is often conflict between the 'Mates Values' – sharing, caring and working together to achieve team goals – and the 'Me Values' – working selfishly and egotistically to satisfy individual needs and personal goals ahead of team goals.

A certain amount of competition and conflict is necessary for good teamwork but when 'Me Values' dominate destructive conflict ensues and forces like greed, petty jealousies, egotism, infighting and political battles disrupt unity, shared vision and common purpose. But, too much harmony can be just as harmful to performance as too much conflict. Balance is needed. The challenge for leaders is to determine how much harmony to encourage and how much conflict to allow.

In some Eastern cultures where the group takes precedence over the individual, it is usually easier to build and maintain good teamwork than it is in the West where we praise and glorify the individual and individual achievement. But in densely populated countries in the East where competition for jobs and places in sports teams is intense, fear of failure and rejection are ever present. 'Me Values' can then take over.

Good leaders build their teams around a sense of purpose and unity. Players unite more easily when they share a common philosophy, have a clear vision of what they want to achieve and are committed to making that vision a reality.

Constant articulation of the team's values and priorities is very important. Everyone in the team should know them. But talking about them is not enough. The leaders must show by example, what the team really stands for.

Leadership should not be confined to the person at the top. People at every level of the team and sports organization should take responsibility for motivating and leading the people around them.

In 1994, I worked with Gamini Dissanayake a Sri Lankan politician who was running for the presidency of Sri Lanka. At the time, he was also the president of the Sri Lankan Cricket Board and had invited me to work with his cricketers on two other occasions. Sadly, he was assassinated during the political campaign by a suicide bomber. A week before he died we had an interesting discussion about leadership during which he asked, 'Who is thus a great leader?' He then answered, 'A great leader is not one who says, "I did this, I did that", or "I did everything." He is one who conducts himself in such a way that when at a particular time his people are asked, "Who achieved these great things for you?" They will answer and say, "We did them together."'

THE LEADER'S PERFORMANCE IS ONLY AS GOOD AS THAT OF THE LED

> If you select a captain who is a follower, do not expect him to be a good leader.
>
> — A cricketer

During war, an army needs good management and administration to function, but it cannot win battles without innovative leadership at every level throughout its ranks. No one has as yet found how to administer or manage people into battle. They must be motivated to fight. The same applies to sport. In sport, the battle is fought with balls, bats and clubs but it is the will, spirit and mental strength of the man who leads and the men who follow that lead the team to victory.

The speed of the leader is the speed of the pack. US general Omar Bradley once said, 'The greatest leader in the world could never win a campaign unless he understood the men he had to lead.'

When I was manager of the West Indies cricket team I witnessed a very interesting event that revealed the importance of Bradley's comments, and demonstrated Clive Lloyd's effective leadership and motivational skills. Clive was a quiet achiever and was often underrated because of what people perceived as an easy-going and laid-back style of captaincy. His greatest asset was his knowledge and understanding of his players and his ability to press the right buttons to get the best out of them.

During Kerry Packer's World Series cricket in Australia, one of the West Indies players went right off in a team meeting and attacked the captain and other team members. During his outburst, Clive Lloyd turned to me and said, 'Look at him. Let him get rid of his steam. Tomorrow morning he will come to see me in my room and will apologize profusely for his conduct. He will then go out on the field and take it out on the Australians.' 'How can you say that?' I asked. 'I understand my players and I know how they will behave in different situations. If one of my other players did the same thing I would pull him up before the team and put him in his place. Every player is different and you have to know how to handle and motivate every one of them to get the best out of them,' Clive said.

I was fascinated and curious about Clive's prediction, so I went to his room early that morning to see what would happen. Soon after I got there, the player arrived. He was clearly very ashamed of his behaviour and he proffered a tearful apology to the captain. Clive accepted his apology and then set out to boost his confidence. The player left the room a relieved and happy man and later that day gave a magnificent performance on the field.

GOOD LEADERSHIP STARTS WITH SELF-LEADERSHIP

> The captain must lead by example to get the trust, respect and support of his team. The people I lead carry the expectations of 1.2 billion people, so I help them by keeping everything as simple as possible and by creating an atmosphere that will give confidence and motivation to each and every one to do his best.
>
> — M.S. Dhoni

> I believe that the captain should be a visionary. He should be able to show his vision to team members so that they will know where he wants to take them. All team members will then move together in the same direction. That is important.
>
> — V.V.S. Laxman

What was my vision for the team? I wanted the team to be a team. I wanted each and every player to enjoy the game. To excel as a team you need to go on to the field as a team, not as a collection of individuals, and you need to hunt in packs.
— *M.S. Dhoni*

A successful leader faces the same complex and challenging situations as everyone else but he doesn't just drift along and allow circumstances to chart his path. Instead, he chooses where he wants to go and finds a way to get there. One of his strengths is his ability to tailor his strategy and resources to 'fit' the important challenges and key contingencies in the situations he faces.

Here are three important questions that the leader should constantly ask himself and his team: 'Where are we going and why – our vision of what we want to achieve and become? What do we stand for and believe in – our values, philosophy and principles? What must we do to achieve our goals – our action plan?' The team's culture and performance are usually built around the answers to these questions.

Leadership is action, not a position. You can't build a team that is different from you. You can't make a team into something you are not. If the leader cannot perform well or make timely and sensible decisions under pressure he should not expect his team to do so. Team members often replicate the values, principles and behaviour of the leader.

The good leader learns from the past, is drawn towards the future by his vision and acts in the present to achieve that vision. Professor Luria, a Russian scientist once said that human behaviour is not only determined by past experiences but also by plans or goals that formulate the future. Not only does the brain create these goals or models of the future it also subordinates its activities towards achieving them.

AGENDA FOR CHANGE

Research findings suggest that the best leaders build their leadership on three strong pillars: an agenda for change, a cohesive network of competent and highly motivated people to implement that agenda, and the eradication of poor excuses, bad habits and outmoded traditions.

In their agenda for change they create a clear and detailed vision of what they want their team to achieve and become. They show that vision to team members, articulate an intelligent strategy to achieve that vision and explain how the players will benefit from it. Implementation of their strategy is key and they carefully select and build a team of highly motivated and competent members, committed to making their vision a reality.

When the leader shares his vision with team members and clarifies their roles and responsibilities, he creates an awareness of purpose, and a feeling of belonging. Team members bring passion and commitment with them when they believe that they can truly make a difference to the performance of the team. And when those energies are correctly directed and focused, a major requirement for success is satisfied.

Errol Barrow, a former prime minister of Barbados once said to me:

This vision thing is very important. You must have a powerful vision of where you want to take your country. That vision must be clear in your mind and you must simplify and clarify it further before you speak about it or show it to the country. Your people will then hopefully be able to see it and identify with it. If you get too far ahead of the people they might not see what you are trying to show them. No matter how good your vision, it will be worthless unless your people can see it, understand it and buy into it.

Johan Goethe, a German playwright, once said that people only listen to what they understand. The greater the understanding of the vision and the strategy the greater are the chances of achieving it.

MOTIVATION AND IMPLEMENTATION

Leaders understand that vision and strategic plans by themselves can only take the team so far. Plans and goal charts do not accomplish performance. It is the players that get things done. Players breathe life into the team's vision, plans and mission. At the end of the day, it is competent, well-trained, highly disciplined and highly motivated players that are the key to the team's success.

The good leader therefore focuses strongly on implementation and spends a lot of his time motivating, communicating, facilitating and monitoring.

He motivates by coaxing, praising, kicking, coaching and inspiring. He communicates by telling and listening, informing each member about his role and place in the team, and by giving and accepting feedback. He facilitates by linking players' aspirations to the common vision, and by building good relationships with them. And he monitors by putting people and systems in place to oversee the process.

Some captains motivate their players by leading from the front. Others prefer to lead from behind and push members towards the goal. Clive Lloyd led from the front. He said, 'My players responded to leadership from the front. Other players respond to leadership from behind. Both methods are effective, and sometimes you have to combine them. It depends on the players, the character and the skills of the captain and the circumstances and situations he has to deal with. Players who lack confidence and don't know how good they are or how good they can become often have to be pushed or pulled to play well.'

Good leaders improve team cohesion and team interaction by setting up a contract of expectations with the players. They tell the players exactly what roles and functions they expect them to perform, and what standards they expect them to meet. They then get the players to articulate their expectations of the leaders. Both sides will then know exactly what to expect from each other. This simple exercise gets rid of many negative forces inside the team, and improves teamwork and team performance.

When Ian Chappell was captain of Australia he used to sit down with the players early in the season and have a chat with them. He would find out what they expected of him and he would then tell them what he expected of them. He said, 'I would define the job and role of every player in the team. For example, Ross Edwards's role as a batsman was to get involved in partnerships with the stroke makers and ensure that they got most of the strike. If he did that the team would invariably score 200 runs while he was at the crease.

'Doug Walters's role was to be an attacking player. He had to play his natural game because he was a potential match winner. If the score was forty for four, Dougie knew that he was free to handle the situation in his own way. This meant playing his shots and attacking the bowling. This allowed him to talk to himself in a positive way instead of saying, "If I get out playing my shots, what will the captain say to me? Will he kick me in the ass and tell me how stupid I am?" This thinking produces self-doubts and indecision, the last thing you want to have on the field when you are in a tight position. I think this is terribly important. Captains and coaches can get a lot more out of their players by going through this simple exercise.'

LEADERSHIP IS NOT EASY

Leadership is a difficult and demanding job. If it were easy there would be plenty of good leaders around. Today's complexity, diversity and rapid change contribute to that difficulty. But even in simple conditions many things are needed to create a clear vision, an intelligent strategy, good motivation and successful teamwork.

These four factors require a sound knowledge of the game, the players involved, and the conditions in which the players are operating. They also require a clear and creative mind, first-class analytical skills, good judgement, and the ability to handle many things at once. The capacity to think simply and clearly and to act sensibly under pressure is critical. So too is the ability to identify the first-important priorities in the situations you face and the competence to tailor your skills and resources to deal with them. The leader should be energetic and highly motivated and should have a core set of values and principles that act as his compass.

To motivate his players to work hard and implement his agenda and strategy, the leader must have credibility, good communication skills and a keen insight into the personalities of his players. Charisma and a quick wit can help but these two things are not enough. Being a leader in a social gathering is not the same as being a leader in sport and business.

CLIVE LLOYD'S LEADERSHIP

Clive had a lot of ability and skill in his side but he knew that talent alone would not be enough to transform the team into a champion team. Other things would be needed – a clear vision, strategic thinking, good preparation, mastery of the basics, first-class leadership, great teamwork, good motivation, strong self-discipline, good mental control and high standards of execution on the field.

When Clive Lloyd was building his champion team, his leadership reflected the research findings that were described above. He built his leadership on three strong pillars: an agenda for change; a group of highly motivated and competent players committed to implementing his agenda; and the eradication of insularity, local prejudices, distrust and bad habits.

He revealed his agenda for change to me over a few drinks in a Melbourne pub in 1976 soon after our disappointing Test series against Australia. He showed me his vision for the team – the best team in the world for the next ten years – and he explained his strategic plan for achieving that vision. He then told me that he would search the Caribbean for players with the 'right stuff' and would mould them into a highly motivated and disciplined unit to conquer all before them.

He wanted his side to be the fittest team, physically and mentally, the best fielding team, the best bowling team, and the best batting team. And he wanted to become the most successful West Indies captain. He would favour players who were hard-working, enthusiastic and professional and would make self-discipline and mental toughness top priorities. Once those things were in place he would execute his plan in a forceful manner, using a quartet of aggressive fast bowlers to 'hunt in a pack' against opposing batsmen.

He thought that eradicating local prejudices or insularity, the curse of West Indies cricket, and getting the players to trust, respect and care for each other were his most difficult challenges. He wanted to make things as simple as possible and ensure that every team member knew his role and responsibilities, and understood the importance of good preparation and high standards. Getting each player to be a leader on the field was another important priority.

Those objectives became the building blocks of his team's amazing success. The magnitude of his achievements has not yet been fully appreciated by the Caribbean people. He brought together a diverse collection of talented individuals who lacked direction, focus, discipline and common purpose and transformed them into a highly professional and all-conquering unit that dominated world cricket for fifteen consecutive years and became one of the most successful teams in the history of sport.

I don't know if Clive was aware of the three questions about teamwork that were posed at the beginning of this chapter: Where are we going and why – our vision or picture of what we want to achieve or become? What do we believe in – our values, philosophy and principles? What must we do to achieve those goals – our action plan? But, he somehow built a champion team around them.

Clive led by example but he also knew what made his players tick and what he had to do to motivate them.

Ian Chappell a former Australian cricket captain claims that any captain could learn how to set a field, change the bowling, write out the batting order, or formulate and explain a game plan. He feels that the most important thing in captaincy is the motivation of players to execute the plan or strategy, particularly under pressure when things get tough and when smart thinking and extra effort are required.

Chappell said that captaincy is a very demanding job. He thinks that a four or five-year period is about the limit for most captains because the pressure sometimes gets to them after that, dampens their initiative and creativity and interferes with their motivation and leadership skills.

Vince Lombardi, a very successful American football coach, thought along similar lines. He once said, 'Coaches who can outline plays on a blackboard are a dime a dozen. The ones who win get inside their players and motivate.'

THE POWER GAP AND THE TWO ROLES THE LEADER MUST PLAY

Leaders are given a great deal of power. When they rely solely on the power of their position to get things done and ignore the management of important relationships inside and outside the team they usually fail because they create a huge power gap that prevents them from reaching their goals. This gap is only bridged when they improve communication and build cooperative and harmonious relationships in the team.

Leaders must play two critical roles. The first is a task-oriented one. In this role, they ensure that members have the training, skills and knowledge to carry out their tasks and that the tasks actually get done. Good execution is a first-important priority. The second role is a maintenance role. Here, the leaders choose the best people, blend their talent and expertise, and manage relationships inside and outside the team. They also communicate frequently and motivate members to work together to achieve the team's goals.

The two roles should be balanced. If the task-oriented role dominates and the other one is neglected, the tasks might get done but harmony and team spirit might suffer. The leader might then be seen as uncaring, tough and autocratic. And if the maintenance role is emphasized at the expense of the other one, standards and performance might decline and the leader might be regarded as a nice but weak person.

If a leader is weak in one role he should appoint someone to the leadership team who is strong in that role to cover for his weakness. For instance, a tough task-oriented captain who is determined to get the job done at all costs should have a vice captain to look after relationships in the group and teamwork. The reverse also applies.

THE HUMAN BODY AS A MODEL FOR TEAMWORK

The embodiment of good teamwork is found in the workings of the human body. These include:

1. *A common vision or a shared goal or purpose*: This is the health
   and survival of the human body and the reproduction of the
   species.

2. *Specialization and structure*: The cells in the body are organized
   into groups or units to form organs and systems. Each organ
   – the heart, lungs, brain, kidneys, gut – and each system –
   cardiovascular, pulmonary, nervous, urinary and gastrointestinal
   – has a unique structure and performs precise functions.
   Specialization improves function and efficiency but only if the
   component units are well organized and closely integrated to
   coordinate and direct their activities towards the common goal.

3. *Cooperation and coordination of effort*: This is one of the
   cornerstones of good teamwork. Competitive struggles amongst
   the cells or units can disrupt performance.

4. *Effective detecting mechanisms*: These police the internal
   environment of the body and the activities of the cells, organs
   and systems. Any change in the environment or deviation of
   function is quickly detected and rectified.

5. *Good communication systems*: These are essential for harmony,
   cooperation and coordination of effort. Poor communication
   disrupts function and teamwork. For example, if the main nerve
   to the lower limb were cut, the limb would be paralysed and
   would become a useless appendage, even though it has all the
   other systems and structures in place. This happens because there
   is no communication between the brain and the limb. What you
   say and how you say it are important in communication but not as
   important as what the listener hears, sees, feels and understands.
   That is why body language and non-verbal communication are
   so powerful.

Cancers

Selfishness, egotistical behaviour, infighting, competitive struggles and
destructive conflict are the enemies of good teamwork. The epitome
of selfishness and egotistical behaviour is found in the cancer. It is not

concerned about the health or survival of the body; it is only interested in itself and its power to grow and spread throughout the body.

When you have cancer, your own cells stop responding to the instructions coded in the genes. They then turn on themselves and begin transforming their energy into rampant and uncontrollable growth. During this rapid growth the cancer destroys the structure and function of the organ in which it arises and does the same thing to other parts of the body as it spreads. Eventually, it kills the body. People usually die from the spread of the cancer cells rather than from the cells that remain in the organ of origin, in the same way that the spread of selfishness, infighting, internal conflict and misuse of power in the team kill teamwork. But in killing the body the cancer kills itself because it can only survive in a living body. It commits biological suicide. Cancers are prevalent in many of today's sports teams and sports organizations.

Peter Brock's comments on teamwork are quite interesting and instructive. He said:

> In motor racing you can't win or have success unless you have a cohesive and strong team behind you. Your life and safety depend on their performance.
>
> The first criterion that is required is that all team members should have a total commitment towards high standards and a common goal or result. Loyalty and discipline are necessary. Team members should have a shared vision, shared beliefs and a common philosophy. Ours was to win fairly. I cannot condone winning by foul means or by rule breaking.
>
> The second criterion is expertise. You have to blend this expertise correctly to produce the best results.
>
> Individual members of the group must respect each other, have a common bond, and have a relatively harmonious existence. They don't have to be bosom buddies. They can be friendly, work well together, and share something that is meaningful without being great mates. Our philosophy was to 'help your team mates'. We cared for each other and if someone was having problems with his job, the others would pitch in and help. They didn't say, 'Tough luck mate, we've done our jobs so we are OK.' Caring for each other and showing respect for each other creates trust and cohesion in teams.

Good communication is essential but it can be difficult to achieve. If it isn't good, teamwork and performance will be poor. Everyone in the team must know what his job and responsibilities are.

Earlier this year, we had a problem with communication in the team. A few petty squabbles broke out and some members claimed that they didn't know what their job and responsibilities were. We ironed them out rather smartly and by the time we got to Bathurst we had an efficient unit. Everyone knew what he had to do, when and where he had to do it. We went to the trouble of putting down job specifications on paper so that everyone could study them. Because they were clearly defined there was no confusion or indecision and it worked very well.

To monitor the system we employed a couple of people to oversee the operation and to make sure that it ran smoothly. They don't necessarily have to know very much about the technical aspects of motor racing but they must be good judges of character, good communicators and they must be strong. They have to spot problems early and nip them in the bud. They are very honest with me and give it to me straight. If they think I am not doing my job properly they tell me so. They might even be insulting at times but you must take it and appreciate the fact that they are trying to help you. They should also acquaint you with important problem areas in the system.

I know that some people are sensitive to criticism and get upset when someone points out their faults or mistakes but that is stupid. You must be honest with yourself and with the rest of the team. You should regard constructive criticism as feedback about what needs to be questioned, improved or changed. If you can't handle this type of communication you should not get involved in professional team sport.

DIFFERENT TYPES OF TEAMWORK

Don't play one game and coach another.

— Rudi Webster

There is no one type of teamwork that is ideal. Three basic forms have been described and in each type leadership, coaching, player management and group interaction are somewhat different. Combinations of these three forms are found in most sports.

In American football, the main objective is to keep possession of the ball and move it down the field incrementally or in one or two great plays to get the ball over the line for a touchdown. Most of the players never even touch the ball and the team generally moves in one direction, forward. Specialist coaches often control their team's tactics in the game by calling the plays for the team.

In this type of teamwork, the coach is king. He has great power and usually calls the shots. The main priority in the team is the implementation of the coach's plan. Conformity is the name of the game and dissent and individuality are not encouraged or tolerated. Leadership and coaching usually have an inflexible and authoritarian flavour.

In basketball and soccer everyone handles or kicks the ball and the patterns for moving the ball are complex. Players are usually more flexible, innovative and creative and constantly interact with each other throughout the game.

Chemistry is a significant factor in this type of teamwork – how the players interact and communicate with each other and with the coach and how they cooperate and coordinate their efforts. In soccer and basketball, the performance of the team is greater than the sum of its parts.

In baseball and cricket, the result of the game is the sum total of individual effort and individual scores. A player can win a game with a good individual performance since the game is really a contest between a pitcher and batter, or a bowler and batsman, with a supporting cast of fielders.

In this type of teamwork performance is built around individual execution, so there is more emphasis on individual effort, style, motivation and achievement than on the other two types of teamwork. Motivation of the individual and management of his assets and weaknesses should be top priority. So should the proper blending of individual talent.

Martin Crowe, the great New Zealand batsman, recently spoke about the importance of individuality in cricket. He said: 'Many play [cricket] because of the unique nature of individual expression, bowler against batsman, all inside a team environment. Eleven-a-side offers plenty of variety in personality and character, which is required, given the different roles and skills that are called upon. Cricket is a fine all-round sport: healthy for the body without direct contact, and healthy for the mind as it makes you concentrate for long periods.'

Good coaches and administrators are flexible enough to accommodate internal differences and individual needs while focusing on the common goal or purpose. Having one rule for all can be counterproductive in this type of teamwork. The simultaneous management of diversity and interdependence is a key to good teamwork,

In a jazz band each member at first plays the same tune but is then given the freedom to improvise and innovate. In a classical orchestra, the conductor is in total control and makes sure that every member faithfully follows the musical score. No latitude is given for innovation or experimentation. Teamwork in the jazz band is similar to that in cricket, and teamwork in the orchestra is like that in American football.

Teams run into trouble when the team plays one game and the coach and administrators play a different game. For instance, when a baseball or cricket coach manages his team like an American football coach most things revolve around him and his plan rather than around the captain and his players. His need for control and conformity and his dislike of any kind of dissent invariably stifle individual talent and creativity and interfere with team dynamics and performance. Similar problems with teamwork and team performance arise in American football if the coach tries to manage his team like a cricket or baseball coach.

LIFE CYCLE OF A SUCCESSFUL TEAM

Everything has a beginning and an ending.

– Anonymous

The life cycle of every successful team is one of conception, growth, optimum performance, stagnation and finally decline. Every successful team dominates for a while, but then strikes a plateau and stagnates. After that it starts to decline and is superseded by another team that is on the rise. But that decline can sometimes be prevented if a second growth curve or a psychological rebirth is created when the team is still performing well. To revive the team and start a new growth curve a reorganization of priorities is needed as well as an infusion of new players and new leaders with fresh ideas, attitudes and agendas for change. New systems, more efficient structures and better allocation and management of resources are also required. The longer the decline lasts the more difficult it is to reverse. Unfortunately, most teams wait until they are in full decline before they act.

When the West Indies cricket team was champions of the world they did not see the need to start a second growth curve and eventually went into a decline in the 1990s. At that stage they were in a state of denial, could not see the reality of the situation that they were in and believed that things would miraculously turn around at any moment. At the time Pat Rousseau, an innovative and forward-looking president of the Board, tried to open the eyes of his members to show them a way to reverse the trend but his short-sighted colleagues literally shot him down. Consequently, little was done to change or adapt to the circumstances they faced. During the last seventeen years the team's failure spiral has intensified as the slope of the decline became steeper. For some time now the team has been near the bottom of the world rankings in both Test and One Day cricket! Recovery will be difficult and painful. The decisions and actions of the leaders of West Indies cricket and the West Indies Players Association are a great example of what not to do in circumstances like these.

After an impressive run as world champions, the Australian cricket team recently went into a state of decline. But, unlike the West Indies team they have already recognized and accepted that decline and are looking for solutions. They are beginning to ask the right questions, are making some difficult and unpopular decisions and are starting to put different personnel, structures, systems and resources in place to arrest that decline and start a second growth curve. Sooner rather than later, they will have a rebirth and climb back to the top tier of the Test and One Day rankings. Psychological rebirth like human birth can be traumatic and painful but in the end it is worth the pain and anxiety.

The Indian cricket team has done extremely well in the last few years and is now at a critical phase of its performance cycle in Test cricket. The authorities must now choose the way forward. They can continue with business as usual, make minor cosmetic changes and run the risk of going into a decline, or they can be bold and innovative and start a second growth curve or a psychological rebirth. The latter approach would at worst prevent any serious decline and at best keep the team in the top two or three positions.

Some boards and administrators find it difficult to start a second growth curve because they frequently do not see themselves as part of the problem. They don't understand that transformation or psychological rebirth of the team is easier when they set the right example and start with themselves. They must also understand that it is difficult for a team to perform consistently well on the field with a poorly functioning administrative and management team behind it. They must lead and motivate.

A New Leadership Model

> The world that we have made as a result of the level of thinking we have done thus far creates problems that we cannot solve at the same level that they were created.
>
> — *Albert Einstein*

Conventional wisdom and old methods of leadership are still valuable and we must capitalize on them. But to improve performance and succeed in today's and tomorrow's complex, competitive and rapidly changing world, we must find better and more innovative ways to lead and perform. We must use our imagination. We need to identify the most important demands and challenges in the situations we face or are likely to face and then tailor our thinking, intelligence, skills, resources, strategies and technologies to meet those dramatic and ever changing challenges. Flexibility and good communication will be important. So too will be the simultaneous management of diversity and interdependence.

Today's scientists tell us that the size of our very distant ancestors' brain – about 700cc – remained static for more than a million years. Then fast, drastic, and recurring cataclysmic climate change in the Rift Valley of Africa changed it. To survive those turbulent conditions and prosper, our ancestors had to adapt. They had to improve their thinking, reasoning, planning, and decision-making abilities as well as their motivation and communication skills. Teamwork and group interaction became priorities. To achieve these objectives brain function improved and brain size gradually increased to its present size of about 1,200cc.

Mankind again faces some very complex, rapidly changing and life-threatening challenges. Like our earliest ancestors we must adapt to survive and prosper. We must utilize the brain's untapped or dormant potential and resources and use it more creatively and efficiently to produce new leadership and performance models.

A new leadership model can be built on four interconnected and interdependent pillars.

The first two pillars, self-mastery – competence, self-belief, self-discipline, self-motivation and good concentration – and team synergy – teamwork, group interaction, communication, and cooperation and coordination of effort – have already been discussed.

Continuous learning is the third pillar. Leadership and learning are indispensable to each other. When leaders and teams stop learning they stop! Smart leaders and teams are always trying to learn new things and find better ways to improve performance. Learning does not stop in childhood; it continues throughout life and brings with it new opportunities, new methods and new levels of performance.

V.V.S. Laxman emphasizes that learning and improvement should be a continuous process and until you play your last game in professional sport, you should always be trying to learn and improve all aspects of your game, not just your skill and preparation but also your mind and temperament.

The fourth pillar is sustainable development. This includes such things as accountability, respect for each other, respect for the game, respect for the fans, respect for the environment in which the game is played, respect for authority figures, respect for the rights of the players, and an awareness of responsibilities to employers, employees, spectators, sponsors, stakeholders and the country.

It is fitting to end this section on teamwork and leadership by quoting Bill Russell who played for the Boston Celtics, one of the most successful teams in the history of the American NBA.

Russell said: 'The main difference between great teams and good teams is not physical skill but mental toughness. That is how well a team can keep its collective wits under pressure. Teams that "can do this under the greatest pressure will win most of the time."'

REMEMBER

Teamwork

1. In sport, groups do more and accomplish more than the individual.

2. Teams should ask themselves, 'Where are we going and why? What do we believe in and stand for? What is our action plan?'

3. Too much harmony can be just as harmful to teamwork as too much conflict. Balance is needed.

4. When players have a clear vision of what they want to become and are united and committed to common goals, a shared philosophy and common standards, they bond easily. Moreover, when they accept co-responsibility for setting and implementing those common goals, their commitment and performance automatically improve, especially when those goals meet their personal needs and aspirations.

5. What you say and how you say it are important in communication, but not as important as what the

listener hears, sees, feels and understands. That is why body language and non-verbal communication are so powerful.

6. The epitome of good teamwork is found in the workings of the human body — a common vision or shared purpose; specialization of cells into organs and systems; cooperation and coordination of effort; good monitoring mechanisms to detect any deviation of function; and good communicating systems.

7. The cancer is the embodiment of selfishness and egotistical behaviour. It is not interested in the health of the body. It gets what it wants but destroys everything in its path. Eventually, it kills the body and commits suicide in the process because it can only survive in a living body. When it kills the body it kills itself.

8. There are different types of teamwork. Don't play one game and coach another. In some sports the result is the sum of the individual parts but in others it is greater than the sum of the individual achievement.

9. All teams go through a performance cycle. Each team has a period of growth, optimum performance, stagnation and then decline. Decline can be prevented or lessened by starting a second growth curve when the team is still doing well. Unfortunately, most teams wait until they are in steep decline before they act.

10. According to Bill Russell, 'The main difference between great teams and good teams is not physical skill but mental toughness. That is how well a team can keep its collective wits under pressure. Teams that can do this under the greatest pressure will win most of the time.'

Leadership

1. Good leadership starts with self-leadership.

2. A group needs leadership, but leadership should not be confined just to the person at the top. People at every

level of the team and sports organization should take responsibility for leading the people around them.

3. A successful leader faces the same complex and challenging situations as everyone else but he doesn't just drift along and allow circumstances to chart his path. Instead, he chooses where he wants to go and finds a way to get there.

4. The clever leader learns from the past, is drawn to the future by his vision and acts in the present to achieve that vision.

5. Good leaders help team members see beyond what the team is at the moment, to what it can become in the future. They are dealers of hope. They show their team a future that it can believe in and benefit from.

6. No matter how good the vision, it will be worthless unless the players can see it, understand it and buy into it.

7. The leader's performance is only as good as that of the led. The speed of the leader is the speed of the pack.

8. Here are three important questions that the leader should constantly ask himself and his team. First, where are we going and why — our vision of what we want to achieve and become? Second, what do we stand for and believe in — our values, philosophy and principles? And third, what must we do to achieve our goals — our action plan?

9. Leaders should constantly articulate their values and priorities to team members and make sure that everyone knows them. But talking about them is not enough. They must practice what they preach.

10. Leadership is not easy. If it were, there would be plenty of good leaders around. Today's complexity, diversity and rapid change contribute to that difficulty. But even in simple conditions it can be difficult and demanding.

11. The best leaders build their leadership on three strong pillars. First, they produce an agenda for change in which they have a clear vision of what they want to achieve

and an intelligent strategy to achieve that vision. Second, they put together a competent, cohesive and motivated team to implement their agenda. And third, they get rid of limiting beliefs, old excuses, bad habits and outmoded traditions.

12. Leaders know that plans and goal charts do not accomplish performance. It is the players that get things done. They breathe life into the team's vision, plans and mission. At the end of the day, it is competent, well trained, highly disciplined and highly motivated players that are the key to the team's success.

13. In sport the battle is fought with balls, bats and clubs but it is the spirit of the men who follow and the man who leads that take the team to victory.

14. The captain must lead by example to get the trust, respect and support of his team. Some captains lead from the front and get their players to follow them while others lead from behind by pushing their players towards the team's goals. In many cases a mixture of the two styles is needed.

15. Good communication is a vital factor in leadership and teamwork so the leader must communicate simply and clearly by word, deed and body language.

16. Good leaders are themselves highly motivated and show their zeal and passion to the team. They have a core set of values that act as their compass and they spend a lot of time communicating those values to the players and motivating them.

17. Vince Lombardi: 'Coaches who can outline plays on a blackboard are dime a dozen. The ones who win get inside their players and motivate.'

18. The leaders, or the leadership, must play two critical roles. The first is a task-oriented one and the other is that of maintenance. These two roles should be balanced.

19. A new leadership model is needed to deal with the enormous challenges in today's complex and rapidly changing

world. This model can be built on four interconnected and interdependent supports – self-mastery, team synergy, continuous learning and sustainable development.

A CONVERSATION WITH CLIVE LLOYD ON LEADERSHIP AND TEAMWORK

Rudi. Not many people realize how culturally diverse Caribbean people are. I believe that a large part of the success of your West Indies team came from your ability to transcend those differences and get rid of the insularity and local prejudices that had plagued our cricket.

From different West Indian islands you brought together a diverse collection of talented individuals who lacked direction, focus, discipline, mental toughness and common purpose – the so-called calypso cricketers – and you transformed them into a highly professional and all-conquering unit that dominated world cricket for fifteen consecutive years.

During an eleven-year period as captain not only did you conceive and develop that team but you also took it to the pinnacle of success. When you gave up the captaincy you handed over a well-established champion team to your successor, Viv Richards, who carried on the winning ways and never lost a series as captain. That team is now regarded as one of the most successful teams in the history of sport. Very few people can boast of such an accomplishment.

In the course of this conversation I trust that you will tell us how you did it.

Clive. I will try.

Rudi. When I was manager of the West Indies team during the Kerry Packer World Series, I was able to observe very closely what you and the team were doing from a very unique perspective. During this chat it will be interesting to see how closely our ideas match.

Early Days of Captaincy

Clive. As you know when I was left out of the team to play against Australia in the West Indies in the early 1970s, I was in Australia playing domestic cricket. The president of Guyana, Forbes Burnham, who was incensed by the decision of the selectors, brought me home and applied some pressure on the West Indies Cricket Board of Control (WICB). As a result, I was selected for the Test match in Guyana and I made a big century there. When Burnham stuck his neck out for me I had to grab the opportunity and capitalize on it. I couldn't let my president down. In life, you have to keep fighting all the time.

After that series I had a very good run as a batsman, particularly in England where I was playing for the County of Lancashire. So I knew that they could not leave me out of the team. They had to pick me.

When they were looking for a new captain to replace Rohan Kanhai, they must have seen some leadership qualities in me because they selected me ahead of players like Deryck Murray and David Holford.

Rudi. Like Frank Worrell you were not universally accepted for the job – Frank because he was to be the first black captain, lots of people at the time didn't think we were ready for a black leader, and you because you didn't have a university education like Holford and Murray. A lot of people felt that the team needed a university-educated leader at that stage. I remember pointing out to your critics that the thinking and intelligence required to pass university examinations are very different from those needed to play sport, captain a cricket team or run a business. Very few academics become good sportsmen or great captains.

Clive. Exactly. I saw my appointment as an enormous challenge and it motivated me greatly. I looked at people like Brian Close of England who never went to university and yet was a very good captain. I thought, 'Chappell didn't go to university either and he was a great captain and I don't know if Richie Benaud went.' I was captaining teams from my school days so I thought that I must have some leadership qualities.

Perhaps my greatest lessons in leadership came from looking after my family. My father died when I was twelve years old and I became the only breadwinner in the family. I put my sisters through school – all levels of school. I looked after the family home, I had to give my mother money to keep things going and put food on the table and I had to look after my sisters and keep them in check. So I was like the head of everything – the leader. I didn't look at it as leadership then but that is what it was. Those roles and responsibilities contributed greatly to my character and personal values. Later on, I was able to take the family values of caring, sharing, respecting and trusting that I acquired during that time to the West Indies team. I believe that imprinting that strong sense of family in the team contributed greatly to the closeness of players in the team and to their performance on and off the field.

When I got to the big stage as captain, my first trip was to India. There, I got a lot of help and close cooperation from the manager, Gerry Alexander, a former West Indies captain. Early on, he realized that I was very serious about my job. I remember we were playing in Bangalore and my friend and Lancashire colleague Farookh Engineer said to me, 'It looks as though the manager is captaining the team from the inside. He sits right to the front and keeps moving players around.' I then went to the manager and said to him, 'Let's get things straight. When I am on the field this is my ball game. If you want to send out a message to me do so, but don't be moving players around, please.' From then on any time he wanted to speak to the players he sought my permission and would ask, 'Can I?' I would then say, 'Fine. Go ahead.' We got on extremely well after that. Gerry had a great cricket brain. I believe he was the first person to write to the ICC requesting neutral umpires because of the umpiring in that series. That was way back in 1974. Gerry was the best manager I ever had.

Rudi. What was your biggest challenge when you became captain?

Clive. When I heard Wes Hall and other former players talking so glowingly about Frank Worrell, I thought that he must have gained their trust and respect. So I said to myself. 'Your first job is to get the trust and respect of your players.' I knew some of the players like Viv

Richards and Andy Roberts suspected that I would favour players from my country, Guyana, but when they saw that I did not, and noticed how even-handed I was in the treatment of players, their attitude changed. They also realized that I was a team man and that I wasn't looking for personal glory. I think that is when trust started to build up in the team and when we began to play really well.

As captain, I used to try to help my players. If anybody had a problem on or off the field I would try to help. I would talk to them about the way they should dress and the way they should behave because I believed that their self-image and the image they projected to the world were very important. Some of them bought briefcases and tried to look like businessmen; others invested their money in houses and began to look after themselves better. Some of those things happened quite innocently. When they came to my house they noticed that I had a good house but lived simply. I would prepare food for them and look after them well. Some of them even stayed with me when they were seeking medical attention. So in me, they saw a captain who cared for them and looked after their interests and welfare. I was like a father figure who lifted their spirits and their confidence. In turn, they helped me by responding positively, giving maximum effort and playing really well.

Rudi. What you did was very important. In leadership, plans and strategies by themselves come to nothing. It is the players who bring those plans and strategies to life and produce results. And this only happens when members of the team care and share and when they are loyal, disciplined, focused, and execute well. It is the spirit of the men who follow and of the man who leads that gains victory.

Worrell the Role Model

Rudi. You and Frank Worrell are considered to be the two best West Indies captains. Yet many people speak of Frank's captaincy in glowing terms and play down your achievements by saying that you were lucky because you had a very good team with four great fast bowlers, and that anyone could have led it to success. But people who saw the two teams play claim that there was hardly any difference between them and if anything, Frank's team was more balanced. Some of the old-timers still feel that the team that Frank and Gary led was better than yours.

How do you account for this disparity and how do you think Frank and Gary's team would have done against your team if both of them were at their peak?

Clive: There was no difference between those teams. All I can say is that it would be a hell of a game.

Rudi. So what was the reason for the disparity in perception between Worrell's captaincy and yours?

Clive. I don't quite know. Perhaps the fact that Worrell spent a short stint at Manchester University gave people the feeling that he had something extra-special. What people don't understand is that you don't have to be bright academically to be a good captain. Captaincy is about good judgement and common sense and about motivating, managing and leading players. An old friend, Fred Wills, once said to me, 'Don't worry about this university stuff. If you have a modicum of intelligence you could become a lawyer like me, or whatever you want to be. But I can get all of the best coaches in the world to teach me how to play cricket but I would never be able to bat like you or Gary Sobers.'

I think that when you have success over a long period and make winning look easy, people don't truly appreciate what you are doing. There was a lot of ability and skill in my side, but I had to develop them and put them together in an effective way. I knew that talent alone would not be enough to build a champion team. I had to have a clear vision, an intelligent strategy, powerful motivation, and good planning and preparation. I also had to lead well, build good teamwork, instill strong self-discipline, improve the players' mental toughness and mental control, and get them to execute their basic skills really well. People don't see these things when you are winning easily, and when they can't see them they tell you that you are just lucky to have four fast bowlers in the team or other things like that.

Rudi. A sign of good leadership is to achieve your goals in a way that looks simple and easy.

Clive. To be a good cricketer you must be able to think, particularly when you are under pressure. Successful players out-think, out-plan and outperform their opponents. Just because someone might use a few green verbs or is not well versed in grammar does not mean that he is not a good thinker. My players won the first two World Cups and should have won the third, and they were world champions for fifteen consecutive years. Not many of them went to university or to any great schools. Nevertheless, they could think and play like champions and that is what is important in sport. That West Indies team was one of the greatest teams in the history of sport.

Rudi. Was there anything that you learned from Worrell and his style of leadership that helped you to do the amazing things that you did with your team?

Clive. Yes. I adopted many of his values and principles and tried to instill them in my players. One incident comes to mind. When we were playing in India there was a riot during the game in Calcutta and many of the players including the senior ones wanted to cancel the tour and go home. I asked myself if going home would be the best thing for the game and I sought the advice of Frank Worrell who was in India at the time. When I told him what was happening he said, 'There was a riot in Jamaica during an England tour, did the England team go home? No they didn't. If there is a riot when next we go to England, will our team go home? No they will not. The people of India love cricket and they love the West Indies players, so you stay on and play. They love you.' I treasured that advice. Unfortunately, Frank died a few months later of leukemia.

Worrell was a man with a vision and was the personification of the quiet achiever. He was a great motivator and in the heat of battle he was able to calm the minds and strengthen the nerves of his young and excitable players. The fact that he almost won the 1960-61 Test series against a very strong Australian team speaks volumes about what he had done to improve the self-belief, self-worth and self-confidence of the players. Once you improve these things, the players will play their natural game and get the best out of themselves.

Worrell was a forward thinker. He didn't just think of the past or the present. That's why he was so good. I tried to do the same thing. I was always looking ahead. You see that ability has nothing to do with what school you attended. It is what you have in your head. I captained the team for eleven years. I knew when it was the right time to introduce new players and what was needed to continue our winning ways. I learned a lot about respecting players and respecting people from the example that Worrell set.

Rudi. So you would say that he had an impact on your leadership.

Clive. Definitely. That meeting alone made a big impression on me. Being just over twenty years of age, my thinking about the riot was closer to that of the other players but when Frank talked to me and told me, 'They love you,' he changed my perspective and my thinking.

Rudi. Do you think that some of those values that you and Frank held so dearly have been lost in recent years?

Clive. Yes. Many of them have been lost. Look at discipline. People don't realize what a disciplined squad we had. Occasionally, our boys would break the curfew but on the field we never lost our discipline, mental toughness or will to win.

You must have a lot of discipline to be strong in every aspect of the game – batting, bowling and fielding. And once you are strong in those three areas you will have a great chance of beating anybody.

Defeat in Australia: A Wake-Up Call

Rudi. After winning the first cricket World Cup, the West Indies team went to Australia with high expectations but you lost the series five Tests to one. Immediately after the series you spent a few days with me at my home in Melbourne and I know that you were very depressed. One day we went to a nearby pub, the Tok H, and drowned our sorrows over a few beers. That visit proved to be a very important one because it was there that you articulated your vision for West Indies cricket to me and explained the strategy you would use to make that vision a reality. It is often said that failure is the father of success. I would like you to cast your mind back to that time and give me your version of what took place in that pub.

Clive. Although we lost the series badly I still felt secure as captain because I had won the first World Cup a few months earlier. But the thing that gave me comfort, great hope for our cricket and the motivation to press on was the fact that we had beaten the same Australian team in the Perth Test in just three days. So I was convinced that we had the players to be a very good team.

At that stage, I knew exactly what I wanted the team to achieve, and become the best team in the world for the next ten years. Our fielding was to be a top priority because we had dropped a lot of catches during the series, and as you know catches win matches. Every player would have to become a top fielder. Andy Roberts was not the best fielder but he worked hard to improve and he eventually became a much better fielder. During the Perth Test the Australians were very uncomfortable against the pace of Holding and Roberts and I decided there and then to get two more like them to make up a quartet. I was not worried about our batting because I thought it had a lot of potential. My aim was to build the best bowling, batting and fielding team. And I wanted to be a successful captain.

Rudi. So you created your vision and worked out your strategy during that time.

Clive. Yes. It was the win in Perth that stimulated me to create my vision and strategy. Fielding was really important because no matter how good your fast bowlers are, they won't get wickets unless the fielders take their catches.

Rudi. I have always said that your fielding team was one of the best ever.

Clive. Yes. People are always talking about our fast bowling but I think the best team that we had was the 1984 team that included Roger Harper.

Rudi. Why do you say that?

Clive. We had everything in that team. We had four fast bowlers and a good spinner. Larry Gomes used to chip in with his spin and I occasionally bowled my right-arm optimistic. So we had variety in our attack. To me that was the perfect side. We had two terrific opening batsmen, a fantastic middle order, a wicketkeeper who was a very good batsman, a spinner who could also bat and four great fast bowlers. Our fielding was very good before Roger Harper joined the team, but when he came the fielding was sensational. Unfortunately, Roger didn't remain in the team for very long after I gave up the captaincy. I think that was a bad mistake.

Rudi. Roger's omission was partly political because he was being touted as the next captain of the team and that didn't go down very well in some quarters.

Clive. Exactly.

Kerry Packer and World Series

Rudi. I want to go back to another period that I think was very important in the development of your team – the Kerry Packer Series. How vital was that series to the team?

Clive. It played a very big part in the development and future success of our team. That is where our professionalism and discipline really started. Just about every day you were playing with or against fifty of the best players in the world. So the standard was extremely high and to do well you had to play in a very disciplined and professional manner. World Series cricket was the toughest cricket I ever played. A few of the so-called great players got caught out in that competition.

Rudi. You did some innovative things during that series that other teams have since copied. For instance, you appointed a full-time fitness coach and used me as a mental conditioner or mental skills coach. And you also changed the format of practice and turned it into an enjoyable, intense and very competitive session, with lots of discipline thrown in.

Clive. You are right. I always believed that the mind and body compliment each other and work together to improve performance.

As far as fielding went there was no one in the team who did not enjoy practice. At practice I often put the bowlers in first to bat and face the new ball, and I gave them the full twelve to fifteen minutes of batting practice. I felt that if we were asking them to make runs for the team they should be made to practise seriously in the nets.

Rudi. What impressed me most was the fielding practice that was at times a bit frightening to watch. You hit the ball so hard to the fielders that I felt that some of them might get hurt. The intensity and enthusiasm at fielding practice were enormous. I think you spent more time at catching practice than teams do today. You knew that your fast bowlers would only be successful if the fielders held their catches and in the matches they didn't drop many of them. The other teams didn't practise like that at the time, but they soon started to copy us.

Clive. I remember Ray Lindwall, the great Australian fast bowler, in London at a Lord Taverners function praising what we had done for Australian cricket. I thought, 'Surely, what we had done really did not go that far.' But he thought so.

Rudi. You changed the way players practised, planned and prepared for the contest and the way they played the game.

Clive. Many of our people at home don't know that but even if they did they wouldn't give credit where it is due. They are more willing to recognize and reward the achievements of people from outside the region. That is the way we are.

You know, Rudi, I am not a motivational speaker but I can still highlight the things that are important and vital for good performance. That is what I missed out doing soon after I finished playing the game. Our young players should have successful people around to motivate and guide them. That is what I wanted to do. Even now I think that I have a lot of knowledge and experience that I can share with the young players.

Rudi. Ian Chappell, the great Australian captain, once told me that for him the most important job as a captain is the motivation of his players. Some experts now say that motivation is a better predictor of future performance than skill and ability.

Clive. Motivation is extremely important.

Rudi. Going back to Kerry Packer, I know that you were very impressed when he and I flew all the way from Australia to Guyana to be at your side when you, Deryck Murray and other players were having some problems with the West Indies Cricket Board. What did that visit mean to you and the players during your time of crisis?

Clive. It had an enormous impact on the players. I remember Kerry saying to me, 'I know you didn't expect me to come to your side but I wanted to because I am with you and your players 100 per cent.' To have the richest man in Australia coming all that way to be by our side took our respect for him to a new level. It brought the players closer together and made us more determined to do everything in our power to make World Series a success. At that stage we would have done anything for him. The icing on the cake took place when, at your suggestion, he flew all the players and their wives and girlfriends to the exclusive Sandy Lane Resort in Barbados for a short period of rest and recreation. I think Kerry's visit also made a big impact on the people in the Caribbean.

Rudi. I have often said that in World Series your team went through a mental transformation and a process of self-acceptance in which players really began to see and appreciate their true worth. During that time, the players developed a powerful self-image and strong self-belief, and started to take great pride in being West Indian.

I have never spoken to you about an interaction I had with Kerry Packer early in World Series, but I will tell you about it now. Our side had a very important team meeting in Melbourne before the first Super Test in which Albert Padmore had us all in fits of laughter. After that meeting, I went to Kerry and said to him. 'We are going to beat the hell out of you.' He laughed at me and replied, 'That's a joke. You don't know how to win. You are weak mentally and you will cower and crumble under pressure.'

I then said to Kerry, 'Something took place in our last team meeting that will change all that. The players went through a process of self-acceptance and have come to terms with something that has been bugging them for a long time. I now expect them to go through a mental transformation. They are not even aware of the significance of what really happened in that meeting and probably never will, but soon, their self-image will change and they will become different players. The team will be tougher mentally and will win the mental battle with the Australians.' Kerry gave me one of his famous looks and told me I was talking garbage and a lot of psychological rubbish. 'What is this mumbo-jumbo about self-acceptance?' he asked. 'It is about knowing yourself and valuing yourself,' I explained. 'Self-acceptance means that you accept yourself as a worthwhile and valuable person whether or not you perform well or whether or not people admire, criticize, abuse, praise or accept you.' Kerry rolled his eyes, pursed his lips and walked away.

We won the first game and eventually the series. After our first win Kerry said to me, 'This is very dangerous for us. You buggers have just learned how to win against us. It will now be very difficult to beat you.' How right he was. It took Australia more than sixteen years to beat us again.

Clive. In that series I think the players improved physically, technically, and especially mentally. They became mentally tough and played with a lot of pride and self-belief.

Rudi. The top cricket teams today have a coach and a large support team behind the players. In your day the captain had to do it all.

Clive. Yes. The captain was the coach, the taskmaster, the father figure, the motivator, the selector, the trainer, the problem solver, and the team builder. He was in charge of everything. Sometimes he got help from the senior players who took turns at coaching the younger players and supervising training and practice. The players were more involved in helping each other. This system worked well.

Rudi. That system did work very well for you. Today, there are many coaches in international teams and they have taken over a lot of the things that captains used to do in your day. Some of them are even dominating their relationship with the captain. But I think that relationship works best when coaches facilitate rather than dominate;

and when they assist and cooperate with the captain to achieve the captain's vision and the team's common goals.

You had to put your foot down in India when the team manager, Gerry Alexander, stepped out of line. Shane Warne recently reflected the feelings of many of the older cricketers when he said that international teams need good managers who act as a facilitator for the captain rather than domineering coaches. That was the way the old system worked. But cricket has changed very rapidly and has become quite complex. I believe that coaches and assistant coaches are essential but their main job should be to help the captain get the best results by mixing and matching the best of the old – values, techniques, strategies and technologies – with the best of the new and at times by guiding and encouraging the captain. My one concern today is that some coaches attach more importance to the tools and methods that improve analysis and planning than they do to the factors that improve execution.

Clive. I agree with you. The captain is the leader but he needs a cadre of coaches and specialist personnel in his support staff to assist him. Those coaches should work closely with him to guide him when necessary and to help him motivate his players to get the best out of them, improve teamwork and achieve his vision.

Vision for the Team

Rudi. In the text I said that successful leaders face the same complex situations as everyone else but they don't just drift along and allow circumstances to chart their path. Instead, they choose where they want to go and then find a way to get there. What was your vision for the team?

Clive. My vision was to be the best in the world in every department of the game. So I always wanted to have good, disciplined and mentally tough players in the team. I wanted them to enjoy what they were doing, and be friends, care and share, and respect each other.

I have the highest respect for what the players did for me and for West Indies cricket. They were very loyal to me. They gave their heart and soul and often played through injuries and pain. I will never forget those things

I wanted the people throughout the Caribbean to be proud of what we were doing on the cricket field. In the Caribbean our people are not like the people from other countries like Australia where they live on one land mass and have the same culture. We are about six million people with different backgrounds, thinking and culture. I had to bring players from those islands together and unify them. It was a challenging task.

Rudi. I believe that you and Frank did that very well. The two of you got rid of local prejudices and insularities and brought the players together in a cohesive and strong unit. I believe that was one of the most significant things that you achieved. No other Caribbean sportsmen, politicians or educators were able to do that.

Just to remind you of what I said at the start of the interview. From different West Indian islands you brought together a diverse collection of talented individuals who lacked direction, focus, discipline and common purpose – the so-called calypso cricketers – and you transformed them into a highly professional and all-conquering unit that dominated world cricket for fifteen consecutive years. That team is now regarded as one of the most successful teams in the history of sport. Very few people can boast of such an accomplishment.

Clive. Getting rid of local prejudices and insularity that held us back was an enormous feat that allowed us to take a giant step forward.

Rudi. When you left the scene insularity slowly crept back into our cricket and it has now reached cancerous proportions. Some people are even calling for the dissolution of the West Indies team and its replacement by individual territorial teams. Going back to discipline, what did you do to improve it in the very early days?

Clive. One of the simple things that we did was to insist that the players be on time to catch the bus to the ground. If a player were late he would be left behind and would have to find his own way to the ground and pay to do so. Bernard Julien was the first to transgress. But very soon after, Viv Richards was late and was left behind, and when he got to the ground his teammates started to tease him and laugh at him. Not many people were late after that. Subsequently, I don't know why, everything seemed to come together and discipline improved in leaps and bounds. I told the players that there was no excuse for being late since they all had watches. I even told them to get alarm clocks or make arrangements at the front desk for early wake-up calls. These were small things but they made a big difference.

You will always have one or two problem players in your team. You must know how to handle them. Most of the time they have a weakness that they try to hide by behaving in ways that do not conform to the norm. You have to get to know them, learn about their fears and weaknesses and help them by addressing those problems and by motivating them in a way that makes them feel important and special. Being tough on them can sometimes work but in most cases you must mix the tender and tough approaches.

Recognition Overseas

Rudi. Clive, I don't think the Caribbean people understand how much you were loved and respected around the world.

In the 1980s when Bob Hawke was prime minister of Australia, you were given Australia's highest award. At the time I believe you were the first cricketer and the only non-Australian to get it. I remember the occasion well. Four of us attended the ceremony. We stayed at Kerry Packer's home in Canberra and went to the governor general's residence where the award was presented to you. You might remember that when Wes Hall, the manager of the team, was presenting you to the governor general, the pressure got to the great champion and he could not remember a simple thing like your name. I had to prompt him.

Soon after that award you were given a contract to resurrect Australian cricket but one or two of their Test players objected to your appointment and nothing happened. Can you remember that?

Clive. Yes I remember that very clearly.

Rudi. When you went to South Africa I believe you met Nelson Mandela. Can you remember that meeting?

Clive. How can I forget it? I went to meet him with Dr Ali Bacher, and as we were approaching him he said, 'This is a sportsman I know.' Dr Bacher then turned to me and said, 'Did you hear what he said?' 'Yes and I will never forget it,' I replied. I have a picture of that meeting in my house, and wherever I go to live I will take it with me. If a man who was incarcerated for twenty-seven years and isolated from almost everything tells you that he knows of you and what you have done, that alone speaks volumes.

When I asked Mr Mandela if he bore any resentment or hatred towards the people who had imprisoned him, he said he bore no malice or resentment for any one. He explained that he had to heal many painful wounds and attitudes and had to unite and develop the country. He said that he would not be successful if he operated in an atmosphere of anger, bitterness and resentment towards the whites; he would be making the same mistake that they made. He said that South Africa had a great future and his job was to set it on the right path. I remember thinking, 'What a great and incredible person this man is.'

Rudi. The fact that Mandela knew of you means that he was following your exploits on the cricket field and must have felt a sense of pride because of your winning ways against all teams, particularly England and Australia.

Clive. Yes. It was because a black man was leading a black team that was beating everyone else in the world.

Rudi. That should have been mentioned in the film, *Fire in Babylon*.

But Mandela was not the only South African leader who admired you. In the 1990s during the transition period in South Africa I was visiting that country when President DeKlerk asked me to come to see him in his office in Pretoria. He was very keen on golf and we talked about the game for a while but he soon took me into the Cabinet room and said to me, 'This is where apartheid was legally born and this is where it will legally die.' I told him that he was doing the right thing and that it was a very brave and courageous act that showed great leadership. He then said, 'Talking of great leadership, I have always admired Clive Lloyd. He was an outstanding leader.'

So Mandela and DeKlerk, leaders on both sides of the huge and extremely bitter racial divide in South Africa, were singing your praises. That is an amazing compliment and an enormous mark of respect.

The Film *Fire in Babylon*

Rudi. Would you care to make a few comments about the film *Fire in Babylon* that highlighted the exploits of your champion team? I know that during an eleven-year span you conceived and developed that team and took it to its pinnacle before you handed over the captaincy to Viv Richards who carried on the good work and did extremely well. I watched the film with Seymour Nurse, the great West Indies batsman, and we both found it entertaining and amusing at times, but we were very surprised about the major reasons it put forward for the team's success. What did you think of the film?

Clive. I don't think the film gave the whole history or a full and accurate picture of what really happened. Our success did not take place in a vacuum. There were other people before us who showed us the way. The Worrell and Sobers West Indies team of the 1960s were world champions before we were. They could have shown snippets of that team and its players. They should have interviewed some of our opponents to find out why they thought we were such a great team. They should also have interviewed journalists like Tony Becca, Reds Perreira and Tony Cozier who between them would have seen all of the games that the team had played. Instead, they spent a lot of time interviewing some people who didn't have a clue about how the team was developed or why it did so well.

People like yourself who were involved with the team from its inception and Wes Hall who was manager of the team during some of its toughest battles should have been interviewed to get your views. Sir Garfield Sobers's thoughts about the team would have been extremely valuable. He could have told us why his team was world champions in the 1960s and why he thought the team of the 1980s was such a good one. I am sure that those two world champion teams had a lot in common. Instead, they completely sidelined the greatest player in the history of the game. What does that say about us as a people?

Our success had nothing to do with Babylon or any fire in Babylon. It was about professional cricket played at the highest standards. It was our talent, self-discipline, mental toughness, winning attitude and strong desire to be the best team in the world that made the difference. Clear thinking, good strategies and high standards of execution also played vital roles in that period of world dominance.

The film started with a lot of people getting broken arms and broken bones. But that was not our cricket. It was not like that. Those are by-the-way things that happen when batsmen face a good fast bowling side. Players today are still getting broken bones and blows to the head from fast bowlers. That is a by-product of fast bowling. We had an aggressive strategy, but our aggression was focused on bowling well and getting the batsmen out, not on knocking them down or injuring them. We bowled with hostility but not with hatred or malice.

To me the film portrayed the wrong concept of what the team did, how it did it and why it did it. It also had the wrong name. Surely, they could have found a more appropriate name.

Rudi. But Clive, they never stressed the things that you just discussed as being responsible for the team's success.

Clive. Rudi, I spent two hours of filming time talking about those things but they never put them in the film. I don't know why. I can only assume that they had their own motives for highlighting the things that they identified as the reasons for the team's success. It was very disappointing.

Rudi. I think that those factors you mentioned were critical to team success along with your leadership – keeping the team together, focusing on a common goal, having a sharing and caring attitude, and imprinting a winning philosophy in the players' minds. The team's aggression and enthusiasm, and its highly competitive spirit and powerful self-belief ensured its success. Your team did not just win the fitness and technical battles but more importantly it won the strategic and psychological ones.

The film highlighted the goal of triumphing over our colonial masters as a major motivating force for the team's success. But the team we wanted to beat most, and had to beat to become the best in the world, was Australia, and they were not our colonial masters. Neither were New Zealand, India or Pakistan.

Clive. That is why I'm saying that the theme and the reasons given for our success were wrong. Everton Weekes is the last 'W' who is still alive. Surely, they could have interviewed him to get his ideas about the team. Seymour Nurse, Wes Hall, Charlie Griffith and Gary Sobers from the 1960s world champion side are still around, and as far as I know they were never asked a single question. Those guys paved the way for us. And I can tell you that I used many of the values and guiding principles that Frank Worrell imparted to those players and his champion team to build my own team and take it to its pinnacle.

When Worrell's team was leaving Australia after its historic series against Australia, over half a million people lined the streets of Melbourne to say goodbye to them. That was in 1961 when the world was a bit different from what it is today. I believe that in my time as captain my team gained the same admiration and respect from the people of Australia and had a similar support base.

Rudi. I don't think the people in the Caribbean understand how much your team and Frank's team were loved and respected by the Australian people, not just for your performance on the field but also for the way you conducted yourselves off the field. I lived in Australia for seventeen years and I can report first-hand that their love and admiration for your West Indies players were genuine and enormous.

Clive. You know we enjoyed beating England but defeating Australia was the thing that motivated us most and gave us the greatest satisfaction. After about sixteen years the Australian team finally beat us and then went on to dominate world cricket for a long time, just as we had done before. The same performance factors that made us a great team helped them to become the best team in the world.

The Mind: Leadership from the Front

Rudi. How important is the mind in performance?

Clive. It is very important. Good thinking, confidence, concentration, discipline and mental toughness are vital things in performance. So too is motivation. I used to motivate my players by leading from the front, challenging them, and leading by example. My performance as the 'old man' of the team occasionally embarrassed the players into doing well. If I batted well, the other players might think, 'The skipper went out there and batted well, so we have to do well too.'

During practice sessions I was always exercising and running with them, bad knees and all, not running behind but in the midst of them. I did everything with them and I didn't ask them to do anything that the 'old man' wouldn't do. That stimulated the players to work harder and it created a lot of discipline and respect in the team. A lot of those things have been lost in recent years, particularly team discipline and self-discipline.

You know some of our modern administrators who never played the game but who should know better are now telling me that those basic principles and priorities are old-fashioned and not applicable today. The fundamentals and the important priorities of the game hardly ever change. If you get these things right you will have a good chance of playing well but if you downplay or ignore them you will be doomed to failure.

Rudi. Do you think that the administrators' misguided attitude and lack of knowledge and understanding of cricket are in any way responsible for the poor performance of our team in the last two decades?

Clive. Maybe. I believe that knowledge, experience, vision, the right attitudes, mindset and values are just as important today as they were in the past and as they will be in the future. They are the keys to success.

Rudi. I agree with you. In West Indies cricket we should focus on simultaneously managing complexity, change, uncertainty and the great conflict that is destroying our game. You might think that our ability to cope would be enhanced by the many new management concepts, techniques and technologies that are available today. The trouble is they there are so many of them available to our leaders and administrators that they don't seem to know which ones to choose or which way to turn. The best administrators, however, understand that it is not good enough merely to discard old principles and fundamentals in favour of the new and the unproven. They mix the best of the old and the new because they understand that conventional wisdom and fundamental principles still have great value today. In spite of everything, the basics are still the fabric of good performance.

Clive, some captains like yourself lead from the front and by example, and motivate their players to follow and strive for the highest standards, while others lead from behind and push their players in the right direction.

Clive. My players responded to leadership from the front. Other players respond to leadership from behind. Both methods are effective, and sometimes you have to mix them. It depends on the character and the skills of the captain and the circumstances and situations he has to deal with.

The Disastrous South African Tour

Rudi. In the 1990s you were the manager of the West Indies team during its disastrous tour of South Africa. The players went on strike before the start of the series and later performed very poorly in South Africa. I believe that the team lost just about every game and experienced all sorts of problems there. Looking back at that period, what would you have done differently?

Clive. That period was one of the low points of my career. I was very disappointed at having to travel all that way to tell the players that not going to Mr Mandela's country was not a smart move. Mandela was one of our best supporters. I know that he got inspiration from our team's exploits on the cricket field when he was incarcerated on Robben Island and that he respected us greatly. I tried to explain to the players how disappointed and let down the great man would be if we didn't go to South Africa and play well, but they didn't seem to understand or care. They were so blinded by the conflict with the WICB and their personal agenda that they could not see the broader picture and the wider implications of their decision to snub the president of South Africa, his country and its cricketing public that were so looking forward to our visit.

The players' refusal to go to South Africa in the beginning hurt me very much. I pleaded with them to go and to sort out their problems with the WICB afterwards. But they didn't listen and only agreed to tour literally in the last hours. I felt that the tour should have been cancelled or made shorter. When we got to South Africa we were not mentally and physically prepared for the challenges we had to face on the field. The tour was in a shambles.

Rebirth of the Team

Rudi. After that disastrous tour you came home to the West Indies to play the best team in the world, Australia. During that series there was a complete reversal in form and we drew the Test and One Day series. We could have beaten them in both of those formats.

Clive. Definitely. We should have beaten them. No one in the West Indies expected us to do well, and at the time they were pouring all sorts of criticism on the team and were mocking the players and showing their contempt for them. That embarrassed us.

We lost the first Test match in Trinidad very badly and the ridicule of the public got worse. I think the embarrassment that the players felt changed their attitude and motivated them to play better. At the time new personnel were added to the squad and that helped the change. We employed a fielding coach, and you were added to work on the mental side of the players' game. After the loss in Trinidad we trained much better and took control of the situation. From then on we played fantastic cricket. We won the second and third Test matches and might have won the last Test had we played young Chanderpaul. Our win in the One Day match in Guyana was denied when the match referee annulled the result because spectators had invaded the field thinking that the match was over when in fact it was not. Eventually, the match was finished but the protest of the Australians was upheld. We would have won the One Day series if the Australian protest had not been upheld.

Importance of Self-belief

Rudi. How important is self-belief at the top level of sport?

Clive. It is very, very important. Self-belief gives you everything. If you believe in yourself, you think you can beat everyone. But you must guard against overconfidence and complacency. Once you believe in yourself and have a good level of confidence you will do well. My team had very strong self-belief and they didn't think that anybody could beat them.

Rudi. How many times did your team escape the jaws of defeat and then go on and beat your opponents? Apart from getting rid of the insularity in the team, the most significant thing I think you did was to instill a powerful self-belief in your players. I strongly believe that eradicating insularity and improving self-belief were the two keys that opened the doors to your winning ways.

Clive. You might be right. I remember playing a match in India and they wouldn't give Gavaskar out, and Andy Roberts started to complain to me and said, 'What must we do to get this man out?' I looked him straight in the eyes and said, 'Bowl him down. Don't you believe you can bowl him down?' Andy then started to bowl with great fire and did just that. Once you know or believe you can do something you will do it when you get the right motivation. Encouragement motivated Andy.

Leadership Style: Planning, Preparation and Strategy

Rudi. Many captains are flamboyant and demonstrative on the field and communicate with the players by waving their arms around, pointing, and shouting instructions. Spectators like that style and often associate it with good leadership. You led your team quietly and effectively from the front without much fuss, like the quiet achiever. Some people mistakenly saw that style as a sign of mediocre leadership. Does the captain have to be flamboyant to be a good leader?

Clive. All good leaders have different styles. Some are quiet and others are vocal and flamboyant. A former CEO of Durham Cricket Club once said to Roger Harper that he didn't see Clive gesticulating or throwing his arms around on the field to direct his players. Roger told him that there was no need to do that because we covered most things in the dressing room during our preparation so when we got out on the field we knew what we had to do and which way we had to go.

People didn't notice the subtle signals and subtle things that we did on the field, nor did they know what we planned and discussed in the dressing room before the game.

Rudi. So what you are telling me is that your planning and preparation were very important.

Clive. Yes. They were extremely important. We used to go through everything in detail. For instance, we used to discuss the top batsmen and the rest. I used to remind the team that West Indies teams often had trouble getting rid of the lower-order batsmen. So we would go through the bowlers we would use against them, discuss how we would bowl at them and decide what fields we would set for them. In most cases when our players went on to the field, execution was the only thing they had to concentrate on.

Nowadays, teams use computers and other technologies to analyse, plan, prepare and get feedback. We had to do all of these things mentally because those technologies were not available then. In many ways, doing things mentally is better because you are more actively involved in the process. The use of computers is extremely valuable and has made a huge difference but when the computer gives you information you still have to know how to interpret it and use it constructively. Many of today's players are passive and detached onlookers when they view things on the computer and are not mentally challenged by them. I believe that the brain is still the greatest computer around.

Rudi. It is interesting that you say that. In visualization, when you create mental images where you watch yourself or other people performing, you are using external or disassociated imagery. This is similar to watching videos of yourself or your team.

But, when you create images where you are actually in your own body looking out, you are using internal or associated imagery. Both types are effective but research has shown that internal imagery is much more powerful and beneficial. In general, coaches are not aware of this and spend most of their time with players watching videos or using external imagery.

In your day, Clive, you and your team used more internal imagery in your planning, preparation and execution.

Clive. That is true.

Rudi. Some captains are so obsessed with tactics that they forget or ignore their strategy. The two things are different. Strategy is the overall intention and way of playing and tactics are moment-to moment moves that have to be made within that strategy. In general, strategy drives tactics; not the other way around. People often criticized your tactics and claimed that sometimes you responded too slowly to changing situations. I noticed that once you formulated a good strategy you stuck to it and didn't fiddle around too much with tactics.

Clive. Having a good strategy is very important and if you stick to it you will succeed even with ordinary tactics. I didn't see the need to chop and change too often in the game because even with the best tactics you will still lose if your strategy is substandard.

Pressure

Rudi. What about pressure? You handled it very well.

Clive. Pressure squashes certain players but the same pressure lifts the performance of other players. I handled it fairly well because I didn't panic. I used to stay calm and think clearly and simply even when I got a bit tense. Having good people around you helps you to cope.

Having a plan also helps you to handle the pressure. When you are under pressure your judgement is affected and you sometimes make the wrong decisions and do the wrong things. But those things are less likely to happen if you have a plan. For example, in a fifty-over game you must know who should bowl the last five overs. You should also make a plan for dealing with the unexpected. You must always expect the unexpected and be prepared to deal with it.

Rudi. You stayed calm, controlled your thinking, suppressed your emotions and played with grace and style even when you were under pressure. You were always the 'Supercat'. But some people who suppress their emotions pay a price and suffer from insomnia, ulcers and other stress-related problems.

Clive. I never had those problems. I feel that my thinking and coping skills on and off the field prevented that from happening to me.

Rudi. Many of today's West Indies players do not cope well with pressure. But we have had this problem before. You corrected it during your time as captain and not only did you show your players how to handle the pressures that were being placed on them but you also showed them how, when and where to apply pressure to the opponents.

Clive. That is true. As I just said, if you don't handle pressure properly, your judgement, decisions and execution will all be negatively affected.

Rudi. You are absolutely right. Under pressure, some leaders show poor judgement, have difficulty making decisions, drag their feet and act too slowly. Others speed up, make decisions too quickly and behave impulsively and incorrectly.

Looking Back on the Accomplishments

Rudi. When you gave up the captaincy you must have looked back on your career with immense pride and a sense of great achievement.

Clive. When I looked back at what we had accomplished over the years I was extremely happy about what we had done. We did what no one else had done before. At one stage I think we played twenty-nine Test matches and only lost one and in those days we didn't have to play against some of the weaker teams that are in today's competition.

Rudi. Taking a group of young men, bringing them together, instilling the right values in them, and then turning them into one of the best ever teams in the history of sports must fill you with great pride.

Clive. Yes. I tried to get them to understand that playing for West Indies was the ultimate. When you saw Viv Richards wrapping the West Indies cricket flag around himself, you couldn't help but feel privileged and proud to be a West Indian.

Looking at monetary rewards, I don't think our players earned the money that they should have. But that was a sign of the times. What I regret is that the WICB was not innovative or forward-looking enough at the time to recognize the monetary value of TV coverage of cricket. They didn't see the opportunity so they couldn't seize it. Had they done so when we were still champions, we would have done much better money-wise. They didn't learn very much from World Series cricket, a battle that was fought over TV rights. The WICB could not see the power of that medium in those days. They were not forward-looking.

Building a Team and Maintaining its Performance

Rudi. What was the difference in leading a team that was just emerging and one that was dominating the game?

Clive. In the emerging team the first thing you must do is to create the right mindset in the players and instill the right values in them. You then have to emphasize the importance of fitness, thinking, and concentration and all the other things that are responsible for winning. Continuous learning and mastery of the basic skills are a must. They must learn how to approach the game and different game situations, know what to do before the game, and learn how to think, concentrate, play and stay in control during the game.

When the team is established you still have to concentrate on those things. But you must remind the players about where the team came from, where it currently is, and what it had to do to get to its present position. You must also show them where you want the team to go and what you want it to become. And it is imperative to warn them how easy it is to slip backwards. So you must alert the players to the dangers of overconfidence and complacency, and be constantly on the lookout for it because complacency will get them in trouble. Overconfidence is a very serious problem.

Rudi. Gary Sobers always used to say that overconfidence and complacency are a prescription for failure. He said when you become overconfident you get arrogant and you put yourself on a pedestal and underestimate your opponent and his ability. That is so true. Overconfidence is psychological fraud. It causes a distortion of reality and dishonesty with self.

A Conversation with M.S. Dhoni on Leadership and Teamwork

Dhoni. I am not a lone wolf. I am a team man. I need to have people around me. If you give me the toughest assignment possible and I have people with me, I would definitely give it my best shot.

Rudi. What are the most important things about leadership and captaincy?

Dhoni. Let me stick to my sport, cricket. I am the captain of the Indian cricket team and I presently lead fifteen players and six support staff. These are the people who carry the expectations of 1.2 billion people, so I help them by keeping everything as simple as possible and by creating an atmosphere that will give confidence and motivation to each and every one to do his best.

I try to learn as much as I can from the senior ones and then pass on that knowledge to the younger players in the best possible way. I don't believe in bossing around people. I try to communicate in a polite way even when I have to give someone bad news after making a tough decision.

I also get to know my players and try to understand what makes them tick. No matter how good a leader you are you will never win or get the best out of your players unless you understand each and every one of them.

Proper communication is very important. I believe it is about making things as simple as possible because the simpler things are, the easier they are understood. There is a lot of talk about good leadership, but leaders are only as good as the players who follow them. Leaders do not usually get much success with poor teams. I feel that if you have a good side and the captain and coaches do the right things there is no good reason why that team should not do really well.

The leader must be able to blend and balance the expertise in the team and create a learning atmosphere. The atmosphere in the team is very important. The leader should try to get most of the players to perform well at the same time. Every one in the team must be motivated to play his part. A part-time bowler who can get a crucial breakthrough at the right time helps the main bowlers to go through the rest of the batsmen. Similarly, lower-order batsmen can contribute to the score and change the momentum of the game by putting their heads down and batting sensibly. I expect each and every member of the team to be a batsman and a bowler.

Rudi. Clive Lloyd, the former West Indies captain, was a good leader who built a team that dominated world cricket for about fifteen or sixteen consecutive years. In 1976, he did the following:

- He created a vision of what he wanted his team to be – the best team in the world for the next ten years – and he showed that vision to all of his players.

- He then designed an intelligent strategy to make that vision a reality, aligned it to his vision and talked about it with his players.

- He searched for players whom he thought had the 'right stuff' and brought them together as a close and energetic unit.

- He spent a lot of time motivating his players to execute his strategy, building and monitoring standards, and creating cooperative relationships in the team.

Ian Chappell, the great Australian captain, once said to me that any captain can learn how to set a field, change bowlers and write down the batting order, but for him the most important part of captaincy is the motivation of the players – getting them to work together as a team, committing themselves to team goals, and putting in extra effort when things get tough.

How important is motivation in your captaincy?

Dhoni. Motivation is very important in team performance. The captain must lead by example to get the trust, respect and support of his team. He must know the strengths and weaknesses of team members, know what makes them tick and know how they are likely to behave in different situations. He must build on the strengths of individual players not only to improve their game but to also inspire them to help to improve the performance of other team members.

When Sehwag opens the innings and plays well it takes a lot of pressure off the middle-order batsmen and makes their job easier. At the same time Sehwag knows that he is free to play his own style of game and that if he gets out cheaply the other six batsmen will do the job.

I try to talk to each player in the team, especially the young ones. Although Test cricket is a tough and gruelling game that tests the character of the players, I try to get them to understand that it is still a sport and should be enjoyed. Enjoyment and love of the game are two of the most powerful motivating forces in sport.

Rudi. When you took over the Indian team, did you have a vision of what you wanted the team to achieve and become?

Dhoni. I wanted the team to be a team. I wanted each and every player to enjoy the game. You know when I was young, four o'clock was my time to play sport and more often than not it was cricket. When I went on to the field I wanted to win but at the same time I wanted to enjoy the sport. These two things seem to compliment each other. If you enjoy playing your sport, particularly the process, you will have a reasonable chance of winning, and if you win you will enjoy the game.

Rudi. In the last four years you have done really well as a team. How did you create such good teamwork?

Dhoni. Over a period of time we gelled as a strong and cohesive team. It was not a quick fix. It was a continuous process where everyone contributed and enjoyed his involvement. If I score a hundred runs for the team and I know that the guy next to me is happier about my success than I am, I know that I have the makings of a good team. If the twelfth man wants to get into the team he should not hope that the person he wishes to replace fails. He should say to himself, 'Let him make a hundred runs and if I get a chance I will make a hundred and twenty runs.' You should encourage teammates to play well and then motivate yourself to perform better. This healthy attitude enables the team to perform well particularly in tough conditions. Over a period of time that is how really good teamwork evolves.

Apart from having a common goal and a strategy to achieve that goal the team should gel well. Team members should back up and help each other, appreciate each other's contribution, enjoy each other's success, and motivate one another to perform better. These are key factors.

Rudi. I have always said that game plans by themselves don't accomplish performance. At the end of the game, players are why the game plan works and why the team succeeds or fails. Skilful, united, well-trained, and highly motivated players are the key to team success.

Dhoni. That's right. To excel as a team you need to go on to the field as a team, not as a collection of individuals, and you need to hunt in packs, not as individuals.

Rudi. During the last World Cup you promoted yourself in the batting order at a very critical period of the game. What motivated you to go into bat before Yuvraj and to play such a magnificent innings?

Dhoni. Two off-spinners were bowling at the time, Muralitharan and Randiv, and I did not want to have two left-hand batsmen in at that time because the ball that is going away from the left-hander often causes him problems. Furthermore, I had played a lot of cricket with Muralitharan in the IPL, so I knew his bowling.

At that stage, I thought it was important to rotate the strike between a left-hand batsman, Gambhir, and a right-hand batsman, myself. Gambhir was well set at the time and I felt that if the two of us could stay at the wicket for a while it would make things easier for the batsmen coming in after us to score the required runs if they had to bat.

Rudi. You rose to the occasion and performed extremely well.

Dhoni. For me it was an opportunity and a great challenge. I believe in living in the moment, not thinking too far ahead in time, and I was taking one ball at a time. Even if you are the greatest batsman in the world your heart rate will go up during the first few deliveries that you face. Being in the moment calms your mind, stops you from thinking about too many things, and helps you to play one ball at a time. In the One Day format of the game you need to rotate the strike with your partner by taking singles. That takes some pressure off each batsman. It also helps the side because it reduces team pressure and maintains a good run rate without either batsman having to take too many risks. That is what I tried to do in that game.

As I said to you before, pressure brings the best out of me. I don't see pressure as a negative force. I view it as a positive force that lifts me to better performance. Pressure to me is just added responsibility. That is how I look at it. It's not pressure when God gives you an opportunity to be a hero for your team and your country. That moment in the World Cup was a great challenge and opportunity that I was happy to take as leader of the team.

I think I also told you earlier that if you give me the toughest assignment possible and I have people with me, I would definitely give it my best shot. That is what I did in the World Cup and it worked out well for the team.

Rudi. You are now a superhero in India. How do you cope with the enormous pressures that you face and the high expectations of 1.2 billion people?

Dhoni. You have visited India and you have seen the high expectations that are placed on the team. What is important is to have realistic expectations for the team and for individual players. You must be honest with yourself and know your strengths and weaknesses.

In 2011 every person in India wanted us to win the World Cup but the people from other nations also wanted their teams to win. Just because it was taking place in India there was no rational reason why we should win it. In fact, until then no host country had ever won the World Cup.

I believe that setting the right expectations for the team and the individuals in the team is very important. Expectations must be realistic. For example, a number eleven batsman should not expect to score a hundred and fifty runs. What he can do is put a price on his wicket and help to build a partnership with one of the other batsmen. So setting the right expectation levels is very important. That is what we have done.

We set long-term, intermediate and short-term goals. They are all very important.

Rudi. After working with you guys in India for a short period before the Champions Trophy in 2006, I had an illness that affected my spinal cord and left me paralysed from my waist down. I had to learn how to sit up, crawl, stand, and walk again, just like a baby. During my recovery I used a lot of visualization techniques to speed up the healing process. A few days after India was knocked out of the 2007 World Cup I saw some clear and detailed images that kept repeating themselves, over and over in my mind, and I said to my wife, 'During the last few days I have been constantly seeing images of Dhoni holding up the World Cup with jubilant team members around him, but India has already been knocked out of the competition.' My wife then replied, 'Perhaps it will happen at another time.' Four years later you won the World Cup.

Dhoni. You want to hear something funny. Before the last World Cup I saw myself holding up the cup and I kept replaying those images in my mind over and over again.

CHAPTER 3

SELF-CONFIDENCE

Self-confidence is vitally important. It comes from belief in yourself and in your ability. It is influenced by practice and preparation – knowing that you have practised hard, that you have left no stone unturned and that you have given everything you have got.

– Rahul Dravid

Self-confidence is knowing what you are doing and being in control of what you are doing.

– Peter Thomson

Far too many players perform below their potential because of bad habits, negative thinking and low self-confidence.

Self-confidence is important in every aspect of our lives, yet so many of us struggle to find it. A certain level of self-confidence is needed for good performance but it does not guarantee success nor does it prevent you from making mistakes and having failures. However, it helps you to deal with them better.

In the team, a sense of identity, a feeling of importance and a feeling of belonging are vital for building and maintaining self-confidence and team confidence.

Confidence can be a self-fulfilling prophecy. Players without confidence often fail because they expect to fail, and players with confidence usually succeed because they expect to succeed, not because of any superior skill.

People who are low in self-confidence often have a negative attitude. They see the cup half empty rather than half full. They underestimate themselves, focus on their weaknesses and magnify their difficulties. They can see other people's assets and strengths but not their own, and in some cases they try to hide their feelings of insecurity and inferiority by wearing a false mask, or by behaving in a falsely confident manner. They fear criticism and failure and are often reluctant to take the initiative just in case they make mistakes or fail.

Confident players on the other hand have a positive attitude and a realistic view of themselves and their challenges. They trust their abilities and expect to be successful. Even when they fall short of their goals and expectations they still remain positive and are not afraid to take the initiative or make mistakes.

Overconfident players think that they are better than they really are. They overestimate their knowledge and ability and underestimate their opponents and their challenges. Overconfidence or false confidence is psychological fraud. It is a prescription for failure.

A lot of time is spent teaching athletes how to cope with failure. I believe that an equal amount of time should be spent teaching them how to cope with success to prevent them from becoming overconfident and big-headed.

Here are some comments about overconfidence from an ultra-marathon runner: 'When you become overconfident you underrate the race and the other runners. So that when simple problems arise they hit you twice as hard because you are not prepared for them. They may be problems that you have handled successfully many times in the past but because of your attitude you are not prepared for them. You put yourself on a pedestal, believe that you are the king, become complacent and just go through the motions thinking that things will be easy. With that mindset you behave foolishly and sometimes pay a heavy price.'

WHAT IS SELF-CONFIDENCE?

Years ago, I discussed self-confidence with golfer Peter Thomson and I told him that Dennis Lillee, the great fast bowler, described confidence as belief in yourself; a positive feeling about yourself and about your ability to cope; an expectation of meeting your challenges and achieving success. I told him that Dennis did two things to maintain his self-confidence whenever it was threatened. First, he would tell himself that he was one of the best bowlers in the world; and second, he would recall his statistics – one wicket every five overs in Grade cricket, one wicket every seven overs in Sheffield Shield cricket and one wicket every nine or ten overs in Test cricket. Those figures assured him that if he continued bowling, success would come to him.

Peter admitted that was one way of maintaining confidence, but stressed that there is more to it than that. For instance, Lillee could have all those things at the back of his mind and be full of confidence, but if he then bowled five consecutive wides or no balls, his confidence could plummet because he would suddenly realize that he was not in control of his bowling.

He believes that the secret to confidence is knowing what you are doing and being in control of what you are doing, or at least thinking that you are. If you don't know what you are doing or if you are not in control of what you are doing your confidence will be compromised.

Peter concluded in the following manner: 'You can't exhort yourself to be confident. It develops as a result of the things you do and feel. Confidence comes from your knowledge and the repeated application of your skills. When you demonstrate to yourself that you know what you are doing and that you are in control of what you are doing, your confidence will be established. It is built on competence, good execution, adequate preparation, your record, your experience, your knowledge of the game and your knowledge of yourself.'

Dravid and Laxman use the analogy of sitting for an examination to highlight the close relationship between good preparation and self-confidence. They say that if you prepare well and read all the chapters in the book from which you will be examined, you will go into the examination room with a calm and clear mind and a healthy level of confidence knowing that you have covered the work. But if you only study three of the six chapters you will have less confidence and hope that none of the questions come from the chapters you had not read.

And if they do, your confidence would suffer and your expectations of passing would fall.

But, having the knowledge does not mean that you will use it effectively to pass the examination. This requires competence in other examination skills – handling examination pressure and anxiety, reading the questions carefully and understanding what is needed, writing out the answers simply and clearly, and doing so within the allotted time. Practising these skills under the same physical and psychological conditions that you will face in the exam will enhance your confidence and improve your chances of passing the examination.

If you want to play a particular piece of music well, you must practise it repeatedly until you get it right. If you want to run well in a 400-meter race you must repeatedly practise running that distance. And if you want to get confidence and do well in your sport you must prepare well and repeatedly practise your physical and mental skills in real and simulated match conditions until you master them. Competence and confidence go hand in hand.

Confidence and concentration are also closely related. Your confidence could be shaky when your concentration wanders into the past on previous mistakes and negative experiences or into the future on the result or on the things you fear might go wrong. Keeping your concentration in the present on the process is a good way to maintain self-confidence.

REMEMBER

1. Self-confidence helps you to play better but it does not guarantee success nor does it stop you from making mistakes.
2. You can't exhort yourself to be confident. It develops as a result of the things you do and feel.
3. When you know what you are doing and are in control of what you are doing, your confidence will be established.
4. Confidence comes from your knowledge and the repeated application of your skills.

Curtly Ambrose, Phil Snaith of Shell, Sir Everton Weekes, Dr Peter Bourne, Pat Rousseau, president of the West Indies Cricket Board, and Sir Garfield Sobers at the opening of the Shell Cricket Academy, St. George's University, Grenada, West Indies.

Batting against Sobers for Warwickshire against the West Indies. Frank Worrell is at first slip.

At Harrison College, Barbados, many years ago. I believe that my record in the 200 metres still stands.

Cartoon by Haddon in the *Melbourne Herald* newspaper.

After winning the Grand Final some of the players from the victorious Hawthorn Football Club team whom I had prepared mentally for the game brought the trophy to my house to show their appreciation.

Discussing cricket, politics and the Sri Lankan civil war with the President of Sri Lanka, Junius Jayewardene.

With Sir Garfield Sobers, Sir Wesley Hall and Clive Lloyd in the dressing room at the Melbourne Cricket Ground after beating Australia.

Visiting a Buddhist temple in Sri Lanka with my wife Lyndi.

Kerry Packer World Series West Indies team. *Front row, left to right:* Viv Richards, Jimmy Allen, Deryck Murray, Clive Lloyd (captain), Bernard Julien, Gordon Greenidge, Roy Fredericks, Wayne Daniel.
Back row, left to right: Rudi Webster (manager), Collis King, Albert Padmore, Michael Holding, Joel Garner, David Holford, Andy Roberts, Lawrence Rowe.

Ambassador of Barbados to the US and to the Organization of the American States.

With Mike Smith, captain of Warwickshire and England.

Bowling for Warwickshire against Worcestershire.

With US President Bill Clinton after his State of the Union Address to a Joint Session of Congress in Washington, DC.

With the US power soccer team. All the athletes were differently abled.

Immediately after graduating in medicine I celebrated by taking 7 wickets for 6 runs against Yorkshire in the first innings and 12 wickets for 58 runs in the match.

Warwickshire team at Lord's with the Benson and Hedges One Day Trophy. Six of these players represented England and one represented Pakistan.

My good friend Gamini Dissanayake and his close friend Rajiv Gandhi, the Indian Prime Minister. This was a picture that kept preying on my mind repeatedly the night I had to leave Sri Lanka in a hurry. A few days later, a suicide bomber killed Gamini. Earlier, Rajiv Gandhi suffered the same fate when he was assassinated by a suicide bomber in Tamil Nadu.

Ian Chappell, Sir Garfield Sobers, Tony Greig, Clive Lloyd and Rudi Webster toasting the start of World Series Cricket in Melbourne, Australia.

The fight between coaches Tony Jewell and Peter Jones during an Australian Rules finals football game. Peter Jones sent me this picture soon after, with a note that read: 'All over you, Rudi.'

Gamini Dissanayake. My visits to Sri Lanka strongly influenced my thinking and attitude towards life.

The two coaches shaking hands and making up with my blessings in a TV studio the day after the fight. Peter Jones is on my right.

With US
President
George H.W.
Bush, Mrs Bush
and Lyndi at the
White House.

he victorious World Series team. *Left to right:* J. Allan, C. King, L. Rowe, B. Julien, R.
Fredericks, G. Greenidge, J. Garner, Sir Garfield Sobers, V. Richards, A. Padmore, C.
Lloyd, R. Webster, D. Murray, A. Roberts, M. Holding, D. Holford (physical trainer).

Receiving the 'Sportsman
of the Year' trophy from
Lord Cameron at the
Assembly Room, Edinburgh
University, Scotland.

Brian Lara talking to young players, emphasizing the importance of having a calm mind and keeping the eye on the ball.

With Sir Garfield Sobers and Clive Lloyd after winning the Sir Garfield Sobers World Series Trophy.

5. Confidence is built on competence, good execution, practice, adequate preparation, concentration, your record, knowledge of the game, and knowledge of yourself.

6. A certain level of confidence is needed for good performance. Loss of confidence and overconfidence are equally dangerous to performance.

7. We need to spend more time teaching players how to deal with success to prevent them from becoming overconfident and swell-headed.

8. Overconfidence is psychological fraud and is a prescription for failure.

9. In the team, a sense of identity, a feeling of importance and a feeling of belonging are vital in building and maintaining self-confidence and team confidence.

HOW IS SELF-CONFIDENCE DEVELOPED IN THE FIRST PLACE?

In the early years, the interaction of parents and coaches with children is very important. So too is the interaction of children with other children in free and unstructured play.

When parents are supportive and accepting of their children and allow them to be kids, they build a foundation on which the children can start to feel good about themselves. Parents who are too hard and critical, or too soft and protective often inhibit their children's capacity to build self-worth and self-confidence. Children must be given the freedom to explore, develop self-reliance, and learn critical social skills by interacting with other kids in unstructured and unsupervised play.

If parents give their kids a certain degree of independence and show them love, respect and understanding, particularly when they make mistakes or have failures, the children will become more accepting of themselves and start to build self-worth and self-confidence.

Parents and coaches often put enormous pressure on their kids by demanding unrealistically high standards from them. Their lofty expectations and their quest for perfection create considerable stress and anxiety. They would be better served if they lower expectations, set challenging but achievable goals, allow their children to be creative and innovative, and reward them for both their effort and success. They should also get into the habit of praising small successes and then challenging their children to strive for higher goals. When small successes are repeated and celebrated they often result in significant jumps in confidence.

Recently, an article in the *American Journal of Play* stated that today overprotective parents and over-controlling coaches often schedule practically every moment of their children's lives. Free or unsupervised play is seldom allowed. In a special issue of this journal experts are confirming that this lack of unrestricted free-time play – not allowing kids to just be kids – is having dire consequences on our children's behaviour and on their physical and mental health.

According to Professor Peter Gray, a psychologist at Boston University, we can draw a clear line connecting the decline in free play with the rise in childhood and young-adult anxiety, depression and suicide.

In 1982, Jack Canfield, an expert on self-esteem and self-confidence, conducted a study to find out how many negative and positive statements a group of young children received during the course of a day. He found that on the average each child received 460 negative or critical comments and only seventy-five positive or supportive comments, six times more negative than positive ones. What would happen to the self-confidence and self-worth of children and young people if that ratio were reduced or reversed?

Years ago some researchers placed a group of timid mice in a cage with a group of confident and aggressive mice. The timid mice huddled in one corner and trembled with fear. They were then removed and placed in an empty cage. Over a few weeks, the researchers gave them simple tasks to perform, and each time they completed those tasks successfully they rewarded them with pieces of cheese. The researches gradually increased the difficulty of the tasks and rewarded the mice each time they completed them successfully. With each small success the mice became more confident. After a while the researchers returned them to the first cage. The group then displayed a newly found confidence and aggression towards the other group that became weary and docile.

In Australia, I was once asked to work with an Australian Rules football team that had come close to winning the championship on a few occasions but somehow could not take that last step. There were many good players in the team, including at least four superstars.

I told the coach that I wanted to do some special work with eight of his least talented players – there are twenty players in each team – and I asked him to tell me what roles he wanted them to play and exactly what he expected of them. I then asked him to praise some aspect of their performance at the end of every game in front of the team and the press. The coach agreed and did a wonderful job in that respect throughout the season. Before, only the stars received praise and attention.

When I started to work with those eight players, I told them that the superstars in the team could not win games consistently without their contribution. I stressed that the team would only win if they did their jobs well and if they fulfilled their roles and responsibilities. I constantly repeated that message and emphasized how vital their input was to the success of the team.

I used ego-boosting techniques to increase their self-worth and then changed their thinking and their self-talk. I taught them various visualization and mental rehearsal techniques and got them to practise them regularly. They identified their first-important priorities, set themselves modest goals and concentrated on mastering the fundamentals of their game. I told them that they were allowed to make mistakes but must learn from them.

With each game their contributions increased, the coach gave positive feedback and their confidence grew. The team reached the Grand Final, the equivalent of the English FA Cup Final and the

American Super Bowl and won it in a convincing way. Those eight players performed extremely well and were among the best players in the game.

I used the same strategy in India with the Kolkata Knight Riders during the 2012 IPL cricket season. I worked quietly and exclusively with the team's lesser-known and lesser-talented Indian players, some of whom were overwhelmed by the presence of the superstars. I tried to change their thinking and to convince them that the team would not achieve success without their contribution and commitment. I stressed that their input would be just as important, if not more than that of the local and overseas superstars and I used some of the ego-boosting and mental-conditioning techniques that I described above to improve their thinking, self-beliefs and self-worth. In the final against the Chennai Super Kings one of these lesser-known players lifted his game to new heights and batted brilliantly. He put the team on the winning path and won the Man of the Match Award for his outstanding contribution. Another one of these local players kept his cool and common sense in the last two overs of the game when the pressure was at its peak and most dangerous. He scored the winning runs with just a few balls to go.

REMEMBER

1. The foundation for self-confidence is built at an early age when parents, coaches and society interact with children and when children interact with other children.

2. Parents and coaches should monitor their interaction with children carefully and ensure that they create a learning environment in which children can build self-worth and self-confidence.

3. Jack Canfield, an expert on self-esteem and self-confidence, found that during an average day a child receives 460 negative comments and only seventy-five positive ones, six times more negative than positive comments.

4. Allowing 'kids to be kids' in unstructured or unsupervised play has become taboo for many parents. In a special issue of the *American Journal of Play*, experts confirm that this lack of unrestricted free-time play is having negative effects on children's physical and mental health.
5. There is a clear line connecting the decline in free play with the rise in childhood and young-adult depression, suicide and narcissism.
6. Small successes when repeated and celebrated result in quantum leaps in self-confidence.
7. Once you get the basics right, your performance will revolve around your self-belief and self-confidence.

SELF-CONFIDENCE AND SELF-ACCEPTANCE ARE NOT THE SAME THINGS

> Self-acceptance is too often a neglected factor in performance. It is a key to good performance.
>
> – *Rudi Webster*

When I am dealing with players I always break down self-confidence into two parts, self-esteem or self-worth and self-efficacy.

Working on the players' self-esteem I try to create a feeling of well-being and a general sense that they will be able to cope successfully with their challenges. The aim is to produce a feeling of readiness, create a positive self-image, and focus on positive self-statements like: 'I am a valuable player even with my faults and weaknesses.' Positive self-talk and creative imagery help to imprint those statements and beliefs into the players' mind.

Self-efficacy is more specific and is about building a sense of competence, creating a feeling of 'can do', and a belief in the ability to master the basics of the game and the challenges in the game.

People often ask me why the Clive Lloyd and Viv Richards West Indies team that dominated world cricket for fifteen consecutive years was such a great team. It was indeed a very talented, fit and professional team. If I had to name a single factor it would be self-acceptance. I believe that at the highest levels of sport where there is not much difference in the talent of the players, or the team, the players' performance is strongly influenced by self-image and self-belief.

Self-acceptance is related to self-confidence and self-esteem but it is slightly different.

Self-esteem and self-confidence in sport revolve around performance. When an athlete rates himself or feels good about himself because he played well or intelligently, he feels confident. This feeling is enhanced when people admire, praise and respect him. But if he plays poorly or stupidly he is likely to feel badly about himself, particularly if people disrespect him and criticize his performance.

In self-acceptance, the player accepts himself as a worthwhile and valuable person whether or not he plays well or intelligently, or whether or not people admire, respect, or praise him.

It is foolish for an athlete to rate his worth as a player solely and entirely on the basis of his performance because as his performance fluctuates so will his confidence and self-esteem.

Good players maintain a sense of worth that is independent of their performance and statistics. Bill Russell, the great American basketball player from the very successful Boston Celtics team, pointed out the importance of self-acceptance in champion players when he said:

> Any good athlete will identify with his score, his statistics and reputation. It is a struggle to keep a sense of self-worth that is independent of these elements. In the Celtics we had an extra feeling of confidence beyond the game itself, because we knew we would be all right no matter how the game turned out. Ironically, this feeling of independence makes you play better and it also helps you to assume what I call the star's responsibility.

Dennis Lillee, the great fast bowler, was also able to separate his worth as a person from his performance. He said: 'If I bowl badly, I don't come off the field thinking that I am a failure or a useless person. I say to myself, "I had a bad day today. It was a bad day's work. Tomorrow is a new day and I will make sure that I do better." On the other hand, if I bowl well and get lots of wickets, I don't walk off the field pushing out my chest, strutting around like a bloody peacock thinking how great a person I am. I say to myself, "That was a good performance. I bowled really well. It was a good day's work. But tomorrow is another day, and I will have to work harder to repeat it.'" Dennis added, 'Being a bowler is not who I am. It is what I do for enjoyment and a living. There is more to me than being a good bowler.'

REMEMBER

1. When dealing with self-confidence you should divide it into two parts — self-esteem and self-efficacy.

2. In sport, your self-confidence is usually built around your performance — how well you play, how you rate your performance and how others assess it.

3. It is silly to value your worth as a player solely on the basis of your performance because as your performance goes up and down, so will your confidence.

4. Self-acceptance is different. In self-acceptance you accept yourself as a worthwhile and valuable person and player, whether or not you play well, or whether or not people admire, respect or praise you.

5. Good players maintain a sense of worth that is independent of their performance and statistics.

6. According to Bill Russell this feeling of independence makes you play better and helps you assume what he calls the star's responsibility.

CONFIDENCE IS NOT STABLE

Confidence can be quite fragile. It can improve after a single shot or small success, or can be lost after a simple mistake or failure.

— Greg Norman

There is an optimum range of confidence within which players give their best performances. That level varies from one person to the other and from one situation to the next. For instance, a batsman might be confident against off spin bowling for most of the game but might lose it against the same type of bowling when the game is on the line and the result depends on his performance.

If two players, one low in confidence and the other overconfident, look at the same game situation they will most likely see different things and think and play differently. The player lacking confidence might see failure and danger, and the overconfident player might see opportunity and an easy victory. That difference of perception causes contrasting actions, caution and conservative effort in one case and boldness and aggression in the other.

Greg Norman, once the world's best golfers, stressed the fragility of self-confidence when he said to me: 'During the final round of the Victorian Open in 1983, I was leading the field by one shot on the seventeenth hole and I was confident that I would win the championship. But I narrowly missed an easy putt for par on that hole and dropped a shot. I was very disappointed and angry when I walked off the green and was in a sort of daze. All of a sudden, I was not as confident as I had been a few minutes earlier. However, all was not lost and I thought that I would still win if I birdied the last hole or at least get into a play-off if I parred it. But I played the hole badly, bogeyed it and lost the championship by one stroke. A certain victory became a failure because I missed an easy putt on the seventeenth green and lost my confidence and composure.'

Many players fall into that same trap. They get negative thoughts and negative emotions when they make mistakes or have bad breaks, then lose concentration and composure and make more mistakes.

Peter Thomson, Australia's best golfer, must have been thinking of that Greg Norman incident when he said: 'In the game of golf you might go along very nicely with everything happening to plan when something unexpected suddenly happens. You might play a wild shot or miss an easy putt, and if you don't know why or have a simple explanation, your confidence can be shattered. If you are in control, you are prepared for most eventualities and you deal with them successfully when they arise. Players often lose control at critical periods if they don't know what they are doing. These players don't have a forward plan. You must be prepared for the unexpected.'

It is not unusual for a player with little confidence to become overconfident and blasé after a successful performance, only to fail and lose confidence soon after. That is exactly what happened to Norman Cowans, an England cricketer.

During England's cricket tour of Australia in 1982-83, Cowans, England's fast bowler, was prematurely thrown into the Test match arena with less than a full season of first-class cricket behind him. Supporters thought he had lots of potential and believed that he would do well in Australia. But in the first half of the tour he performed disastrously. Some commentators claimed that he was the worst fast bowler ever to play Test cricket.

Just before the fourth Test in Melbourne he asked me to help him. At that time he was a very dejected young man and had grave doubts about his ability to play Test cricket. I had never before seen such low confidence in an elite athlete.

I used the same approach that I had employed with Viv Richards a few years earlier and immediately set out to lower his anxiety, improve his self-esteem and confidence, work on his concentration and go through a simple goal-setting process for the upcoming Test match. I asked him to break down his bowling into small simple segments and encouraged him to select a few simple goals that he knew he was capable of achieving. He then set himself two goals, the 'result goal' of getting two wickets in each innings and the 'process goal' of a smooth relaxed and rhythmical run-up and of bowling a good line and length for at least four balls in every over.

I showed him how to relax and gave him helpful ego-boosting ideas. I imprinted the two simple goals in his mind with powerful suggestions and then got him to mentally rehearse them using clear, vivid and detailed imagery. He was asked to see and feel himself walking back to his bowling mark and just before turning to start his run-up he was instructed to take two relaxing breaths to remove any tension from his neck and shoulders. His main goal then was to run up to the wicket smoothly and rhythmically and to be well balanced at the crease to bowl exactly where he wanted it to go.

He repeated that imagery during the session and I taught him how to replay and practise it for the game. Before he left my house he thanked me for my help and said. 'I feel so much better now. I know what I have to do and I believe I can do it. I am sure that I can get two wickets. I am also certain that I can run up to the wicket smoothly and bowl a good line and length.'

In the first innings of the Test he bowled extremely well and got his two wickets. In the second innings he bowled even better and faster and collected a match-winning haul of seven wickets. He won the match for England and was given the 'Man of the Match Award'. Suddenly, he was hailed as a new and exciting find.

A few days later he went to Sydney to play the next Test, an extremely confident young man with very high expectations. Before the Test started I told my wife that he would perform poorly in the game because I knew that he was on a high and that he would abandon the planning and preparation that had brought him success in the previous Test. As expected, he bowled badly and performed way below his expectations. After the game he was totally deflated. In a matter of two weeks his confidence went full circle.

A day after the game finished he phoned me and admitted that he set his sights on winning the Man of the Match Award again, and did not use the approach and mental techniques that he had practised a week earlier.

THINKING AND SELF-TALK

> For one who has conquered the mind, the mind is the best of friends. But for one who has failed to do so, his very mind will be the greatest enemy.
>
> — *Bhagavadgita*

> Talk and listen to the 'little man'. Make him your best and most trusted friend and work with him closely to perform your tasks

and reach your goals. If you make him your enemy he will
sabotage your performance.

– *Rudi Webster*

When your confidence falls, the three most common refrains are: (1)
I can't do it. I am not good enough. I will mess it up. (2) It's too hard.
He is too good for me. There is no point going on. (3) They will hate
me if I let them down, and will think that I am useless.

But when your confidence is high and you are faced with identical
situations that self-talk changes to: (1) I can do this. I can beat him.
I can win; (2) This is easy. He is not that good. Just keep going; and
(3) I will show them how good I am. I don't need their advice or their
praise. I will rely on my own opinions and judgement.

Many players describe self-talk as talking to the 'little man' inside
the head.

A few years ago an Australian Rules football player became very
dejected when he was unexpectedly dropped from the team. He
thought the selectors had lost faith and confidence in him and was
concerned about his future with the team. However, he was chosen
for the next game and was determined to play well. He came to see
me and asked me to help him with his mental preparation.

I put him in a light hypnotic trance and instructed him to talk to
his 'little man', make friends with him, and ask him to help him find a
solution for his performance problems. Fifteen minutes later he woke
up with a broad smile on his face.

'Why are you so happy?' I asked.

'All is well, I will play well in the next game,' he replied. 'I made up
with the "little man". We've been fighting each other for the last six
weeks but we shook hands and became friends again. We even shared
a couple of beers.'

'What did he look like?' I asked.

'He is a leprechaun. He is about one foot tall and was dressed in
a colourful outfit. He wore green shoes with large gold buckles, plus
four tartan trousers and long red socks, a green coat and a large red
Uncle Sam hat. He had a silver goatee beard. He was standing on the
mantelpiece in my house when he spoke to me.'

Incidentally, that player was of Irish descent.

In the next game he played extremely well and was the best player on the field. His good form then continued in subsequent games.

Another footballer came to see me soon after with a more serious problem. He had damaged the posterior cruciate ligament in his left knee and had been in plaster for eight weeks. Before his injury he was a key player in his team. So he was desperate to recover because the season was almost over and his team was leading the competition and was certain to play in the finals.

He became terribly depressed when the plaster was removed because his thigh and leg muscles had wasted terribly and were half their normal size. Furthermore, he could not bend his knee. I was able to bend it past ninety degrees but he could only manage ten degrees by himself. His doctors told him that there were some fibrous adhesions inside his knee and that it needed lots of physiotherapy to break them down and more time to heal. They also told him that his chances of playing again that season were almost zero.

In the past, I had taught him self-hypnosis, so I asked him to put himself into a hypnotic trance, talk to the 'little man', go into his knee joint with him and examine it to see how they could speed up healing and improve its function. He controlled and directed the session all by himself and after about twenty minutes he ended his trance and woke up smiling.

I asked him what had happened and he told me that he spoke to the 'little man' and then went inside the knee joint with him. The joint was very rusty and dirty and the surrounding muscles were dry, withered and weak. While they were inside the joint looking at the mess, twenty tiny men appeared with oil cans in their hands and told him that they had come to help him fix the joint. They proceeded to lubricate the inside of the joint as well as the surrounding muscles. Immediately, the joint became clean, smooth, white and shiny and the muscles enlarged and came to life.

We both had a good laugh and while we were laughing I told him to bend his knee. He did so quite easily and to his surprise bent it past ninety degrees.

'This is incredible!' he exclaimed after bending it several times. 'How did that happen?'

I told him I didn't know and asked him not to tell his doctors or physical therapists about what we had done because they wouldn't believe him. 'Let them think that their therapy was responsible for the sudden improvement,' I instructed.

Within a few weeks he was playing again and later went on to play in the Grand Final that his team easily won.

Years ago, the Australian golfer Greg Norman asked me to come and see him at his hotel on the morning of the last day of the Australian Masters Golf Championship. Greg hadn't been playing well and was about eight or nine shots behind the leader of the tournament at the end of the third day's play. We didn't have time for a lengthy session, so I started to speak to him about the importance of communicating with the 'little man'.

I explained that he has a 'little man' inside his head and that he is in constant conversation with him, but that most of the time he is not aware of that interchange. I told him that the 'little man' plays an important role in building and maintaining confidence and in controlling concentration. I advised him to make him a close and trusted friend and ally, not an opponent or enemy. I told him that if the 'little man' were his enemy he would sabotage his performance. 'Befriend him and ask him for his help and cooperation. You won't play well today unless you do so,' I explained. Greg found all of this quite amusing and I didn't know if he would pay any attention or give any credence to what I had said. Before I left the hotel I gave him another suggestion – concentrate on playing to position, not on the score.

I followed him on the course that afternoon and hid in the background for most of the round. On the second hole, a par four, he played a magnificent drive down the middle of the fairway and was about to play a wedge to an undulating green that was surrounded by many large bunkers. He addressed the ball and was about to start his backswing when he suddenly pulled away and shouted, 'Come on man. Don't talk to me like that. You're supposed to help me. You know what you have to do.' He then addressed the ball again, played a wonderful shot to within two feet of the hole and sank his putt for a birdie. That birdie gave him great confidence and he went on to play a fantastic round to win the championship.

On the eighteenth fairway he spotted me, ran up to me and exclaimed, 'You wouldn't believe what happened on the second hole! I had to have a serious chat with the "little man" who was being very difficult. Before I played my second shot, I was confident that I would hit the ball close to the pin. But, just as I was about to start my backswing the little man said, "You can't do it. You are going to mess it up," and I could see the ball going into the bunker. All that happened in the matter of a split second and I became tense as a result. After I spoke to him everything changed, my confidence returned and I knew I would play a good shot. I could see the ball coming to rest next to the hole before I actually played the shot. I executed the shot perfectly and birdied the hole. That gave me great confidence. Throughout the rest of the round I told the "little man" what I wanted to do and I concentrated on hitting the ball to position. I wasn't aware of my score until I reached the tee on this hole."'

The importance of self-talk – talking to the 'little man' – in managing confidence and improving performance cannot be overemphasized. Equally important though is listening to what the 'little man' says to you. I am acutely aware of how vital this is because my 'little man' saved my life a few years ago in Sri Lanka.

Just before I finished my term as Barbados' ambassador to the USA, I went to Sri Lanka as a political advisor to my friend Gamini Dissanayake during his six-week political campaign for the presidency of Sri Lanka. At that time he was president of the Sri Lanka Cricket Board and had invited me to Sri Lanka on two previous occasions to work with the Sri Lankan cricket team to help team members improve their mental skills and to assist the board in designing a development programme.

During the campaign, I stayed at Gamini's home and wherever he went I was by his side. Every night we attended three political meetings and I always sat close to him on the political platform. Occasionally, he would introduce me to the crowd as the person who had helped Sri Lankan cricketers with the mental part of their game.

Three weeks after I got there, I was awakened one morning at three o'clock by my 'little man'. He was talking to me. He said: 'Leave Sri Lanka right away. Go back to Washington. You have done what you came here to do.' At first, I didn't pay him any attention but for the next three hours he kept repeating that message and just would not stop. At seven o'clock that morning I went into Gamini's bedroom and told him that I had to return to Washington immediately. He was very disappointed and said: 'You are not going to desert me now, are you? As long as you are here with me I feel safe. Go back to Washington, attend to your business and come back for the last two weeks of the campaign.' I promised to do so.

I flew out of Sri Lanka that evening and went back to Washington via London. Before I left Gamini's house to go to the airport I was extremely anxious. My anxiety was so high that I thought I was going crazy; I couldn't understand why I was feeling that way. The one thing that stuck in my mind was a beautiful picture of Gamini and his friend Rajiv Gandhi that was on the wall in the lobby. That high level of anxiety stayed with me until I arrived at the airport. The moment I set foot in the terminal building my anxiety vanished completely and I became perfectly calm and relaxed.

Soon after I returned to Washington, I received a telephone call from Sri Lanka informing me that a suicide bomber had just assassinated Gamini at a political meeting. Sixty-three people were killed including everyone on the political platform. Had I not left Sri Lanka I would have been on the platform close to him. I couldn't believe what I heard and later realized how lucky I was. I also learned that the same people who murdered Rajiv Gandhi, the Liberation Tigers of Tamil Eelam, had claimed responsibility for Gamini's assassination.

Scientists call this phenomenon precognition. Sportsmen refer to it as premonition or intuition and claim that they sometimes get intuitive flashes on the field that often result in success when they follow them.

Some people seem to be quite sensitive to this phenomenon. In 1987 Errol Barrow, the prime minister of Barbados, came to see me at my home and spent the entire Sunday morning with me. We talked about the old days, about his vision for Barbados and about the future leaders of the party and country. When it was time for him to leave, my wife and I accompanied him to his car and as he got into it he had a very sad look on his face. While he was driving away I said to my wife, 'Wave goodbye to him. This is the last time we will see him alive.' She shouted at me and told me to shut my mouth and that she didn't want to hear anything about my thoughts or feelings.

Next day, I was very uncomfortable at work in the prime minister's office and left early because I was extremely anxious and didn't know why. I had lunch at home and soon fell asleep on a couch in the verandah.

Sometime later, my wife woke me up in a state of fright. 'What's wrong with you?' she asked. 'Were you having a nightmare? You were groaning and clutching on to your chest as though you were having a heart attack. You scared the daylights out of me.' I wasn't aware of that and didn't know what she was talking about. Half an hour later we got a phone call informing us that the prime minister had just died of a heart attack.

Many years ago, an Australian Rules football player came to see me on the eve of an important game for help with his mental preparation. I put him in a light trance, gave him ego-strengthening suggestions and asked him to visualize and mentally rehearse the way he wanted to play during the game. Near the end of the procedure he told me that he could see his team's final score: 12-10-82. 'What is the opponent's score?' I asked. 'I can't see it,' he replied. In Australian Rules football a major goal receives six points and a minor goal one point, so his team would have to score twelve major goals and ten minor goals to get to a score of eighty-two.

Immediately after the session I told my wife to write down those numbers on a piece of paper and asked her to give it to me when I was leaving home to go to the game. As soon as I entered the team room I gave the paper to the team manager and told him that our team score at the end of the game was written on the paper. Most of the players in the team referred to me as the 'Witch Doctor' and I could see from the look on the manager's face that he was thinking, 'What on earth is the "Witch Doctor" up to?'

We lost the game by a narrow margin. Soon after the manager brought the paper and said, 'Look at those numbers.' 'What about them?' I asked. I had completely forgotten about them. 'They are supposed to be our team score,' he replied. 'What was our final score?' '12-10-82,' he said. 'And you are truly a bloody witch doctor,' he added.

REMEMBER

1. Smart self-talk is a good way to build and maintain self-confidence. The three common types of refrain when confidence is high are, 'I can; it is easy; I will show them how good I am.' When confidence is low they are, 'I can't; it is too difficult; they will criticize me and put me down.'
2. Some players refer to self-talk as talking to the 'little man'.
3. Talk to the 'little man' nicely and listen to him carefully.
4. Make him your best and most trusted friend and work with him closely to execute your tasks and achieve your goals.
5. If you make him your enemy he will sabotage your performance.
6. For one who has conquered the mind, the mind is the best of friends. But for one who has failed to do so, his mind will be the greatest enemy.

DEALING WITH LOW SELF-CONFIDENCE

When confidence is low, anxiety, fear, self-doubts, negative thinking, tension, impatience, and poor concentration set in. These symptoms are usually caused by a distortion of perception. You overestimate the difficulty of your tasks at the same time that you underestimate your ability to cope with them.

Reduce Anxiety

Lowering anxiety should be your first-important priority because anxiety gives strength and power to fear, impatience and all of the other disruptive symptoms of low self-confidence. Being calm and relaxed negates self-doubts and low self-confidence. You can reduce anxiety by using simple breathing and relaxation exercises that are coupled with smart and positive self-talk or by more advanced techniques like the ones that are described in the chapter on pressure.

Correct Perceptual Distortion

You can reduce your distortion of reality by seeing the challenge and your ability to cope in their true perspective without getting them out of proportion. Redirecting concentration to the process or task at hand is the first step in correcting that distortion. It takes your mind away from yourself, your weaknesses and the result of the contest. The next step is to break down your goals into sub-goals or smaller challenges. These two steps often calm your mind, strengthen your nerves, and allow you to talk positively and encouragingly to yourself.

If You Lose Confidence in One Area of Your Game Focus on Another You Can Control

When you lose confidence in one aspect of your game it is not unusual for you to lose confidence in others as well. This can result in a total breakdown in performance. For example, in golf if you play badly with your driver and get worried and uptight about it, you might lose confidence, then play poorly with your irons and your putter and finish with a very high score. But if instead you control your ego and emotions, leave the driver in the bag, use a long iron off the tee and are successful in keeping the ball in the fairway you will feel that you are in control of your game off the tee. You would then be able to stop the decline in performance and rebuild confidence. Small successes are very important in building confidence particularly by maintaining control over other areas of your game when they are repeated and rewarded.

Don't be Greedy; Lower Expectations

Recovery does not happen all at once, nor does it occur in a straight line. It takes time. Too many players expect to get back to the top of their form in one great leap. That is the exception rather than the rule. Lowering expectations reduces pressure and improves concentration but too many players are reluctant to lower their goals when their confidence is low. They are not aware of the power of small successes in restoring confidence. Some players get really greedy when they are down and often gamble and take unnecessary risks during the game. They don't play the percentages.

Focus on the Basics

Execution of the basics is usually one of the first casualties of anxiety and low self-confidence. Since they are the building blocks of performance you should pay particular attention to them and take pleasure in executing them well. If you ignore them or don't get them right your confidence will stay low and your performance will continue to be weak.

Be Patient

Impatience can be a killer when your confidence is low. Normally, your psychological clock runs faster than the real one. That difference increases when you are anxious or low in confidence. A fast psychological clock speeds up thinking, tempo, rhythm and actions.

Try this exercise. With a watch in your hand, ask a colleague to estimate when twenty seconds have elapsed. Tell him not to look at his watch or count; just guess when twenty seconds have passed. If he is like most other subjects he will give his answer well before the twenty seconds have elapsed. The more anxious he is the earlier his guess becomes.

All the great players value patience because they know it will bring them success, particularly when they are under pressure. They get rid of their impatience by taking slow deep breaths, relaxing their mind and bodies, slowing down their movements, and talking to themselves simply and positively.

Keep Your Concentration in the Present

When confidence is low, your concentration often wanders off to the past on previous mistakes or negative experiences or to the future on the result or the things you fear or don't want to happen. If you must go back to the past, think about your successes rather than your failures. Keeping your concentration in the present by focusing on the process rather than the result reduces that wandering and improves confidence.

Practise Sensibly; Prepare Well

The importance of practice and good preparation and their close relationship with self-confidence have been discussed earlier.

Use Smart Self-talk

Few things change negative emotions and behaviour more than smart self-talk, and the elimination of limiting beliefs. If you change your beliefs you will change your perception; if you change your perception you will change your self-talk; and if you change your self-talk you will change your emotions and performance.

Years ago, five of America's best golfers made the following comments about coping with low self-confidence.

Ben Crenshaw said that most of the problem is mental – when you start to lose confidence, fear sets in and you worry about posting a high score. He claimed that fear undermines confidence and breaks concentration. To overcome fear and anxiety he recommended that you focus your concentration in the present and not get trapped in the past or caught up in the future.

Johnny Miller stressed that when your confidence drops, you speed up mentally and physically. First your mind starts racing and anxiety follows. This leads to speeding up of your tempo – you walk faster, play faster and swing faster. Not only does your backswing quicken but it also shortens. He advised that you should slow down and play your best shot, one shot at a time.

He stated that if you make a bogey five when you think you should have had a four you tend to press yourself on the next hole and try to make up for the lost shot by getting a birdie. You then take chances and try to play shots that are not on. He advised that the best way to deal with this situation is to back off, play conservatively and try to make a quiet par or bogey if that is your usual score. And once you trust yourself and your swing, and start to get a little bit of success everything else will fall in place.

He said that the problems are usually mental but most people mistakenly believe that they are physical in nature and start to fiddle with their swing – this can be disastrous.

Bill Kratzert said that when you are in a slide you tend to get too greedy and impatient. He explained that when he came to a relatively easy hole after making a couple of bogeys he would have the urge to get the shots back all at once. He said that the key is to hang on to your concentration and be patient.

Tom Weiskopf said that keeping yourconcentration in the present is key. He added that the quality of your concentration should be the same for each shot. He said that when you are playing badly you think that you have to find a concrete cause but you can't always find one.

Raymond Floyd explained that when some people get into a tough situation they expect the wheels to fall off and they do. He said that some players get problems because they haven't had the experience of recovering from desperate situations. He stressed that if you have pulled off something once, then you have more confidence to do it again and you might say, 'I've turned it around once and I can do it again.'

These five players made the following recommendations: (1) Play your round one shot at a time; (2) Expect a few bad shots every round; (3) Give each shot an equal amount of effort and concentration; (4) Be patient. Don't be greedy. Play the percentages; (5) Slow down; (6)

Draw encouragement from the past; and (7) Check your fundamentals. Keep it simple and don't overanalyse.

Tony Rafferty, an Australian ultra-marathon runner, offered this advice to players who are low in self-confidence:

- Be sensibly motivated and set yourself reasonable goals and sub-goals. The sub-goals are very important because they enable you to concentrate on the step-by-step process that will take you to your major goal.
- Stick to your basic skills and execute them well.
- Try to improve your concentration.
- Slow down your psychological clock and be patient.
- Talk positively and encourage yourself.
- Expect to encounter setbacks and obstacles and learn to cope with them.
- Each time you are confronted with an obstacle and overcome it, or come through a moment of crisis, you should compliment yourself. That creates pride and satisfaction in your achievement.
- Give yourself the best physical and mental preparation possible.
- Take on competitive challenges at practice and during the game.
- Rely more on yourself. Pay less attention to the expectations and judgements of other people. You cannot please everyone.
- Learn to cope with tiredness, discomfort and pain.

REMEMBER

What would happen to your confidence if:

1. You don't know what you are doing or are not in control of what you are doing;
2. You think that you are not good enough to beat your opponent;
3. You don't feel competent enough to do the job because you don't have the right skills;

4. You focus on your weaknesses, on past failures and mistakes or on future failures;

5. You think that the challenge is too great or your opponent is too good for you;

6. You think that your preparation is substandard;

7. You think you can't cope with the pressures of the game;

8. You think you won't be able to reach your goals or live up to your own expectations or the expectations of the people around you;

9. You make a fool of yourself and behave stupidly and incompetently;

10. You think people around you don't like or respect you or don't recognize or appreciate your effort and contribution;

11. The coach doesn't think much of you and constantly criticizes, humiliates or punishes you;

12. You feel you don't belong or will not be accepted by the team;

13. You think you can't control your emotions and behaviour during the game; and

14. You don't have confidence in your teammates?

SLUMPS

> In most cases of slumps, players believe that the cause of their problem is mechanical or technical in nature and spend a lot of their time fiddling with their technique. But that often makes matters worse. The slump might be started by a mechanical fault but in the end it is always due to poor mental functioning.
>
> – *Sir Garfield Sobers*

A slump is a dramatic and prolonged loss of confidence that is always accompanied by anxiety, poor concentration and poor performance.

When players and teams go into a slump they usually become anxious, tense, dejected and sometimes depressed. They are easily confused and lose sight of priorities, unable to differentiate between what is important and what is not.

The signs and symptoms are similar to those of low confidence but are more intense. Players in a slump get trapped in a failure spiral where they fail, expect to fail and fail again. Getting back on to the success spiral is often difficult. The longer the slump lasts, the more difficult it is to fix.

In the failure spiral players are severely lacking in confidence. Ian Chappell, the great Australian cricket captain, had this to say about slumps: 'Your confidence and concentration are messed up when you are in a slump. Players in this state often do a thorough analysis of the physical aspects of their game. They examine their technique very carefully and pick it apart bit by bit. The people around them then offer all sorts of advice and often suggest that they change important aspects of their game that worked well for them in the past. They must learn to protect themselves from that type of advice. In those people who have a reasonable history of success, a slump is usually due to poor mental functioning rather than to any great technical problems.'

Sir Garfield Sobers reiterates Chappell's comments: 'Your thought patterns change when you are in a slump. You doubt yourself, you worry about things that might happen to you, you make your job harder than it really is and you put yourself down. You become anxious and confused and you don't cope very well with the situations you face because you approach them badly and don't use your common sense to apply your skills. You tend to fiddle around with your technique. When you do this you usually make matters worse. Believe me, you don't find the cause or solutions in the body very often. You must look into the mind, in particular, your thinking and concentration.'

BREAKING THE SLUMP

The treatment of a slump is similar to that of low self-confidence but is more urgent and intense. The best way to escape the failure spiral is:

- Lower your anxiety, take pressure off yourself and clear up your mind. Simple breathing and straightforward relaxation and meditation techniques can help in that respect.

- Keep your concentration in the present, stick to the fundamentals, and enjoy the process. Focusing on the results, or past failures and mistakes often cause performance anxiety and tension. Staying in the moment calms your mind and strengthens your nerves.

- Lower your goals and expectations. Set clear, specific, simple and achievable goals and targets. Unfortunately, many athletes do the opposite and set goals and expectations that are too high.

- Start thinking simply and rationally. Talk to yourself in a positive and encouraging way.

- Plan and prepare properly. Know what you are doing and try to control what you are doing.

- Make mastery of the basics a first-important priority.

- Celebrate small successes. When small successes are repeated they often produce great leaps in confidence.

- Slow down your psychological clock and be patient. In the anxious state your psychological clock works much faster than the real clock, so everything speeds up. Recovery takes time. Unfortunately, too many people are in a hurry to recover and become reckless with their game.

- Play your own style of game. If you play a style that is foreign to you, you will make matters worse.

- Approach the situations you face in a sensible way, identify their first-important priorities and adjust your skills and strategies to deal with them.

- Use mental methods like visualization and mental rehearsal techniques to speed up recovery.

- Sometimes the best way to break a failure spiral is to have a short break from the game to recharge your batteries and clear up and refresh your mind.

CONFIDENCE-BOOSTING TECHNIQUES

Hypnosis

The secret of our success lies within us. At an unconscious level, we have the inner resources and the inner potential to solve our own problems and bring about beneficial changes in our lives and our sport. Going into a relaxed, hypnotic or trance-like state opens the doors to the imagination and the unconscious mind that in turn bring about these changes.

In hypnosis, attention is focused on an object, thought or image. The critical or analytical part of the mind is silenced or by-passed and suggestions go directly to the unconscious mind. In this state, the unconscious mind is very sensitive and receptive to images and suggestions about new feelings and behaviours, and for some time after, the player will feel a compulsion to carry out those behaviours.

Suggestions can be given indirectly or directly. Examples of both methods are described below.

Indirect Suggestions to Build Confidence

When a player comes to me for help I ask him to:

- Give a detailed account of his loss of confidence and his poor performance – when it started, how it started, how it is affecting his thinking and concentration, and the negative emotions it is creating.
- Tell me what advice he would give to a young player to solve the identical problem that he has.
- Take the same advice that he gives to the young player.

I then ask him to close his eyes and allow himself to go into a relaxed state. I tell him to repeat his story again from start to finish, in detail, and to highlight the solution to his problem. I then say to him, 'Now that you are deeply relaxed the things you are saying and visualizing will stimulate your unconscious mind to implement your solution and bring about the change you desire.' When he finishes this segment, I ask him to open his eyes and discuss his experience with me.

After that, I tell him to silently think about and visualize the things in his story, replay them in his mind, and speak to me only to tell me when he is finished. We do not discuss content. I then put him in a hypnotic trance and suggest to him that in this relaxed state those images and silent thoughts will be imprinted deeply in his unconscious mind and will automatically bring about the changes in confidence and performance that he desires.

After several minutes of silence, I wake him up and tell him that in the future these changes will happen automatically and he won't have to think about them. I then repeat the whole process one or two times.

In a second method negative influences in the mind and body are exchanged for positive ones.

Our inner potential and resources are often suppressed by negative thoughts, fear, anxiety, self-doubts, old excuses and bad habits. When these obstacles are removed this potential comes alive and performance automatically improves.

To make that exchange:

- I place the player in a relaxed or hypnotic state and guide him into a beautiful garden where he feels perfectly calm, perfectly relaxed and perfectly safe and secure.

- After an ego-boosting session, I ask him to visualize those obstacles leaving his mind and body and see them flowing into a nearby stream, a fire where they are burned, or into a hole where they are buried.

- I stress that once those obstacles are removed the inner potential and the untapped inner resources will immediately come alive.

- I then ask the player to visualize himself playing his game at a very high standard with confidence and self-assurance, mastering the basics and successfully achieving all his goals and objectives.

- He is then asked to mentally replay those success images in the following days, weeks and months.

Direct Suggestions to Build Confidence

I have used a modification of John Hartland's confidence-boosting technique with great effect with players who were low in confidence.

After putting the player in a relaxed or hypnotic state the following ego-boosting suggestions are given:

As you become more relaxed and less tense each day so you will remain more relaxed and less tense when you are on the field during the game and even before you go on to the field no matter who you are playing, no matter how difficult the game or the situation.

You will be able to meet your opponents on equal terms, and you will feel more at ease and confident in their presence without the slightest feeling of inferiority or self-doubt, without becoming self-conscious, without becoming confused or feeling embarrassed in any way, without magnifying the difficulty of the task or the challenge.

The moment you go out on the field all your nervousness will disappear completely, and you will feel completely relaxed, completely at ease and in control of what you are doing. Once you know what you are doing and are in control of what you are doing your confidence and self-belief will grow. Your performance will then revolve around your self-belief.

As you become and remain more relaxed and less tense each day, even when you are not with me, you will become so deeply interested, so deeply absorbed in what you are doing, the presence of your opponents and the reputation of your opponents will no longer bother you in the slightest, and you will no longer be uncertain, confused or intimidated in any way.

Your nerves will be stronger and steadier and your mind will be calmer and clearer, so calm and steady and so focused and involved in the moment on what you are doing, that you will no longer worry about how you are doing it. You will play freely, naturally and sensibly without worrying in the slightest about your mistakes, your opponents, the score or the result of the game.

If you make a mistake or become distracted, you will immediately shift your concentration back to the task at hand, and will no longer experience the slightest nervousness or discomfort.

No matter how difficult things become you will continue to believe in yourself and remain calm, patient, confident, and in control of what you are doing.

Eye Movement Desensitization and Reprocessing (EMDR)

EMDR is a relatively new but poorly understood technique that has nevertheless proven to be very effective in restoring confidence and resolving many emotional problems. I have used it with some success in the treatment of anxiety, low self-confidence and poor performance. It is a very simple technique that is quite impressive when it works.

I ask the player to focus his attention on the images, thoughts and physical sensations that he gets when he is low in confidence and is playing badly. While those thoughts and images are in his mind I move my hand from side to side in front of his face and ask him to follow it with his eyes. We don't know exactly how these lateral eye movements work but they seem to reprocess the negative thoughts and perceptions the player has about his worth and his ability to cope with the situation and its challenges.

I then get him to imprint positive thoughts in his mind by using positive self-statements like, 'I'm a worthwhile and valuable person, even with my faults and limitations; I'm in control, so relax and let it happen,' and success images of himself mastering his tasks and reaching his goals.

Clinically, this technique has been used successfully to treat phobias and post-traumatic stress disorders in war veterans, victims of sexual abuse and survivors of natural disasters.

Balanced Breathing: Writing New Brain Programmes

Balanced breathing is based on an old meditation technique that has been used to reduce anxiety, promote relaxation and increase self-confidence. Recently it has been adapted to write new programmes in the subconscious mind.

I ask the player to identify the negative beliefs, thoughts and habits that are holding him back and sabotaging his confidence and performance. As an example, he might say, 'I don't like pressure; it makes me nervous and messes up my confidence and concentration.'

I then get him to sit in a chair and place his left ankle over his right ankle and his right wrist over his left wrist. I then ask him to close his eyes, and relax the muscles in the face, jaws, neck and shoulders and pay attention to his in- and out-breathing. When breathing out he focuses on the word balance. As he continues to breathe he becomes relaxed.

He then sets about imprinting new beliefs and new thoughts in his subconscious mind to replace the old ones, by repeating self-statements that reflect those beliefs. For example he might say, 'I enjoy and look forward to pressure. It brings the best out of me and helps me to play with confidence and flair.' Not only does he repeat that statement over and over, but he also creates images and feelings of himself playing well and achieving his goals under pressure conditions. The more detail he puts into those images the more powerful they become.

He stops the process in his own time and opens his eyes. I then get him to look straight ahead and roll his eyes full circle clockwise and then anticlockwise, keeping his head steady. He uncrosses his ankles and wrists and touches the fingertips of his right hand to those of the left. This is supposed to save the new programme in the mind in the same way that information is saved on the computer when the save key is pressed.

The player is then asked to repeat this process several times a day to strengthen those new thoughts, beliefs and behaviours.

INTERVIEWS

PETER THOMSON

Rudi. What are your thoughts about self-confidence?

Peter. Self-confidence is necessary for good performance. However, it isn't something you can adopt. You can't exhort yourself to be self-confident. It develops as a result of the things you do, experience and feel first as a kid and later as a sportsman. It must be built on a sound basis – knowing what you are doing and being in control of what you are doing.

When you lose your confidence its place is taken by self-doubts and indecision. The doubts arise when you suddenly become aware that you are not in control of what you are doing or if you think you are not. This usually occurs when something happens unexpectedly or when things don't go according to plan. The whole basis of your self-confidence is then destroyed.

Self-confidence goes back to a very thorough knowledge of the game, your job, yourself and your capabilities. It is often affected by how well you practise. Practice is the repetition of your skills in an effort to maintain or improve them to become competent. Confidence and competence go hand in hand. If you don't think you have the competence to do your job you won't be too confident. When assessing competence you must consider your capabilities, your successes and failures, the preparation you have put in, the odds of success and failure, the nature of the opposition and knowledge of the situations you are likely to face.

Rudi. A lot of players use past performances and records to help them maintain confidence and persistence when they are playing poorly. Dennis Lillee stressed the importance of this during our discussion. He said that if he was beginning to lose confidence in the game he would think about his record and say to himself, 'I get a wicket every six overs in Grade cricket, every eight overs in Sheffield Shield cricket and every ten overs in Test cricket; so if I keep bowling, the wickets will come.' He said that often helped him to maintain his confidence.

Peter. That is one way of doing it, but there is more to confidence than that. For instance, Lillee might have all these things at the back of his mind and be full of confidence, but if he proceeded to bowl five consecutive no balls or wides his confidence would suddenly vanish, because of the realization that he wasn't in control of his bowling. I believe the secret to the whole thing is being in control or at least thinking you are in control of yourself and what you are doing.

In the game of golf, you may go along very nicely with everything happening according to plan, when something unexpected suddenly happens. You may hit a wild shot or miss an easy putt, and if you don't know why or have a simple explanation your confidence can be shattered. If you are in control, you are prepared for most eventualities and you deal with them more effectively when they arise. Players who don't know what they are doing, or what the game is all about, will often lose control at critical periods. Those players don't have a forward plan. You must be prepared for the unexpected.

Rudi. What advice would you give young sportspeople about developing confidence?

Peter. As I said before, confidence is self-generating and, to be honest, I wouldn't stress it too much, because it comes as a result of your knowledge and the repeated application of your skills. When you demonstrate to yourself in a convincing way that you are in control of what you are doing, your confidence will be established. It is built on competence, good execution, adequate preparation, your record, knowledge of the game and knowledge of yourself.

RAHUL DRAVID

Rudi. It has often been said that at the top levels of sport performance revolves more around self-image and self-belief than around ability or talent. How important is self-confidence?

Rahul. Self-confidence is vitally important. It comes from belief in yourself and in your ability. It is influenced by practice and preparation – knowing that you have practised hard, that you have left no stone unturned and that you have given everything you have got. Good preparation is sometimes ignored but it can be a source of great confidence.

If you are doing an examination, have prepared well, and have read all the chapters in the book, you will go into the room with a certain amount of confidence knowing that you have covered the subject. If, however, you only studied three of the six chapters, you will go into the room hoping to get questions from those three chapters and worry about questions that might come from the other chapters. You will then have grave doubts about passing the examination if none of the questions come from the three chapters that you have read.

When a team is confident its chances of doing well are automatically increased. If confidence is low the team can get trapped in a failure spiral that is difficult to escape from. It often requires strong individuals to take the team with them to get it out of the rut. When you reach a critical point where three or four players demonstrate enough strength and self-belief, the performance of the team usually improves as other members of the team feed off the confidence of those players and find their own confidence.

Rudi. Peter Thomson, the Australian golfer, often said that although confidence is influenced by self-belief, experience, practice and preparation it boils down to two things in the heat of the contest during the game – knowing what you are doing and being in control of what you are doing.

Rahul. What he says is correct. If you know what you are doing and have the skills to do it and are in control of the process or of what you are doing, your confidence will be good.

M.S. DHONI

Dhoni: I think practice makes you perfect and the more you practice the more self-confidence you will get. If I bowl ten yorkers in the nets I know I will be able to bowl at least four in the game. If I practice hitting sixes in the nets against the spinners and hit twelve sixes in fourteen tries, I know that I will be able to hit at least three in the game. What is important here is having the confidence to clear the field when you need to. Net sessions help you to build on your strengths and improve your weaknesses.

Rudi. Peter Thomson, the great Australian golfer and five-times British Open champion, once told me that self-confidence is about knowing what you are doing and being in control of what you are doing. He said that it is built on practice, preparation and competence.

Dhoni. That is a very good description.

Rudi. What about overconfidence?

Dhoni. Overconfidence is dangerous. I have never taken any sides lightly or any bowler for that matter, even if he is a part-time bowler because I know that it only takes one delivery to get me out.

It is not unusual for some of the best teams in the world to be beaten occasionally by lower-rated sides. On the day, any team can beat you, especially if you underestimate them.

Rudi. How do you make the transition from T20 and ODI cricket to Test match cricket?

Dhoni. I have the habit of going hard at deliveries if I play too much T20 cricket and ODI formats. Technically, I am not the most gifted batsman and when it comes to Test cricket I have to adjust to suit the Test format. So I practise hard to make those adjustments to be ready for the game. Going back to the basics and trying to improve them is critical.

Good net sessions are very helpful. I am usually very specific about the things that will need extra work. Once I start doing well in the net sessions I gain confidence, knowing that day after day I have been doing things correctly. The challenge is then to replicate these things in the game. When you are in the nets you must play as though you are in the game. If you get out, you should start afresh. Net sessions should be simulation sessions for the real game.

When you go into the nets you should focus on the first fifteen deliveries. Once you get over them your heart rate goes back to normal and you become more relaxed. This practice will help you to deal with the first fifteen deliveries in the match and will allow you to settle down after that.

That is the procedure that I follow when I am in the nets.

The practice facilities in the West Indies need to be improved. If you improve the quality of the nets and have serious net sessions you will see an improvement in the players' games.

SIR GARFIELD SOBERS

Self-confidence

Rudi. How did you get your confidence?

Sir Garfield. My ability gave me confidence. I knew there weren't many situations I couldn't handle. I knew what I had done and what I could do. Once you are aware of your ability and you know how to use your skills to cope with the situation, you won't have too many problems with confidence. So to maintain your confidence you must know yourself, your capabilities, your game and the things that can happen during the game.

Once you are in control of yourself you will be confident, but if you are not you will lose it. Fear then sets in and you start to worry about all sorts of things. Fear destroys confidence and concentration because it messes up your thinking and stresses you out following which you lose initiative and your free-flowing movements. Suddenly, the ball seems to come at you faster, bounce higher, and move off the wicket. That happens because you are thinking incorrectly and because you are stiff and can't get into position quickly enough. To play well you must have a bit of tension but not fear. Fear paralyses your mind and body.

Rudi. I know you got confidence from giving the batsman at the other end confidence. How did you give him confidence?

Sir Garfield. People told me that I batted too low in the order and that I would run out of partners. I have never run out of partners. When I was batting I was usually in control of the situation and this seemed to motivate the batsman at the other end and give him confidence. If you make things look easy, the other fellow will then say, 'He is making it look so easy. It can't be too difficult. I'll apply myself and try to do my best.'

I never gave many instructions to the batsman at the other end. I hardly ever interfered and I never criticized him. I tried to encourage him to use his common sense and play his own style of game. If he did something that was absolutely ridiculous, I would speak to him firmly. I wouldn't tell him off or abuse him. I would say, 'There's no need to play those risky shots. You are becoming too ambitious. You can do better. I know you can. Just put your head down and play sensibly. Watch me and see how it is done.' If you tell him off for making a mistake while he is batting you create fear or anger and you will interfere with his batting. He will either stiffen up and be afraid to play his normal game, or he will do something stupid and get out. You have to give him encouragement. There is no need to talk all the time because a smile, a nod, or a clap can be just as effective.

In 1966 West Indies was struggling against England in the Test match at Lord's and were only twenty runs ahead in the second innings after wiping off a first innings deficit with five wickets down and two days to play. I was batting with Holford at the time. I can imagine what the Englishmen were thinking: 'With two days plus to go there is no way they can save the game. Gary might hang around, but Holford is a youngster, he is not a good batsman, and there is no way he could survive the pressure for very long.'

At that stage, I said to myself, 'I can handle this situation. The bowlers are bowling well but I don't think they will give me any problems. All I need is someone at the other end to stay with me.' So I went down to the other end to speak to Holford and said to him, 'This is a very good wicket. It is like our wickets at home. Just think about yourself batting on a Kensington wicket in Barbados and imagine yourself batting well. How could they get you out? The only way they could get you out is if you do something very stupid. They won't get me out today because I don't see any problems out here. Cowdrey is trying to crowd us to put pressure on us, but this will make it easier for me to play my shots.'

As soon as I started to play some shots, Cowdrey, the England captain became defensive and took the pressure off us. We batted well and the longer we spent in the middle the more our confidence grew. Sometime later, I declared the innings closed at 369 for five. We were both not out. I made 163 and Holford made 105. On the last day we almost won the match. England's last batsmen hung on by the skin of their teeth to draw the game.

Overconfidence

Rudi. Were you ever overconfident?

Sir Garfield. It is only human to be overconfident at times. But I tried not to be because overconfidence is very dangerous and is a prescription for failure. No matter how good you think you are, there is always somebody who might be better on the day or some bowler who can produce the unplayable ball. You court disaster if you allow yourself to become overconfident. I was always aware of this. I never underestimated my opponent or the situation. I never thought I was too good for the opposition.

I have seen teams get out of tough situations because of overconfidence in the opposing teams. This is quite common. In 1966 West Indies played a Test match at the Oval and at one stage we had control of the game because our bowlers were on top. The last two English batsmen were in and we were sure that it was just a matter of time before one of them would get out. But they didn't until they had scored over 100 runs.

The same thing happened to us in Australia a few years earlier in a Test match in Adelaide when the last man, Kline, batted with Mackay for two-and-a-half hours to save the Test match for Australia. We thought, 'Surely Kline can't bat for two-and-a-half hours against Sobers, Gibbs and Hall. It is not possible. All we have to do is wait and he'll get out.' It is very difficult to avoid this type of thinking. Instead of pressuring him into making mistakes we waited for him to make the mistake. The more professional the team, the less likely this is to happen. But it still does happen, no matter how good your attitude. Whenever you are in a good position you must always guard against complacency and overconfidence – it is very dangerous.

Slumps

Rudi. What do you think about slumps?

Sir Garfield. Your thought patterns change when you are in a slump. You doubt yourself, you worry about things that might happen to you,

you make your job harder than it really is and you tend to put yourself down. You become anxious and confused. You don't cope well with the situations you face because you approach them badly and don't use your common sense to apply your skills.

The longer the problem lasts the worse you become. Most people start to recover when they hit rock bottom. They start to reverse the slump when they say to themselves, 'This is ridiculous. I can still play. Let's go back to the beginning and start from scratch. Get back to the basics and start thinking sensibly.'

Rudi. So you think the cause of slumps is usually in the mind?

Sir Garfield. Yes. They may be started by something physical like an injury, but in the end poor mental functioning is the cause. There is no doubt about that. When you fiddle around with physical technique you usually make matters worse. Believe me, you don't find the cause or solutions in the body very often. You must look to the mind, in particular, your thinking and concentration. Only after you have done this should you look at other areas.

You must play your own style of game. If you try to change it and start doing things you are not used to, you won't play well. Some people try to work out their problems at practice. It is the best place to do so. You can often find the solutions there and then start to build up your confidence. Other people try to find the answers during the game. Another group may sit quietly and try to analyse their problem.

The cause of the problem is often trivial. A slight change in your thinking or concentration can be responsible for major slumps. Personal problems off the field can also be a cause.

When you are trying to recover, you must look at your current situation and think about what you are doing. You should then cast your mind back to the things you used to do when you were playing well. Chances are you will then be able to spot the changes that have taken place and identify the problem areas. You must then go back to the basics of your own game and play your way back gradually.

DENNIS LILLEE

Self-confidence and Self-belief

Rudi. Do you ever lose self-confidence or self-belief when you are under pressure?

Dennis. No, I don't lose my confidence. No matter how difficult things are, I always believe that I have a chance of succeeding. Sometimes the chances are better than at other times, but I always think that success will come my way. The slimmer the chance, the harder I try. If you throw in the towel, you have no chance.

Sometimes I tell myself that the job is going to be very hard and probably overestimate its difficulty, but I use this to spur me on to try harder. It focuses my mind on the job and improves my concentration. If the job looks too easy, I don't play well. As I said before, the greater the challenge, the better I apply myself and play.

Rudi. Tell me a bit more about your confidence.

Dennis. The newspapers and television have created a myth about me and have built up my ability and reputation much higher than they really are.

Rudi. Do you find that difficult to handle? Does it put extra pressure on you?

Dennis. No. I use it to my advantage. I don't try to change it, although I believe that it is wrong to be built up like that. Sometimes, I say to myself, 'That's not right but if the batsmen think that I am better than I really am, that's good for me. Why not let them continue to think that way. If they believe it, that is one more thing in the back of their minds that they have to worry about.' Once the seed is planted in their minds it is very difficult for them to stop it from growing. All it requires to make them uneasy is a good ball or a simple remark like, 'I enjoy bowling to you. It's just a matter of time.' Sometimes you play little games and put on an air of superiority that tells them, 'I'm in charge, I will get you soon. I am better than you.'

Rudi. The other day I was doing some visualization exercises with a few players and got them to imagine that they were batting really well with lots of flair and confidence. They didn't know who the bowler was because he was in a clown's outfit. After a while, I said to them, 'You are now set and you are in control but look and see what is happening. The bowler is taking off his outfit. He is Dennis Lillee. He will continue to bowl to you.' 'Oh my God!' they exclaimed. 'It can't be. We are wetting ourselves. We can't bat against Lillee.' So Dennis, you see what your reputation can do to players.

Dennis. If the newspapers and television help you to get the upper hand and put the batsmen under pressure why not use them? Deep down you know how good you are and what you can do.

But if you start to believe in your own publicity you will run into trouble because you won't apply yourself to practice, training or the game as hard as you should. Your expectations are then too high and you start to believe that everything will happen easily for you. The moment you believe in what the press guys are writing or saying on radio and television you are in trouble.

If you are good, you don't have to boast to anyone about it. If you have to, you can't be very good. You don't need the press people or the fans to tell you how good you are.

Rudi. Many sportsmen have difficulty handling their success. You seem to handle yours well.

Dennis. You must separate your self-worth from your performance. Being a bowler is not who I am. It is what I do for a living and enjoyment.

If I bowl badly, I don't come off the field thinking that I am a failure or a useless person. I say to myself, 'I had a bad day today. It was a bad day's work. Tomorrow is a new day, and I will make sure that I do better.' On the other hand if I bowl well and get lots of wickets, I don't walk off the field pushing out my chest, strutting around like a bloody peacock thinking how great a person I am. I say to myself, 'That was a good performance. I bowled really well. It was a good day's work. But tomorrow is another day and I will have to work harder to repeat it.'

Rudi. You used a lot of quotations in our discussion. They must be important to you.

Dennis. Your thought processes influence everything you do. A lot of people pay lip service to these quotations but they are just words to them. In my case I believe them and when I use them they really mean something to me. The way you think and talk to yourself is extremely important.

CHAPTER 4

CONCENTRATION

In any sport you will at times be distracted, sometimes by the opposition, sometimes by the crowd, sometimes by the way you are batting and sometimes by negative thoughts in your mind. As soon as you recognize these distractions you should immediately bring your attention back to the present and focus on the process.

— *V.V.S. Laxman*

Concentration in batting is the ability to play one ball at a time and not get too far ahead of yourself or get caught up in the past. I guess that would be concentration for me.

— *Rahul Dravid*

You become what you concentrate on, and in a real sense you are where your concentration is.

— *Anonymous*

What is Concentration?

Concentration is a mental skill that can be learned and improved with training and practice. It is a key to good performance and is a major strength of every good player. Good concentration helps you to make the best use of your ability and sometimes gives you an edge over players who might physically be more talented than you.

It is about focusing attention on interesting or important factors in the situations you face. Sometimes you have to narrow it to one thing and at other times widen it to deal with many things at once. You can also direct it inwardly to thoughts, images and feelings, or outwardly to the task at hand and to things that are happening around you. You can even focus in the past on previous events; in the future on upcoming events; and in the present on the task at hand.

The mind is like an unruly child. It has a will of its own, and can be difficult to control. Players have trouble concentrating: (1) When they are under too much pressure and are too tense, hyped up or anxious – too tight a grip and tense neck and shoulder muscles often interfere with concentration; (2) When they are not hyped up enough and are bored or disinterested; and (3) When they are mentally tired or mentally fatigued.

Yet some players claim that they play better when they have to struggle with their concentration. Ian Chappell is one of these players. He said, 'Concentration is a funny thing. You seem to have your bad days and your good days. I often made my best scores when I was having trouble with it. I played best when I had to work hard at it and had to struggle to get it right. On the days when it came easily, I would start my innings really well but would usually get out for a low score. I suppose I got a bit overconfident on these occasions. Overconfidence spells danger. As soon as I noticed it, I would say to myself, "Be careful, it is not as easy as you think. Get your mind back on the job." This often helped.'

Most mistakes in concentration are made when it is directed and focused incorrectly, when it is trapped in the wrong time, and when it loses its flexibility.

Many coaches believe that they give sound and constructive advice when they tell their players to put their heads down, pay attention, and concentrate. But those instructions are too vague and general. For instance, what do they concentrate on? How many things do they concentrate on? When do they concentrate and when do they relax? How do they turn it on and turn it off? How do they change from one focus to another? How do they lock in their concentration at critical moments of the game?

When players are in good form and are in control of their game their concentration sometimes lifts them to superior performance and gives them an exhilarating feeling that they describe as 'being in the zone'. Concentration is then sharp, instinctive and spot on. But getting into the zone is very elusive and only happens on the odd occasion.

There are many people who think that concentration is just about single-mindedness – narrowing attention to a single detail, task, thought or event. This is an important aspect of concentration but it is only a part of it. Having a narrow focus of attention is a plus in some situations but is a minus in situations where a broad focus is needed to deal with many different things at once.

Other people think that concentration is about shutting out distractions. Many athletes feel that they would concentrate better if they could deliberately shut out or ignore the distractions in their mind and on the field. But, they place so much emphasis on these distractions that they end up concentrating harder on them.

Years ago in Melbourne, Australia, I was discussing concentration with a group of Australian Rules footballers who felt that way. I said to them, 'I want you to concentrate on the cup on the table in front of you and give it your undivided attention. I will talk to you while you are doing that to make it easier for you. Now focus on the cup and ignore the ashtrays and the cigarette lighter next to the cup. Ignore the telephone that is ringing, the noise of the cars outside and the persons on either side of you. There are a few thoughts in your mind at the moment. Forget them. Try to put all of those distractions out of your mind and see how much better you will concentrate on the cup.'

After a while, they admitted that they couldn't keep their concentration on the cup because my instructions were distracting them. The best player in the team then chipped in and said, 'You were trying to trick me but I didn't fall into your trap. You see, all the time you were trying to take my mind away from the cup, I was locked into it and was busy reading the words on it – Good Cricketers Never Die They Just Get Run Out. I read them over and over and after a while

I concentrated on the size, shape and colour of the cup. You didn't break my concentration.'

In competitive sport not only must you be able to control your concentration but you must also know how to distract your opponent and break his concentration. In cricket, this often happens when fielders get stuck into batsmen verbally and psychologically during the game.

For some time, that tactic worked well against the West Indies players, but in the Clive Lloyd era this changed. Instead of allowing opponents' comments to break their concentration they used them as reminders to stay calm and to zero in on the next ball or the next play. They even used opponents' remarks to motivate themselves to play better. Tony Greig's incendiary comments that he would make the West Indies 'grovel' in the Test series between England and West Indies when he was captain of England was a huge mistake because the West Indies players lifted their game to new heights and easily defeated his team. Wise coaches warn their players not to say or do anything to their opponents that they could use to improve their concentration or motivate themselves to play better.

I once worked with an Australian Rules football coach in Melbourne who was a master of distraction techniques. If his team were losing he would send out a message to start a fight. The objective was to break the opponents' rhythm and concentration. The result of the fight was important but was not as important as what his players were trained to do immediately after the fight – stay calm and refocus concentration on the next play and on the execution of the basic skills – attacking and controlling the ball. His team usually won.

REMEMBER

1. Concentration is a key to good performance and strength of every great player. When a good player plays badly it is often due to poor concentration.
2. Concentration helps you to make the best use of your skills and to play well enough to beat opponents who are more skilful than you are.

3. It is about identifying important priorities in the situations you face and focusing attention on them. As situations change, your concentration must change to match the new requirements.

4. You become what you concentrate on, and in a real sense you are where your concentration is.

5. Advice to put your head down and concentrate is not specific enough. What do you concentrate on? How many things do you concentrate on? When do you concentrate and when do you relax? How do you turn it on and turn it off? How do you lock it in at critical moments?

6. In the game, your concentration is usually at its best when you keep it in the present on the process or the task at hand. If you allow it to wander to the past or to the future when it should be in the present, you will make simple mistakes.

7. Your concentration suffers: (1) When you are under too much pressure and are too tense, hyped up or anxious; (2) When you are not hyped up enough and are bored or disinterested; and (3) When you are mentally tired or mentally fatigued.

8. Concentration has direction - internal and external – and focus – narrow and wide.

9. In competitive sport not only must you know how to control your own concentration you must also learn how to distract your opponent and break his concentration.

How Flexible is your Concentration?

Adjust the direction and focus of your attention to match the concentration requirements of the situations you face.

— *Anonymous*

Your capacity to change direction and focus is vital for good concentration. In sport, situations change rapidly and concentration must in turn adjust quickly to fit those changing demands.

It usually takes about one-tenth to one-fifth of a second for that switch to occur, but it might be prolonged if you are too anxious, if you are bored and disinterested and if you are mentally fatigued. Flexibility functions best when arousal is in the optimum range – not too high and not too low.

Peter Brock, the racing car driver, always highlighted the importance of this flexibility in motor racing. He said that motor racing is a fast and exciting sport – like a high-speed game of chess – in which situations change very rapidly. To drive well in those conditions, he said that his concentration has to change rapidly and constantly to fit those shifting demands. He added that this change happens unconsciously, almost by reflex at times and stressed that the penalties for inflexibility or slow adjustment might be disabling or even fatal.

CONCENTRATION, SELF-TALK AND SELF-QUESTIONING

Your thinking and self-talk control your concentration.
                                                    – *Rudi Webster*

You are constantly in conversation with yourself but most of the time you are not aware of it. This internal chat not only controls your concentration but also your self-confidence, emotions, actions and performance. You can improve concentration by tuning into these conversations and changing them when necessary.

In today's world, you receive more negative than positive comments in a ratio that exceeds five to one. During the chats that you have with yourself that ratio is even greater. In general, you spend more time talking to yourself about your deficiencies and weaknesses and about the things you fear or want to avoid than you do about your strengths and the things you want to achieve. This habit gets worse when you are under pressure.

The questions that you ask yourself and the questions people ask you control the direction and focus of your concentration.

At the moment you are focusing on the words that you are reading, but if I ask you about the chair in which you are sitting, your attention would leave the book and go to the chair. If I then ask you about the paintings on the walls, you would redirect your attention to the walls and the paintings. If you started reading again and I asked you about what you read in the last five pages, you would redirect your concentration inwardly to recall the information from those pages.

If you had to open the batting in a cricket game against two very fast bowlers, your concentration and performance would not only be determined by your talent, skill and motivation but also by the way you talk to yourself and question yourself about the situation. For instance, if you ask, 'What is my goal? What must I do to achieve it? How will I do it?' you might come up with these answers: 'My goal is to see the shine off the new ball to make it easier for the batsman who is next in. I want to play in the "V" early and try to bat until lunchtime so I will have to watch the ball out of the bowler's hand, pick up its line and length quickly and get into position to play my shot. I have to be mentally alert but I must also be patient.'

If instead you ask, 'Why is this wicket so green? How will it play? What sort of field will the bowlers set? What will happen if I lose my wicket early?' you would concentrate more on the possible difficulties in the wicket, short-pitched deliveries, the position of the fielders, and the likelihood of getting out than you would on watching the ball closely, judging its direction and length, and getting into position to play your shot.

REMEMBER

1. The questions that you ask yourself and the questions people ask you control the direction and focus of your concentration.

2. You spend a lot of time talking to yourself in a negative manner.

3. Your talent, skill and motivation affect your performance. So do your self-talk and self-questioning.

4. Flexibility is a key to good concentration. If you lose it your concentration will suffer.

5. It usually takes about one-tenth to one-fifth of a second to switch from one focus to another, but it might be delayed if you are too hyped up and too anxious or if you are not hyped up enough and are bored or disinterested.

THE EYES, THE BRAIN AND CONCENTRATION

> Concentration is always slightly [100 to 250 milliseconds] ahead of the eyes and as soon as it moves to a new position, the eyes will want to follow.
>
> — *D.A. Hoffman, psychologist*

The eyes and ears play an important role in concentration because they search the environment for the answers to the questions that the brain asks. They collect information from the environment and send it to the brain for processing and interpretation. It is the brain that sees and hears.

In ball games, some people have trouble seeing and tracking the ball with two good eyes so imagine what it would be like if you only had one eye. But that is exactly what the Nawab of Pataudi had to do. Yet he excelled as a batsman, fielder and captain of the Indian cricket team.

At the age of twenty, soon after commencing his cricket career, a car accident permanently damaged vision in his right eye. Where other batsmen saw one ball Pataudi claimed that he saw two, seven inches apart, so he had to learn to pick the right one to hit – the inner one. He certainly did that successfully. Six centuries, including a double century, along with sixteen half-centuries, bear testimony to that.

In order to see, the eyes must move. These movements are complex and serve different functions. Some of them are small and fast, others are large and slow.

These eye movements produce distinctive visual scanning patterns that are influenced not only by the nature of the situation, but also by your beliefs, values, experience, expectations and interest in the situation. They are also influenced by the questions asked, the instructions given and the tasks that are to be performed. Eye movements reflect your thought processes, so positive thoughts create different scanning patterns from negative ones.

In 1967, A.L.Yarbus asked subjects to look at a detailed photograph of a family in a living room and recorded the scanning pattern of their eyes as they examined the picture. He then asked them different questions about the photograph and recorded the scanning patterns. In every case the visual scanning pattern was different.

This study (http://sstetson.files.wordpress.com/2010/07/702px-yarbus_the_visitor.jpg) is often referred to as evidence that shows how the questions asked or tasks given influence eye movements and concentration.

The sense organs collect information and then send it to the brain in a complex code for interpretation. This process varies from one person to another and is affected by genetic and hereditary factors, cultural influences, beliefs and expectations. This might explain why people who witness the same event see and hear different things.

Recent research at the University of Sussex in England revealed some interesting findings about the movement of the eyes when players are batting against fast bowlers. At the point of delivery, the eyes focus on the bowler's hand and the ball. But as soon as the ball leaves the hand and the eyes pick up its trajectory, they leave the ball and focus ahead of it to a spot on the wicket where they think it will land – its length. The eyes then stay focused on that spot until the ball catches up and again move ahead of the ball before it reaches the bat. These things happen in a split second.

The researches found that the quicker the batsmen took their eyes off the ball and focused on its anticipated length on the pitch, the better they played. They concluded that against fast and medium pace bowling, the best batsmen take their eyes off the ball much quicker and focus them on the pitch much earlier than the lesser batsmen. According to Hoffman, concentration is always slightly (100 to 250 milliseconds) ahead of the eyes, and as soon as it moves to a new position, the eyes will want to follow.

Brian Lara was one of the world's greatest batsmen. I used to watch him very closely, particularly his mannerisms and micro-movements while he was batting. When he was getting ready to receive the ball he would look in the direction of the bowler for a short time and would then focus on an area on the wicket for a second or two as if he was anticipating or previewing where the ball might pitch – its length. He would then shift his attention back to the bowler again. When I asked him why he went through that routine he said he was not conscious of it. I have noticed the same mannerism in other great players.

If you see an object and then look away, its image remains in your mind for a short time – the after-image. When the batsman looks down at the pitch while the bowler is about to run in, is he programming his brain to pick up the length of the ball more quickly?

Golfers go through a similar routine. When they are getting ready to hit the ball they usually have a final glimpse at their target just before they start their backswing. I am sure that the after-image of their target influences the way they swing the golf club. If that after-image is disrupted by negative self-talk or negative mental images, the tempo and the mechanics of the swing often change and the ball flies way off target.

PROCESSING INFORMATION

> The brain can only process a small part of its information consciously.
>
> — *Anonymous*

Some people can process information well, handle lots of information and do many things at once while others cannot. Overloading yourself with information will lead to confusion, anxiety and loss of concentration. You should therefore learn your limits and stay within them.

The brain is a great initiator, receiver and controller. It transmits and receives millions of impulses every second. But it has a limited capacity to deal consciously with all of them so it processes most of the signals at an unconscious level. Only a small number are handled consciously.

When a batsman is facing a fast bowler, most of his information is processed unconsciously because his conscious mind reacts too slowly to deal with the speed with which he has to make decisions and react to the ball.

It takes a baseball player 400 milliseconds to see the ball leaving the pitcher's hand, track it, decide whether or not to swing the bat and then swing it. When he picks up the line, trajectory and speed of the ball, he has 30 milliseconds to select his stroke, less than the time it takes to blink. The same thing happens in cricket. If the player makes batting too much of a conscious or an intellectual activity and focuses too strongly on the mechanics, his performance will suffer because his concentration would be focused incorrectly and he wouldn't be able to see or track the ball properly.

Efficient execution of movement occurs when the mechanics are automatic. Then, you don't have to think about what your hands and feet should be doing, you just do it.

Although most of the information in the brain is processed unconsciously, there are mechanisms that allow information to flow to the conscious level when it is required. For instance, you are not normally aware of the position of your big toes because it is monitored unconsciously. But if I ask you where they were you would immediately become aware of them.

When I was living in Melbourne, Australia, an Australian Rules football player used to come to my house every Friday night to prepare himself mentally for the game on the following day. One evening he was late and after waiting for an hour, I joined my wife in the television room where I soon fell asleep. I was in a deep sleep for a while and then woke up suddenly and said to her, 'Smithy is here. The doorbell just rang.' She laughed at me and told me that I had been snoring and must have been dreaming. I asked her if she didn't hear the doorbell, and still laughing, she said, 'No!' I then left the room and went to the door to let Smithy in and took him to the television room with a broad smile on my face.

Even though I was deeply asleep my unconscious mind must have been programmed to hear the doorbell and alert my conscious mind as soon as it received the signal.

This is not an unusual happening. A mother can sleep through the loudest noises and yet be awakened by the first sounds of her crying baby.

REMEMBER

1. The eyes and ears play an important role in concentration. They collect information and then send it to the brain for processing and interpretation. It is the brain that sees and hears.

2. Eye movements and patterns reflect your thoughts and concentration.

3. Concentration is always slightly (100 to 250 milliseconds) ahead of the eyes and as soon as it moves to a new position, the eyes will want to follow.

4. Researches at the University of Sussex in England found that players focused on the ball as it left the bowler's hand and as soon as the eyes picked up its trajectory, they left the ball and focused ahead of it to a spot on the wicket where they expected it to land – its length. They concluded that the best batsmen take their eyes off the ball much quicker and focus them on the pitch much earlier than the lesser batsmen.

5. Most of the time concentration takes place automatically and unconsciously.

6. There are mechanisms in the brain that allow information that is normally handled unconsciously to flow to the conscious level when required.

7. When you are concentrating well, you are not usually aware of it. Everything seems to flow.
8. You can only consciously deal with a certain amount of information at any given time. Information overload and task overload lead to confusion, loss of concentration and poor performance.
9. Pressure can improve or disrupt concentration depending on the level of the pressure and your ability to cope.
10. Preoccupation with technique during the game results in concentration errors.
11. Movement is best executed when it is automatic. Then, you don't have to think about or concentrate on what your hands and feet should be doing, you just do it.

What to Concentrate on

> Where is my mind? Where should it be? What should I be focusing on and doing right now?
>
> – *Anonymous*

Knowing what to concentrate on is very important. You must focus on the correct cues or signals and the right aspects of the task.

Off the field, the athlete can allow his concentration to move between the past and the future but at critical moments of the game he must keep it focused in the present on the task at hand. Baseball pitchers say that when they are pitching they pitch one ball at a time and focus on three things: the type of pitch, the direction of the pitch and the target – the catcher's glove. They say that if they find themselves thinking of anything else, they step off the mound and start again. The same could apply to bowlers in cricket. For instance, the bowler could bowl one ball at a time, focus on his rhythm in his run-up, his line and length, and his target – the stumps, the batsman's body or the wicketkeeper's gloves. And in batting, the batsman could play one ball at a time and focus on picking up the ball out of the bowler's hand, getting into position to play his stroke, and targeting the area of the field where he wants to hit the ball.

Mistakes occur when attention is incorrectly focused. That often happens when you think negatively, when you lose confidence, when you become overconfident and when you experience powerful emotions like fear, frustration and anger.

A talented woman was preparing to make it to the the Australian team for the Brisbane Commonwealth Games, and the week before the national trials she came to see me. At that stage, her self-confidence was low and she had grave doubts about her ability to defeat her main rival whom she had never beaten. After a long discussion, she set herself two goals. The first was to qualify for the team and the second was to beat this other woman.

She then went through a relaxation and visualization procedure to prepare for her upcoming race, the 400-metre hurdles. She described the race this way:

> The race is about to start and I am feeling uptight. My stomach feels funny. I don't think I can beat this girl. She seems so confident, strong and relaxed. She looks unbeatable. She is in the third lane to my right. We are now on our mark... set... the gun has gone. She got a very good start, she is over the first hurdle and I am just about to go over mine. She is over the second and running well. She is really burning. I am going over the second. All I can do is follow her now because I can't catch up.

The race continued in that manner and near the end she said, 'She is over the last hurdle and is two yards in front of me as she goes through the tape.'

'That was very good,' I said. 'I want you to run the race again but I want you to run it differently. Just concentrate on two things, your lane and your rhythm. Everything else is unimportant. Just focus on your lane and rhythm and allow your body to do its job. When you get over the last hurdle glance to your right to see who is ahead of you. Let us see what happens.'

This is how she described her second race:

We are ready to start and I am feeling a bit nervous but I know this is normal. I know what I have to do and I am sure I can do it. I will just concentrate on getting a smooth rhythm. I am on my mark... set... the gun has gone. I am out of the blocks quickly and I am approaching the first hurdle. I am over it and I am settling down into a good rhythm. I am over the second and going really well. My body feels good and relaxed. I am over the third and I am burning.

The race continued like this and as she approached the last two hurdles she said, 'My rhythm is very good. I am over the second last hurdle and there is just one more to go. I am moving towards it now and I am over it. There is nobody ahead of me. I've won!'

'Where did your rival finish?'

'I don't know but she was somewhere behind me.'

'What was your time?'

'56.6 seconds. It's my best time.'

At the end of the session she said, 'All this time I have been concentrating on my rival and the things she was doing instead of my own running. In the past I used to say to myself, "Forget her, forget her," but it didn't work.' 'You are absolutely right,' I replied. 'You were concentrating on the wrong things and you didn't have a clear picture in your mind about what you wanted to do or how to achieve it.'

She went to trials and won her race just as she had run it in her mind and she was now confident she would win gold at the Commonwealth Games.

A week before the Commonwealth Games she again came to see me. She had set herself two goals, breaking fifty-six seconds and winning gold. She thought she could break fifty-six seconds, but had been unsuccessful because she couldn't get in sixteen strides between the last two hurdles. She did that quite easily between the other hurdles but somehow couldn't do it between the last two. Up to this point her best time was 56.6 seconds.

Under relaxation and visualization therapy she ran the race in her mind and concentrated on rhythm, and staying relaxed in the last 100 metres of the race. She won the race in 55.9 seconds.

A few days later at the Commonwealth Games she demolished the opposition and won the race by about ten yards in a time of 55.9 seconds.

As soon as she returned to Melbourne, she brought her gold medal to show me. Just before she left I said, 'Incidentally, did you get in your sixteen strides between the last two hurdles?' 'I don't know. But who cares? I won and broke fifty-six seconds.'

Years later, that athlete travelled to the Seoul Olympic Games to compete in her race. A few days before she left Australia her sister died suddenly. She was devastated and was uncertain whether she would compete in the games. Her father, who knew how close we were, telephoned me in Barbados, gave me the bad news and asked me to contact her and help her. I sent her a telegram and reminded her about the things we had practised in the past.

I was confident that if she followed that process she would get so involved and focused on what she was doing that she would temporarily put the disaster to the back of her mind. She did compete and went on to win gold in the 400-metre hurdles.

It is amazing how easily great players can sometimes forget what they are supposed to concentrate on. Such was the case with Greg Chappell, one of Australia's greatest batsmen. He went in to a dreadful slump in the 1981-82 series against the West Indies. Everyone was giving advice and all sorts of diagnoses were made. These ranged from technical things like incorrect grip, wrong stance and poor footwork. Other problems suggested were staleness, lack of sleep and burnout. At that stage he was confused and depressed and was considering quitting the game.

I was certain that I knew the cause of his problem and that I had the solution to end his slump. But, there was no way I could help him then because Australia was fighting a mighty battle against my team, West Indies. Had I intervened at that stage, I would have been very unpopular with the West Indies players.

But in the last Test match, Greg left the field and went back to the dressing room and I thought that the time was right to see him.

When I entered the dressing room he was alone in the room, sitting dejectedly in a chair with his feet in a basin of water. We were friends and because of this I was able to make a few facetious remarks about his problem. But after a while we became serious. The conversation went something like this:

'Greg, I think I know what your problem is and I think I can help you.'

'I hope you can because I don't know what the hell is happening.'

'You normally make batting look so easy because you always get into the right positions to play your shots. But recently you have been playing your shots from some weird positions. This suggests to me that you are not seeing the ball early enough in its flight, otherwise your body would automatically move into the right positions. Are you watching the ball?'

'Of course I am watching the ball.'

'Are you seeing the ball early in its flight? Are you picking it up from the bowlers hand?' After a pause he said, 'I'm picking it up somewhere along the line but I am not watching it out of the bowler's hand. Sometimes on the way back to the pavilion I would say to myself, "I didn't see that ball. How could I forget something so basic? I am not watching the bloody ball!"'

'I suggest that you go into the nets for a short practice and find out if that is really your problem,' I said to him.

It was indeed the problem and he quickly recovered from his slump. In the next Test series against New Zealand that followed immediately afterwards, he played exceptionally well and produced some of his best innings. During that series a reporter asked him what had caused his slump and what helped him to recover so quickly after the series against the West Indies. He told the reporter that he was not watching the ball closely and was not picking it up out of the bowler's hand. But once he corrected that, his problems disappeared. The reporter did not believe him because he felt that the answer was too simple.

REMEMBER

1. To find out what you should concentrate on, ask yourself three simple questions: Where am I? Where should I be? What should I be doing?

2. Knowing what to concentrate on is very important.

3. You must focus on the correct cues or signals and on the right aspects of the task.

4. If you are a bowler, you should concentrate on bowling one ball at a time and focus on the type of ball you wish to bowl, your line and length and your target.

5. If you are a batsman, concentrate on playing one ball at a time and focus on seeing the ball out of the bowler's hand, getting into position, and targeting the area where you want to hit the ball.

6. Your thoughts, mistakes, opponents, the score or the state of the match might break your concentration. As soon as you notice this you should refocus your concentration on the task at hand.

7. As situations in the game change, you should adjust your focus to adapt to the changing circumstances.

8. You make mistakes when your concentration is focused on the wrong cues or events and when the shift from one signal to another is delayed.

9. Strong emotions like anger, fear and frustration are often responsible for that slow response.

FOCUS YOUR CONCENTRATION IN THE RIGHT TIME

The point of power is the present. The game of golf starts from where the last ball finishes.

— *Greg Norman*

Off the baseball mound is for thinking about the past and the future. On the mound is for thinking about the present.
— *H.A. Dorfman, psychologist*

Focusing concentration in the wrong time is a very common mistake in sport. It happens when your mind is trapped in the past on previous mistakes, failures or successes, or when it is directed to the future on imaginary results, instead of the present on the process or the task at hand. If your mind is in the past or the future, how can you then concentrate on the things that are going on in the present? Remember that you are where your concentration is.

Yet, good concentration sometimes requires you to revisit the past and look to the future in order to act correctly in the present. Managing that change of direction and focus between the past, the future and the present is very important.

When I was working with the Sri Lankan cricket team a Buddhist priest reminded me about the importance of staying in the present. He said, 'Much suffering comes into the life of those who try to be anywhere but here in the present moment. Are you satisfied with where you are right now because "right nows" are all you have?'

Years ago, two Australian Rules football teams were locked in combat during a most important and close game. In the dying moments of the game Phil Carman, a brilliant footballer, took a mark at point-blank range and had an opportunity to win the game if he kicked what appeared to be a very easy goal. Even though he was under pressure, there was no way he could miss that goal, or so we thought. If he kicked the goal his team would win but if he missed they would lose. He took his time, pulled up his socks, went through his routine in a slow and deliberate manner, took the kick and missed the goal!

A few weeks later, I asked him why he missed the goal. He said: 'As I was about to take my kick, I could see the headlines in the next day's newspapers. *'Carman turns on his magic and kicks the winning goal.'* I could also see my teammates embracing and congratulating me for winning the game. I can't remember when I took the kick but it was dreadful. Normally, I would have picked out a target between the goal posts and kicked to it, but I didn't do it. It never crossed my mind. I was thinking only of the result and the praise I would get.'

Just before you perform your task it is important to bring your concentration back to the present, on the task at hand. Some batsmen do so by looking at their feet just before the bowler starts his run up. Others focus on the feelings in their knees, the in and out movement of their abdomen as they breathe, the feelings and pressure in their hands as they hold the bat, the relaxation in their neck and shoulders or the relaxation in their jaw and lips. Yet others whistle or hum a tune or watch the bowler's chest or face as he runs in. Having refocused their attention to the present the batsmen immediately concentrate on seeing the ball the moment it leaves the bowler's hand to pick up its line and length. The feet, arms, hands, head and body then automatically do what they have to do – receive or hit the ball.

When these players break their routine, their concentration and performance often suffer.

REMEMBER

1. Having your concentration in the wrong time is one of the commonest mistakes in sport.

2. When your mind is in the wrong time, your attention is usually focused on the wrong things.

3. The game of golf starts from where the last ball finishes.

4. You are where your concentration is. If it is in the past or the future there is where you will be. How then can you deal with things happening in the present?

5. A key to good concentration is staying in the moment and enjoying the process or the journey that leads to your goal.

6. Buddhist priest: Much suffering comes into the life of those who try to be anywhere but here in the present moment. 'Right nows' are all you have.

DIRECT YOUR CONCENTRATION TO THE TASK AT HAND

> Under great pressure your concentration is often directed
> internally on your worries and fears instead of externally on
> the task at hand.
>
> — *Rudi Webster*

A common error occurs in sport when attention is directed internally on the things that are going on inside your mind and body instead of being directed externally on the critical things that are happening in the game.

A young female golfer from Australia who was trying to break into the professional tour in the USA once came to me for help. Every week she struggled to qualify for the tournaments. Once she had to sink a relatively easy eight-foot putt in two strokes on the eighteenth green to qualify but the pressure got the better of her and she messed up.

During relaxation therapy she used her imagination to recreate the events on the eighteenth green and I asked her to think aloud during the mental replay. She admitted that as she was about to take her putt she became very nervous and was full of self-doubt. 'I can't get down in two,' she said. 'I'm going to miss it, and I will again have to phone my parents to tell them that I blew it.' While those thoughts were in her mind she putted and missed.

Instead of directing her concentration outwardly and focusing on striking the ball to the hole she directed it inwardly on her parents, doubts and deficiencies.

During the 1999 Australian cricket tour of the West Indies, an Australian batsman asked me to help him with the mental part of his game but I told him that I was working with the West Indies team and could not accommodate him. He had a relatively poor tour and just before the last Test in Antigua he again approached me and I relented and agreed to talk to him.

He was a great worrier and when he was batting he spent a lot of time inside his own head thinking about what he should or should not do, and about what might or might not happen. During his innings his concentration was at times so stuck inside his head that he could not redirect it outwardly to watch the ball and get into position to play his shots. Consequently, he made many simple mistakes and gave his wicket away too often.

To keep him out of his own head and focus his concentration outwardly on the task at hand, I asked him to pay special attention to everything that was going on around him, between overs, and even between balls if he was batting against the fast bowlers. He was to look at the crowd, listen to the loud music, admire the colourful clothes in the crowd, examine the colour of the grass, notice the weight of his bat etc. But as soon as the bowler started his run-up he was to narrow his concentration to see the ball the moment it left the bowler's hand, to quickly judge its line and length and get into position to play his shot. I then showed him a few things to help him with those simple tasks.

He batted extremely well in the match. He scored fifty-one runs in the first innings and 127 in the second and helped his team to win the game and square the Test series. He won the Man of the Match Award.

REMEMBER

1. When you are under great pressure your focus of concentration narrows considerably and is often directed inwardly on negative things going on in your head.

2. Under these circumstances, flexibility is impaired and your concentration remains locked in that internal space.

3. Performance suffers because you have difficulty refocusing externally on the task at hand.

4. To unlock that internal space and focus, you should take a few deep breaths, relax your shoulders and neck, talk to yourself simply and positively and pay attention to the things that are happening around you, on and off the field.

ADJUST YOUR CONCENTRATION SPAN TO MEET YOUR CHALLENGES

Attention can be too wide or too narrow. You can broaden your concentration to deal with many things at once and become overloaded, confused and easily distracted or you can narrow it too much and focus on too few signals. In the latter case you develop 'tunnel vision' and become partially blind and deaf to a part of the environment. You will then miss important things going on around you.

INFORMATION OVERLOAD: DON'T CONCENTRATE ON TOO MANY THINGS

> My worst performances as a coach occur when I give too many instructions, when I interfere too often and when I try to play the game for the players.
> — *Alan Jeans, Australian football coach*

As I stated earlier, the brain receives and generates millions of impulses every second and can only process a small percentage of that information consciously. Some people can concentrate on many things at once and cope with lots of information while others can only deal with small amounts of information. You ought to find out what your capabilities are and stay within their boundaries.

When you overload yourself with information you make everything important and lose your sense of priorities. You then have difficulty differentiating between what is really important and what is not, and concentration inevitably suffers.

If one of two letters, A or B, were flashed on a computer screen and you were asked to press a specific key as soon as you recognized the letter, you would react quickly and there would not be any difference in the recognition times between the two letters. But if the examiner tricked you into believing that one of twenty-six letters would be used but used the same two letters, A and B, you would take longer to recognize them. This is why performance improves when priorities are limited and are clearly identified.

Pre-match Overloading

This is now quite common in sport. Some coaches overload their players with information at this stage by giving long motivational and instructional talks and by going through game plans and tactics in great detail. Many of these coaches mistakenly believe that the more information they give and the higher they psyche-up the players the better they will concentrate and play. But giving too much information and psyching up the players too highly is a sure way to mess up their concentration and performance.

Coaches get the best out of their players in the early part of the game when they highlight the first-important priorities and limit the amount of information they give to the players in the pre-game period. At this stage, psyching down the players is usually more productive than psyching them up.

Allan Jeans, a successful Australian Rules football coach in Melbourne once said to me: 'My worst performances as a coach occur when I give too many instructions, when I interfere too often and when I try to play the game for the players. The best thing you can do is to remind them about what is important and what is required, give them support and direction when they need them, and allow them to do their jobs. You can't play the game for them. Coaches who stay on the sidelines and try to play the game for their players are only fooling themselves. The simpler and more basic the instructions and demands, the better they usually play. Too many complex instructions are a sure way to destroy performance.'

When players are 'ready' for a game the last thing they need is to be overloaded with information. They cannot handle it at this stage. Over-arousal interferes with their ability to understand, remember and carry out simple instructions.

I once expressed those opinions to the coach of the Richmond Australian Rules football team. He didn't take too kindly to my suggestions and looked at me in disbelief. 'How could this bloke be so stupid!' he thought. 'And he is supposed to be an expert in this area.' He pointed out that this type of pre-match preparation had been successfully employed for years by all the coaches in the game. But, I stuck to my guns and told him that many of the players didn't really listen to or understand what was said to them during this crucial period.

At my request he agreed to carry out a simple experiment to see how much information his players would recall five minutes after his pre-match address. I asked him to limit his address to fifteen minutes and to repeatedly emphasize three key aspects of play that he wanted his players to execute on the field.

He did a great job. He repeatedly stressed the three key tasks and at the end of his talk he was convinced that he had got his message across. During the talk I watched the players closely and noticed that some of them were quite restless and were exhibiting signs of anxiety. The game was an important one and they couldn't wait to get out on the field.

Five minutes after the coach finished, I questioned the players and asked each one to repeat the three important things the coach wanted them to do in the game.

Of the twenty players only two remembered the three tasks. Half of the team remembered two of them and the other eight players could only remember one. The coach was very surprised and a little angry but he changed his pre-match routine afterwards, and his team's performance in the first quarter of the games improved considerably.

His team later went on to win the Grand Final and the championship against arch-rivals Collingwood after finishing near the bottom of the table the previous year.

In a team meeting two days before the Grand Final the coach went through his game plan and game strategy in great detail with the players but on Grand Final day he did not give the usual pre-match address. Instead, he asked me to divide the team into two groups, to sit in with them and let them decide how they would play the game. The players then held short but very constructive meetings. They identified three or four of their first-important priorities, discussed how they would execute them and made powerful commitments to each other. Their main goal was to hunt and defend in packs, establish physical dominance early in the game by being extremely aggressive to the ball, and break their opponents mentally. After the meetings the coach asked me how things went and I told him that the players were united behind a common goal and were totally committed to beating their opponents in the key contests and key areas of the game. I assured him they would win the psychological battle with their opponents and would outplay them during the game. That is exactly what happened. They demolished the opposition in the first quarter and went on to win the game by a record score.

REMEMBER

1. Information overload and task overload disrupt concentration and performance.

2. These are common mistakes of overenthusiastic and perfectionist coaches and players.

3. These mistakes often happen in the dressing room in the immediate pre-match period.

4. When you overload yourself you lose your sense of priorities and have difficulty differentiating between trivial and important things.

5. In the immediate pre-match period you should make things as clear and simple as possible, identify your first-important priorities, limit the information you attend to, and mentally rehearse your jobs and responsibilities on the field.

6. Allan Jeans an Australian football coach once said that his worst performances occurred when he gave too many instructions, when he interfered too often and when he tried to play the game for the players. He said that coaches who think they can stay on the sidelines and play the game for the players are only fooling themselves.

WHEN TO TURN ON AND TURN OFF YOUR CONCENTRATION

Like other parts of the body, your brain cells need time to rest and recover from their activities.

— *Anonymous*

If you try to concentrate for long periods without taking the odd breaks, you will get mentally tired and concentrate poorly. To maintain concentration for long periods you must learn when to turn it on and when to turn it off.

Sir Garfield Sobers supports that view. He says, 'It is impossible to concentrate deeply for long periods. You must have breaks, otherwise you will get tired and make silly mistakes. Mental fatigue is the enemy of concentration and good performance. I used to take breaks in between overs or even in between balls. I used to take my mind away from the game and think about other things. The moment I was ready to face up to the bowler again, I would turn on my concentration. A good spin bowler will cause you some trouble in that respect because he is always coming at you and you don't have much time to rest. To counter this, you must find other ways to break his rhythm. Going down the wicket to have a chat with your partner or patting down the wicket in between balls are two common ways of doing this.'

Peter Brock says, 'My concentration is very intense when I am approaching and negotiating corners. These are critical points on the track and you must give them your total and undivided attention. I concentrate on going into the corner at the correct speed, following the correct line and coming out at the fastest speed. Distractions at this stage will interfere with that exercise and you will lose valuable time. When I go through the corner and I am on my way down the straight I relax. These breaks are very important and I regard them as little holidays that I take during the race. I am convinced that you can only maintain the necessary levels of concentration for the hard parts of the circuits and the hard duels during the race if you take those breaks. If you don't, you get tired and lose concentration.'

Talking during a contest serves many purposes but it is often used to turn off and turn on concentration. Lee Trevino the golfer was good at this. He used to relax and turn off his concentration in between strokes by talking and joking. But as soon as he was ready to play his shot, the talking stopped and he became dead serious as he willed his concentration on the shot at hand.

When I was studying medicine in New Zealand, I used to play cricket for the province of Otago. The best batsman in our team used to talk incessantly when he was batting and was known all over New Zealand for his chatter in the middle. That was his way of relaxing, turning off and turning on his concentration.

One day we were playing against Auckland and the members of that team decided not to talk to him while he was batting. When he started to bat he tried to talk to everyone but nobody took him on, not even the umpires and after a while he became anxious and nervous. He wasn't batting well and he realized that he was in danger of losing his wicket so he had to do something quickly to ease the pressure and improve his concentration. He signalled to his colleagues in the pavilion that he wanted to change his bat and started to walk towards the dressing room. One of his team members met him on the field with three bats. He tested each bat while he was talking to his colleague and then chose the one he had been using earlier. This surprised his teammate, who said, 'You've just taken the bat you were using before. That is the one you wanted to change.' 'I know,' he replied. 'I was going mad out there and I was losing my concentration. I had to come down here to have a chat. Those bastards out there won't talk to me.' He went back to the wicket and started to play much better.

REMEMBER

1. It is difficult to concentrate deeply for long periods without getting mentally tired.
2. You must have breaks otherwise you will get mentally tired and make silly mistakes.

3. You must know when to turn on your concentration and when to turn it off.

4. Mental fatigue is the enemy of concentration and good performance.

5. Sir Garfield Sobers said he turned off his concentration in between overs and even in between balls if he was facing a fast bowler. But as soon as the bowler started his run up he would turn it on again to focus on the ball.

6. Just like the muscles in the body, the cells in the brain need time to refresh and recharge themselves.

BLOCK OUT DISTRACTIONS BY LOCKING IN CONCENTRATION

When a batsman tells himself to watch the ball and play it on its merits, he might have other thoughts like scoring runs or not getting out in his mind. Those thoughts can break his concentration and prevent him from watching the ball.

— M.S Dhoni

Many different thoughts pass through my mind when I am batting but as soon as the bowler is about to deliver the ball, my concentration focuses sharply on the ball for that fraction of a second.

— V.V.S Laxman

During the execution of your tasks there are critical moments when you must lock in your concentration. If it is broken or if you get distracted at these times you will make mistakes and perform badly. These lapses in concentration occur in a split second and can be quite devastating. It is amazing how many negative thoughts can flit through your mind in such a short time.

When you are playing golf you might go through your pre-shot routine, take up your stance correctly, align your body accurately and be focused on playing your shot. But as soon as you are about to start your backswing, a negative thought, an uncomfortable feeling, a noise from the crowd or the movement of your opponent might distract you and break your concentration, which will automatically make you play a bad shot. When professional golfers get distracted like that, they often stop their swing, walk away from the ball and start their routine all over again. Tiger Woods has enormous powers of concentration but even he has had some trouble recently locking in his concentration on the tee. Photographers and the noise from their cameras occasionally break his concentration in the middle of his backswing.

Sir Garfield Sobers stressed that being mentally alert is very important in maintaining concentration. He said, 'I see a lot of players stop the bowler in his run-up because someone moves near the sightscreen. Others are distracted by crowd noise or remarks from the opposition. When I am batting, the moment I face up to the bowler, my concentration is zeroed in on him and the ball. Everything else is shut out. A lot of players fail to do this and allow too many irrelevant things to distract them.'

When I asked Greg Norman how he locked in his concentration, he said, 'I do this very easily. I look at the ball and just as I am about to start my swing I think, "Rhythm, get good rhythm." Once I put that thought in my mind, everything else is blocked out. It is like putting a protective shield around my head to keep out distractions. Other golfers do the same thing with different thoughts or instructions.'

Norman added, 'When I am putting, my breathing is very important particularly on fast greens. It helps me to lock in my concentration. Whenever I putt well I always follow a routine of taking two breaths. This is the length of time I spend over the ball, until I stroke it. I take a deep breath looking at the hole and I breathe out slowly as I look back at the ball. I then take another deep breath when I look at the hole again and I breathe out slowly and completely as I focus on the ball. Then I wait for a fraction of a second. At this stage I feel solid and relaxed. I then stroke the ball to the hole. If I break this routine I often hit a bad putt.'

Some batsmen improve their concentration and lock it in by whistling, humming or singing when the bowler is in his run-up.

Lawrence Rowe, the great West Indies batsman, whistled when he was facing up to the bowler and usually played quite well. But when he stopped whistling, his batting deteriorated. M.S. Dhoni sings when the bowler is running in to bowl. He claims that it keeps him calm, clears his mind and improves his concentration. Humming, singing and whistling stimulate right brain activity, the part of the brain that is active in sport, particularly with awareness of the body's movement, and its position in space.

There is a very amusing story about a South African player who was once batting against a very powerful Australian cricket team. The fielders around him were sledging him constantly and tried everything to break his concentration, but he ignored them. Frustrated and angry, one of the fielders shouted, 'What the hell is the matter with you, you silly bugger? Are you deaf?' The batsman did not respond, and a fielder repeated himself several times in a more emphatic and aggressive manner: 'Are you bloody deaf?' Some time later, the batsman turned to the fielder and asked, 'Were you saying something to me earlier? I am sorry mate. I didn't hear you.' The batsman's concentration was so locked in to the task at hand that he was able to shut out the distracting comments of his opponents.

REMEMBER

1. People make simple but costly concentration errors when they get distracted at critical moments during the execution of their tasks.

2. These periods might only last for a split second but the damage to concentration and performance can be enormous.

3. Most good athletes devise their own methods to lock in their concentration on the task during these critical moments.

4. It is easier to lock in your concentration when you are mentally alert.

CONCENTRATION TRAINING: HOW DO YOU IMPROVE CONCENTRATION?

To improve your concentration you must:

- Work on it at training, practice and during the game. You can even improve it with simple breathing technical, meditation, visualization and mental rehearsal techniques. You must train and practise in situations that physically and mentally resemble those you will face in the game.

- Preserve its flexibility by keeping your arousal level in the optimum range – not too high or too low.

- Know what to concentrate on, how many things to concentrate on, when to concentrate and when to relax, and how to lock in concentration.

- In the game you must learn how to keep your concentration in the present and not allow it to wander off to the past or the future.

- If it wanders, as soon as you detect it, you should refocus it to the task at hand.

- Learn how to fit your concentration style to the changing concentration demands of the situations you will face.

- Practise controlling your concentration in different pressure situations.

There are many mental exercises you can practise to improve your concentration. Some of these are outlined in the chapter on self-confidence and others are discussed in the next chapter on pressure. They are breathing exercises, progressive muscular relaxation, biofeedback, thought restructuring, visualization and mental rehearsal techniques, exposure techniques, hypnosis and self-hypnosis. Centering and meditation are described below.

Centering

This simple technique was borrowed from the martial arts. It produces quick and effective relaxation and is a good method for improving concentration and controlling pressure.

Begin by standing with your feet shoulders' width apart, with one foot slightly ahead of the other. Then allow your arms to hang loosely by your side and bend your knees ever so slightly.

Now inhale deeply and slowly through your nose and hold your breath for a moment. Notice the upward movement of your upper body, particularly your shoulders and head and feel the tension in your neck, shoulders and upper chest. Exhale slowly, releasing that tension and allowing your neck, shoulders, arms and fingers to relax completely. During exhalation notice how solid your body feels, as if its weight is pushing down between both your feet.

Inhale deeply and slowly again keeping your shoulders relaxed and down, using your lower chest and abdomen to breathe. Notice the absence of tension in your neck, shoulders and upper chest. Now exhale slowly and completely through the mouth and focus on a spot just below your navel. Notice how much more relaxed, grounded and balanced you feel.

Inhale slowly and deeply for the third time keeping your shoulders loose and relaxed and breathe with your abdomen. As you exhale slowly and focus on the spot below your navel you will feel more relaxed, balanced and centred.

You can also do this exercise when you are sitting down.

During this exercise you keep your concentration in the present by focusing on your breathing and on a spot below your navel. At the end of your third breath you can redirect your concentration to the important task at hand. It is a very handy and quick way to eliminate distractions and to refocus concentration. The more you practise this technique the better you will use it.

Martial arts practitioners tell their students that one of the ways to stay calm and improve concentration is to breathe easily with their abdomen and focus on a point two inches below the navel, the site of the body's centre of gravity. They say that when a player breathes properly and focuses attention on this point he becomes more balanced and alert and concentrates better.

Your balance and centre of gravity are affected by the state of your mind. When you are under pressure, and are uptight, tense and cluttered in your mind your centre of gravity seems to shift upward, away from your abdomen. You can then lose balance and become unstable. But when your centre of gravity stays below your navel you are less likely to sway and lose balance.

Try this exercise. Pretend that you are playing golf and take up your stance. Now put both hands, one on top of the other, palms in, a couple of inches below your navel. Turn your body a few times the way you would in the golf swing and feel how easy it is to maintain balance and stay stable. Now repeat the process with your hands on the top of your head and notice how easy it is to sway and how much harder it is to stay centred and balanced.

Here is another exercise to show how your state of mind affects your balance. You will need a friend to help you. Stand upright and take up the posture that you used in the centering exercise. Focus on your neck, chest and upper back and imagine that most of your weight is in your upper body. Breathe normally, and as you breathe out imagine that most of your weight is moving down to your lower chest and upper abdomen. With the next breath feel it settling down in your lower abdomen. With the next breath feel it in your legs and feet. Now ask your friend to gently push one of your shoulders backward. Your shoulder will give in a bit but your lower body will remain stable and centred.

Now take up your original stance and concentrate on your forehead, clench your jaws tightly and stretch the muscles in your neck and shoulders as if you were under great pressure and imagine that most of your weight is in your head, neck and shoulders. Again ask your friend to gently push one of your shoulders backward. Notice how easily you lose balance and stability.

When you become negative, anxious and uptight – a tight upper body – your centre of gravity seems to move upwards. But when you are calm, relaxed and in control it stays in the abdomen just below the navel.

Meditation

To many people, meditation is a somewhat mysterious process that has spiritual and religious connotations. In sport, there is little doubt that meditation improves concentration and performance. Instead of meditation I prefer to use the term 'attention or concentration training'. In this technique attention is focused in the present on a specific thought, object or activity, like breathing, repeating a mantra, performing a movement or executing a sports skill. And whenever the mind wanders it is immediately brought back to the present and refocused on the object of meditation.

Meditation is not straining or striving. It is relaxation and concentration. It calms and disciplines the mind, disconnects you from your negative and disruptive thoughts, and detaches you from what is happening around you. It lowers arousal, decreases anxiety and promotes relaxation. And it makes the mind more receptive to suggestions and self-statements.

Before starting a meditation exercise I describe the most effective way to breathe. I then tell the player that he must expect to meet with several failures in the beginning because his mind will automatically wander away from his object of concentration or meditation. But as soon as he notices this wandering he has to gently and quietly bring it back to the object of meditation. I stress that each time he does this successfully he will increase his powers of concentration and improve his capacity to meditate.

This is how I ask him to breathe:

Close your eyes and let yourself relax. Take a deep breath and then let it out slowly. Now do that again but this time with a much deeper breath, and at the top of your inspiration hold it for a while and then let it out slowly. I asked you to breathe like this because I wanted to show you how not to breathe in meditation.

I now want you to breathe easily and quietly without any effort. Let your breathing be effortless and automatic. Just relax your jaw, cheeks, lips neck and shoulders and let it happen. Each time you practise this it will get easier. Sometimes your breathing will be shallow and sometimes it will be deep. Just observe it and let it happen.

Sitting Meditation

After explaining that breathing technique, I commence the meditation exercise:

Go to a quiet place and sit in a comfortable position with eyes closed and back upright but not tense. Feel the sensation in the muscles of your jaw, lips, cheek, forehead, neck and shoulders as they get loose and relax completely; and breathe quietly.

Your abdomen is always moving when you breathe. Feel its natural in and out movements and be aware of its rising and falling. As you get better at feeling and following these movements you will notice that your breathing is sometimes deep, sometimes shallow, sometimes rapid, sometimes slow and calm. Be aware of these variations, don't try to control or interfere with them in any way. Let them happen and just feel the movements as they occur.

While you are feeling the rise and fall of the abdomen your mind may automatically go towards other things, such as thoughts, feelings or bodily sensations. Be aware of them as soon as they arise. If a thought comes into your mind, be aware of 'thinking'; if you hear a sound make a mental note of 'hearing'; and if you become aware of a sensation in your body make a mental note of 'feeling'. In these cases you should then calmly return your attention to the rising and falling of your abdomen.

As you get better at this you will quickly detect distractions as soon as they arise. At times your mind will follow these distractions and sometime later you might think that you were daydreaming.

As soon as you notice your concentration drifting away from the present moment and from your focus of attention, note that your mind is wandering. Then return your concentration to the rising and falling of the abdomen. Eventually, these things will happen automatically and there will be less need for making mental notes of your distractions.

This exercise should go on for at least ten to fifteen minutes.

You can clear your mind, relax your body and improve concentration and performance during the day by starting the day with a long version of the meditation technique above, then supplement it with at least five two-minute mini-meditations during the course of the day, and finish the day with the long version.

Mini-meditations can be done anywhere and at anytime. In sport you can use them during the game. For instance in cricket, you can do so during the breaks or even in between overs:

Keep your eyes open and carry on with whatever you are doing. Allow your shoulders, arms, fingers and jaw muscles to relax, and breathe normally through your mouth. Feel the movement of air as it passes across your lips and tongue when you breathe in and out. Do this for ten to fifteen breaths. That's all.

If you don't want to focus on the movement of air over your lips and tongue you can pay attention to the expansion and contraction of your lower chest and feel the in and out movement of your abdomen as you breathe. Just do this for ten to fifteen breaths.

Mini-meditations are supplementary exercises and should be done routinely at least five times a day in a wide variety of situations.

When you master the basics of these types of meditation you can make things more difficult by meditating in an uncomfortable posture or in noisy places.

You should fill out a sheet recording how many major meditations and mini-meditations you do during the day. Your goal should be two major and five mini-meditations.

Walking and Movement Meditation

As well as meditating in the sitting or lying posture, you can do so while standing, walking, or practising specific technical movements. You should divide your time equally between sitting and moving meditation.

In walking meditation, allow your shoulders to fall and go loose and feel the lifting and forward movement of the feet and the placing of each foot on the ground. With the head upright, look at a spot on the ground about six to eight feet ahead, walk at a slow pace and maintain your balance by taking normal-sized steps. Feel each part of the movement as it occurs.

Instead of focusing on just foot movements you can pay attention to and feel the movements of the right leg and right arm or the left leg and left arm when you walk. As the right leg moves forward the right arm moves backward, and as the right leg moves backward, the right arm moves forward.

Let these movements happen automatically and just feel them as they occur. Don't try to control them.

If you don't want to focus on your limbs when you are walking, you can instead focus on the feelings of air passing across your lips and tongue as you breathe in and out through your mouth while you walk.

Whatever your focus of meditation, bring your attention back to that focus whenever you notice that the mind is wandering.

INTERVIEWS

JACQUES KALLIS

Rudi. How important is concentration?

Jacques. It is massively important. It is a key to good performance. I've seen many talented players with lots of potential fall by the wayside and fail to fulfil their promise because of poor concentration and a lack of desire. But I have also seen less talented players outperform the more talented ones because they work harder at their game, concentrate better and toughen up mentally. Good concentration often helps you beat players who are more talented than you are. It is one of the things that separate the great players from the rest.

Rudi. What is concentration?

Jacques. In batting, concentration is about having a clear mind, focusing on the ball and trusting your instincts. It is focusing attention on one thing at a time and not allowing too many thoughts to cloud your mind. It is something that you can turn on and off.

When the bowler gets back to his mark I try to clear my mind, pay attention to the rhythm of his run up and pick up the ball as soon as it leaves his hand.

Rudi. How do you clear your mind and stop yourself from having too many thoughts?

Jacques. I just watch the ball. Once I focus on the ball everything else is shut out.

Rudi. What are the common concentration mistakes that you make?

Jacques. I make mistakes when too many thoughts creep into my mind and when I don't watch the ball closely enough. The most dangerous distractions arise in the mind not from the things that are happening in the game or are being said during the game. For me, fighting distractions is an inner battle. Sledging and things like that don't usually break my concentration. It is the things that go on between my two ears that occasionally cause me problems.

Rudi. In golf, a player might do all the right things before he starts his swing and might know exactly where he wants the ball to go but just as he is about to start his swing some thought or noise might distract him and he might then play an awful shot. The best golfers avoid that mistake by locking in their concentration and locking out distractions during their swing. Greg Norman used to do this by saying, 'Rhythm, get good rhythm.' How do you lock in your concentration when the bowler is about to deliver the ball?

Jacques. Once I focus on the ball, harmful thoughts or distractions are automatically blocked out. I believe that the contest is between you and the ball. The bowler delivers the ball but it is the ball that gets you out. When I tell myself to watch the ball my concentration is locked in to the ball and nothing else enters my mind during that critical split second when the ball is about to come to me.

Rudi. How does pressure affect concentration?

Jacques. Sometimes it improves concentration but at other times it can mess it up. Pressure tightens you up and prevents your muscles from working freely. It also creates tension in the mind and you then start to worry about the outcome or result or about what might or might not happen, particularly when things get tough. Worrying about the outcome creates a lot of the players' pressure. Their concentration is then in the future. But when they keep it in the present by giving their full attention to the next ball most of that pressure disappears.

Players also create a lot of pressure by worrying about what people might say if they don't play well. You can't control what people say when you don't play well but you can control the things you say to yourself. If I don't play well on a particular day I would say to myself, 'I didn't play well today. Things didn't work out today but when I bat in the next game I will make sure that they work out better.' It is easier to adopt that approach after you have played for a while and have some experience dealing with these situations. But if you are inexperienced or are trying to hold on to your spot in the team it can be quite difficult.

Rudi. When do you find it most difficult to concentrate?

Jacques. When I am tired, particularly mentally, after playing a lot of cricket, I am not as focused as I should be. At times like this I like to take some time off from practice and training to rest and refresh my mind for the next game. If your coach trusts you and understands the dangers of mental tiredness he won't object to giving you the time off.

Cricket games go on for hours each day and it is impossible to hold your concentration on the game all the time. If you try to do this you will get tired mentally. You must have breaks during the game and must learn when to turn off your concentration and when to turn it on.

Rudi. I agree with you. Mental tiredness is the enemy of concentration. What is this thing that people refer to as the zone?

Jacques. It is a strange thing. It is like being in a bubble. It is a wonderful feeling. When you are in the zone you are at your best. Your concentration is spot on and you don't have to think about anything. You just watch the ball and play by instinct. You don't think at all about what you have to do, you just do it.

V.V.S. LAXMAN

Rudi. How important is concentration?

Laxman. Concentration in sport is extremely important. It is about committing yourself to a particular task or a particular target or goal. Many different thoughts pass through my mind when I am batting, but as soon as the bowler is about to deliver the ball, my concentration focuses sharply on the ball for that fraction of a second. For me, that is concentration. It's about focusing attention on a particular object, task or goal. Watching the ball out of the bowlers hand is the key to my concentration.

Rudi. What are the things that break your concentration?

Laxman. Overconfidence is one of them. When I am dominating and am in total control of my game I sometimes make concentration errors. So I try to guard against overconfidence by staying calm, focusing on the process and staying in the moment. Overconfidence can be very dangerous because it encourages you to underrate your opponent and the situation you face at the same time you overrate yourself and your ability. I try to stick to my plan and focus on the ball.

I sometimes get into trouble when my mind wanders from the present to the past on previous mistakes and failures or to the future on anticipated results. Many players get out in the nineties because they get anxious and think about a hundred instead of focusing on playing the next ball on its merits. I occasionally lose concentration for a short time if a bowler beats me with a few good balls and start to worry about what might happen next. Focusing on technique in these circumstances makes matters worse.

The best way to concentrate when you are batting, fielding or bowling is to keep it focused in the moment on the process.

In sport, there are certain times when you are distracted by the opposition and the crowd, by the way you are playing and by negative thoughts. As soon as you spot these distractions you should immediately bring your attention back to the present on the task at hand.

Rudi. I agree with you. In sport, the present is the point of power. Greg Norman who was once the world's number one golfer often said the game of golf starts from where the last ball finishes.

RAHUL DRAVID

Rudi: What is concentration, how important is it and what are the common errors that players make?

Rahul. Concentration in batting is the ability to play one ball at a time and not get too far ahead of yourself or get caught up in the past. I guess that would be concentration for me.

It is a critical factor in performance. The common mistakes people make, I guess, are to get too far ahead of themselves or focus on the wrong things. This can happen when they become overconfident, when they get too tense or nervous, and when they start worrying about the result rather than focusing on the next ball or the process.

I think that the ability to consistently focus on the ball day in and day out when you are batting is vital. You may not be able to do it every time but constant repetition and practice helps in that respect. People always ask me what I do to improve my concentration. I don't have a specific method or mantra I can recommend other than constant practice.

The way I work on my concentration is to practise and practise in the nets. You should do the same things there that you do in the match, playing one ball at a time. Net sessions should be simulation training for the real game so you should invest a lot of time to practise in the nets, not just to improve your technique but also your mental skills, particularly your concentration.

Rudi. What do you concentrate on?

Rahul. You must know what to focus on to concentrate well. For me, that is the ball. I try to see the ball as early as possible in its flight and gauge its length quickly. Most of this happens unconsciously. You don't have time to think. It is like a reflex action. If you allow too many thoughts to creep into your mind at that time you won't see the ball early enough and won't get into the right positions to play your strokes.

Watching the ball closely keeps your concentration in the present. If you are facing a really quick bowler and you worry about getting hit or getting runs, think about what the last ball did, or about what the next ball might do, you will run into trouble because your concentration will not be in the present.

Rudi. In the longer version of the game some players set themselves the goal of batting in units of ten runs and try to accumulate as many units as they can. Others concentrate on batting in units of five or ten overs. Still others train themselves to bat for two-hour periods, the usual length of a session. Do you set yourself targets like these?

Rahul. When I go in to bat I try to get over the first five or six overs and then set myself the goal of batting for at least thirty overs which works out to about two hours of batting.

Rudi. Some people claim that their biggest distractions do not come from the game but from inside their own heads. Do you agree with that?

Rahul. Yes. Sometimes the entire contest is a battle with yourself. Most of the time, it is not the bowler who gets you out – you get yourself out. You often make a mental error that leads to your dismissal. This happens to everyone but the more you practise and think about what you are doing the quicker you will learn to cope, and the fewer mistakes you will make.

For me the vital things about concentration are focusing on the right things, staying in the present, and constantly bringing myself back to the present whenever my mind wanders. Everyone is different, so you need to work out what is best for you and do it your own way. We all have different values, beliefs and cultures and that is why knowing and understanding yourself is so important.

You must learn how to recognize and deal with different game situations. You must also be aware of the situations that normally put you under pressure. You must spot them early, and deal with them before the pressure gets out of hand.

Rudi. Training in meditation can be very helpful. It keeps your mind in the present and stops it from wandering. But if it does wander it allows you to immediately bring it back to the present to the object of meditation. This is similar to what you just described, focusing on the right thing, staying in the present or constantly bringing yourself back to the present when your mind wanders.

A lot of players have difficulty locking in their concentration at critical periods and make simple mistakes as a result. How do you lock in your concentration?

Rahul. This is something that the great players have learned through practice. The more you practise holding your concentration on the ball or whatever you choose to focus on, the better you will get at it. I don't have a magic formula other than practice, repetition and more repetition. Breathing is sometimes helpful in that respect. It centres and calms me and enables me to stay in the present and lock in my concentration on the task at hand.

Rudi. There is a technique called centering in martial arts that uses breathing to improve concentration and reduce pressure and nervousness. I have described it in the text.

―――――――――――

M.S. DHONI

Rudi. Concentration plays such a pivotal role in our lives and performance and yet we find it so hard to control or master. How important is concentration in performance.

Dhoni. You cannot play well unless you concentrate well.

Switching on and switching off concentration is very important. A game of cricket goes on for six to seven hours and it is very difficult to be tuned into the game all the time. If you try to do so you will get mentally tired and make mistakes. You have to learn when to switch on your concentration and when to switch it off. If you do this well you will remain mentally alert and hold your concentration.

Rudi. Sir Garfield Sobers makes the same points. He said he used to turn off his concentration between overs or even between balls, if he was batting against a fast bowler. He said mental fatigue is one of the things that interfered with his concentration. What do you concentrate on when you are batting?

Dhoni. When I am batting I focus on the ball. Sometimes my mind wanders off to places where it is not supposed to be but as soon as I notice it I bring it back to the ball.

Singing helps me to stay focused. When the bowler is running in to bowl I start to sing but as soon as he gets to his delivery stride I focus on the ball. Singing when the bowler is running in empties my mind of unwanted thoughts.

Rudi. Lawrence Rowe, the great West Indies batsman, used to whistle while he was batting. He claimed that whistling kept negative thoughts out of his mind and helped him to relax and concentrate better. What are the common concentration errors that you make?

Dhoni. I make them when I get ahead of myself and worry about what the bowler might bowl, and when I get trapped in the past on previous mistakes. Deciding what shot I am going to play before the ball is bowled is an error I sometimes make. Smart bowlers can at times read your intentions and deceive you.

Rudi. Some batsmen concentrate on watching the ball but as the bowler is about to deliver the ball, a random thought might pop into their heads and break their concentration. Does this ever happen to you?

Dhoni. Yes. When it happens I usually play a rash shot. When I am not in the moment I make silly mistakes like that. I sometimes get away with it if I am lucky but I often pay the price and lose my wicket. If I survive, I make a deliberate attempt to lock in my concentration to prevent it from happening again.

I feel that the difference between a great batsman and a good batsman is often the interval between mistakes. Both players might be equally talented but it is the interval between mistakes that usually separates them. The good batsman will make a mistake and repeat it soon after but the great batsman will eliminate it for the rest of the game. That is what makes him great.

SIR GARFIELD SOBERS

Rudi. Did you ever have any trouble concentrating?

Sir Garfield. As long as I am mentally alert, I can concentrate well. But if I become tired because of mental or physical overexertion, or if I am not interested in what I am doing, my concentration will waver. Being mentally alert is very important.

I see a lot of players stop the bowler in his run-up because someone moves near the sightscreen. Others are distracted by crowd noise or remarks from the opposition. When I am batting, the moment I face up to the bowler, my concentration is zeroed in on him and the ball. Everything else is shut out. Too many people fail to do this and allow too many irrelevant things to distract them.

It is impossible to concentrate deeply for long periods. You must have breaks otherwise you will get tired and make silly mistakes. Mental fatigue is the enemy of concentration and good performance. I used to take my breaks between overs or even between balls. I used to take my mind away from the game and think about other things. The moment I was ready to face up to the bowler again I would turn on my concentration. A good spin bowler would always give you trouble in this respect because he is always coming at you and you don't have much time to rest. To counter this you should try to break his rhythm. Going down the wicket to have a chat with the other batsman or patting down the wicket between balls are two common ways of doing this.

Many batsmen get into trouble because they don't rest their minds. In addition to getting mentally tired they run into other problems. If a ball beats them they think about it while the bowler is going back to his mark, and worry about what might happen next. They start looking for problems that aren't there. They create them in their own minds. You have to learn how to focus your thoughts on the next ball. And play it on its merits. If you can do this you will forget the last one and the one after.

Rudi. What do you concentrate on when you are facing up to the bowler?

Sir Garfield. I watch the ball leaving his hand and try to pick up its trajectory as early as possible. I used to practise this in the nets and I would play games with myself to see how quickly I could see the ball and get into position. I would experiment and look at different things. I would try to see the position of his fingers on the ball and pick up what the bowler was doing with them. I would notice the point in the delivery at which the ball was released. I would watch the position of the bowler's feet, his head, his left shoulder, and his left arm – all sorts of things. These experiments helped me to bat better in the middle.

To be the best you must be one step ahead of the opposition. To master the bowlers you must learn their tricks. Good bowlers are very clever and they are always trying to work you out. You must get the upper hand. That is why experimentation in the nets is so important.

Rudi. Why do players have trouble in the nineties?

Sir Garfield. This happens because they are thinking about a hundred instead of the next ball. Some of them try to score ten runs off the next ball. You must stick to your game plan when you reach ninety. If you change it you will run into trouble. Some players get very nervous and do silly things; others become too cautious and may even freeze up and do equally silly things. When I got to ninety I went on batting normally. I didn't think about a hundred because I was concentrating on the next ball. If you concentrate too strongly on the hundred you might get confused and might not even see the ball when it is delivered.

Rudi. One of your greatest Test innings was played in Jamaica against England on a wicket that was described as the worst and most dangerous Test wicket ever. How did you score a century on that wicket? You must have had some negative thoughts about your chances of doing well. How did you concentrate so well?

Sir Garfield. It was the worst Test wicket I had played on. Before going out to bat I thought that I would have to be lucky to do well. I realized that I would have to put my head down and use all my skills in the best manner possible. I remember saying, 'This is a great challenge but I think I can overcome it. The wicket looks difficult but I won't allow its appearance to get me out because I know I can bat on it. If the bowlers want my wicket they will have to earn it. I am not going to give in and hand it to them on a plate.' Most of the other players were psyched out by the wicket and got out in their minds before they went in to bat. My attitude was different. I said to some of them, 'I can bat on this wicket and will do so until proven otherwise.' I went out there and I played each ball on its merits. I concentrated on every ball. The ball did some unusual and dangerous things from time to time but that didn't worry me. You see, I was only interested in the next ball and I didn't think about the one before or the one coming after. If something unusual happened, I forgot about it the moment I faced up to the next ball because that is what I was concentrating on. If I hadn't done this I would have been saying, 'This is ridiculous. Did you see what the last ball did? I wonder what the next one will do. How can I bat on this wicket?' As I faced up to each ball, I assumed that it would behave normally. If it didn't, it would miss my bat or I would leave it alone or alter my shot.

Rudi. So you thought the best way to handle the situation was to play down the difficulties of the wicket and approach each ball as if it was going to be a normal delivery?

Sir Garfield. But that was the only sensible thing I could do. If I went out to bat thinking about all the terrible things that could happen I wouldn't have made any runs. If I had told myself that I couldn't play on it, I wouldn't have. I worked out a plan of action and felt that I had a 60 per cent chance of carrying it out. They were great odds under those conditions. I have always enjoyed difficult and challenging situations. They motivate me to do well and that is when I think I concentrate and play best. In these conditions I often say, 'Now this is the test. These are the conditions that sort out the players and separate the greats from the merely good players. I believe that if you face up to challenging situations with negative thoughts and worry about the things that may or may not happen, you won't play well.

Rudi. So pressure improves your concentration?

Sir Garfield. Yes. The team position and the situations I faced influenced my concentration very strongly. I think that if you are a team man, concern about the position or situation your team is facing is a great way to build and hold your concentration. Selfish players are different because they are only concerned about their own score. When you are batting you have to help the fellow at the other end and the other batsmen who are coming in after him. This responsibility improves my concentration.

I try to teach young cricketers that there is more to cricket than physical technique. They must learn how to approach situations and how to think, concentrate and play when they face different situations. If the team position demands that they stay there and get a given number of runs, they must be able to apply their mind and their skills to achieve that target. The batsman can then say, 'OK, We need another 100 runs to get out of trouble. I will get them. I will stay here until I get them and when I do, I will then think about my next target. Until that time comes I won't take any chances, not even a fifty-fifty one. The odds will have to be 75 per cent in my favour before I chance my hand.' If you get out doing something silly and put the responsibility and pressure of getting the team out of trouble on to your teammate, you haven't done your job.

There are lots of things you must do to concentrate well. Many of these happen automatically. When I go in to bat, I sum up the situation. I look at the score, the team position, the wicket, the bowlers, the field placing and the weather conditions and I say to myself, 'Now, what's required of me? This is what I have to do.' I try to get over the first situation and when I have done so, I concentrate on something else because that situation is no longer important. It has passed. It is no longer present. To play well you must use your mind and your skill to meet and overcome the important demands in the situations you face.

Rudi. I have always said that concentration is a matter of choosing what is important in each situation you face and focusing your attention on it.

Sir Garfield. That is absolutely correct. That is the best way of putting it. If you can pick out the important factors in each situation you face, and deal with them, you will concentrate well.

PETER BROCK

Peter. Motor racing is a fast and exciting sport in which situations change rapidly. You constantly have to make adjustments to cope with these changes. It is mentally and physically demanding; so clear thinking and good concentration are very important. The penalties for negative thinking might be disabling or even fatal.

A fierce desire to succeed and be the best, a sense of achievement and pride in doing your job well and enjoyment of the contest are the things that help you to concentrate better.

Before the race, I like to take a few moments to visualize what I want to do. It then becomes a natural progression from thinking about it to doing it. Visualization programmes my mind for action and when I get out there I am relaxed, confident and motivated and I concentrate well.

Setting goals and challenges during the race helps me to concentrate better. I try to drive the car smoothly and efficiently and at the same time try to pressurize my opponents as much as I can.

I must be relatively relaxed to concentrate well. If I am too tense, my concentration suffers. I stay relaxed by loosening my neck and shoulder muscles, exercising my hands and fingers, taking some slow deep breaths and talking to myself clearly and positively.

When I am too tense, I am less aware of what is happening around me. Sometimes I lose a bit of 'the feel' in my hands, and the fine movements in my hands and fingers then suffer. Once that happens

I tend to grip the steering wheel too tightly and my driving becomes clumsy. When your grip gets too tight, your arms become very tired and you then have to fight with the car to drive it.

My concentration is intense when I am approaching and negotiating corners. I don't allow anything or any thought to distract me during those few seconds. These are critical points on the track and I give them my total and undivided attention. When I get through the corner and I am going down the straight I relax and unwind. These breaks are very important. I am convinced that you can only maintain good levels of concentration for the hard parts of the circuit and the hard duels during the race if you take these breaks or rest periods. If you don't use them you get mentally tired and concentrate poorly.

GREG NORMAN

Greg. Sometimes I have problems with my concentration when I am under great pressure or when I get mentally tired.

My mind often wanders at crucial times. For instance if I play five shots on an easy par five hole I say to myself, 'Damn it, you should have birdied that hole.' Then I worry about it for the next two or three holes and my game often gets worse. I then have to talk to myself firmly to get my concentration going again.

Rudi. Players often make that mistake when they get trapped in the past on previous mistakes or get too far ahead of themselves in the future thinking about the final score or result. You must keep your concentration in the present. During the contest, the present is the point of power.

Greg. That is so important in golf because your game starts from where your last ball finishes. You can't change what happened behind you, and the best way to influence what lies ahead is to take care of the shot at hand. You should try to play the entire course shot by shot. If you concentrate on playing each shot to position you will stay in the present and play much better.

Rudi. You say that your mind often wanders. This is not always a bad thing because you can't concentrate intensely for four hours and not get mentally tired. You must rest your brain during the game.

Greg. After I hit a shot I sometimes walk over to the crowd and have a chat with a friend. They say, 'Don't worry about us, go back and play your golf.' A lot of people criticize me for that. But those breaks take my mind away from my last shots and stop me from worrying about them or gloating about them. As soon as I am ready to play my next shot I turn on my concentration again.

Rudi. Some people lose their concentration at critical periods when they are playing their shots. That period only lasts for a split second but mistakes during that time can be devastating. How do you lock in your concentration at these vital times?

Greg. I handle this very easily. I look at the ball and just as I am about to start my swing I think, 'Rhythm, get good rhythm.' Once I put that thought in my mind, I block out everything else. It is like putting a protective shield around my head to keep out distractions.

Rudi. You are one of the longest drivers in the game and lots of the fans come to see you boom the ball down the middle. How much importance do you attach to that part of the game?

Greg. I love to hit the ball long and hear the gasps of the fans. I like to impress the fans. But recently, I found out that hitting the ball to position is more important and helps you score better and win more often. Impressing the crowd with my drives is no longer a priority. I now concentrate harder on other parts of my game, particularly the short one. That change of focus has got me better results.

IAN CHAPPELL

Ian. Pressure can improve your concentration but it can also mess it up. Concentration is a funny thing. You seem to have your good and bad days. I often made my best scores when I was having trouble with it. I played best when I had to work hard at it and had to struggle to get it right. On the days when it came easily, I would start my innings really well but would usually get out for a low score. I suppose I got a bit overconfident on these occasions. Overconfidence spells danger. As soon as I noticed it, I would say to myself, 'Be careful. Get your mind on the job. It's not as easy as you think.' This always helped me.

Having a routine is most important. Not only does it help you cope with pressure but it also helps you concentrate better. You will notice that when players break their routine, their concentration is affected. Basketball and tennis players bounce the ball a certain number of times before taking their shot or serving the ball. If they change this routine, their concentration is often upset and they make mistakes. Every player should work out a routine. It is very important.

The biggest problems with concentration don't usually come from the events in the game because distractions on the field are not as devastating as the negative thoughts that originate in your mind. Your biggest enemy as far as concentration is concerned is the one within. Negative thoughts can be very difficult to handle. I used to have problems with them and I tried desperately hard to eliminate them. They mess up your concentration and your performance. I would often say, 'Get rid of them, make them go away,' and they wouldn't. Later I adopted another tactic and I would say to myself, 'Don't fight them,' and I would fight them harder. After a while I worked out a fairly effective method of coping. My attitude was to let them come, go through my mind, and then pass out. I thought, 'It's normal to get negative thoughts. No matter what happens I am always going to get them. Other people have the same problem, so I am not alone.' This approach often eliminated them because other thoughts invariably entered my mind and took their place. I always followed a negative thought with a positive one.

I learned a more important lesson about concentration during the early part of my career. You can't concentrate deeply for long periods. If you try to do so, you will mess up your concentration. You must take breaks and allow your mind to have rest periods.

GREG CHAPPELL

Greg. Concentration is the key to good performance. Players fold under pressure because they lose their concentration and self-confidence. Anytime I play poorly it is nearly always due to poor concentration. There are three conditions under which my concentration suffers:

1. *Mental fatigue.* That is when I make the most mistakes and play poorly.
2. *Anxiety.* Fortunately, I don't get this very often when I am on the field.
3. *Lack of challenge.* Lack of interest in the game.

I can only concentrate deeply for about half an hour at a time. If I try to go beyond the half-hour period, I get tired. During the game I concentrate for a while, have a break and then concentrate again. When I am in the slips, I start to concentrate the moment the bowler starts his run-up. In between balls, I try to relax by talking to the other fielders, listening to the crowd, or thinking about things other than cricket.

Rudi. I refer to this as 'turning on' and 'turning off' your concentration. You have to learn when to concentrate and when to have a break. How do you concentrate when you are batting?

Greg. I talk to myself. I remind myself to concentrate when I am preparing to face the bowler. I concentrate on watching the ball out of the bowler's hand and when I am concentrating well I see the ball very clearly and very early in its flight.

At the start of my innings I concentrate on playing the ball in the 'V' sector of the field between mid-on and mid-off. This makes me play straight. This is the routine I have followed for many years and it has worked quite well.

Rudi. What happens when you are not concentrating well?

Greg. I break my routine. During that terrible slump against the West Indies in 1981-82 I became very anxious and confused and couldn't keep my mind on the job. The last thing I thought about was watching the ball out of the bowler's hand or playing in the 'V'. I worried about getting a score and avoiding another failure. I said to myself, 'I must do well today, I must get a score, and I mustn't score another duck. When am I going to get some runs?' My thinking changed and negative thoughts and instructions were always in my mind. I made many ducks in a row and couldn't work out what was happening. When you told me I wasn't watching the ball out of the bowler's hand, I knew you were correct. On my way back to the pavilion after getting out, I would say. 'Gosh. I didn't see that ball. I must have lost it in the background.'

I started to rationalize about not seeing the ball because of the dark background and the black hands of the bowlers. But you reminded me of the basics. You got me back to my routine of watching the ball out of the bowler's hand and playing in the 'V' early in my innings.

Rudi. When you are batting, are you aware of the crowd?

Greg. Yes. I am aware of the crowd but the moment I focus on the bowler and the ball, I don't hear it. I block it out. After the ball has been bowled, I hear it again. It can distract you but it can also work in a positive way to help you relax and have a mental rest.

Rudi. How did you deal with the nervous nineties?

Greg. A lot of batsmen work hard to get to sixty runs and when they realize that they have a chance of getting a century, they lose patience and try to get the next forty runs in a great hurry. They then do stupid things and get out.

I never knew what the nervous nineties were. I used to plan my runs in units of ten. When I reached ninety, I knew that I had achieved nine units and it was just a matter of getting the next one. Many batsmen become impatient and greedy when they get close to a hundred. I knew that if I looked after those units I would get my century eventually.

Greg, 2002, Facing the West Indian Attack

Greg. I have always prided myself on my ability to concentrate for long periods. I found it important to develop a mental routine – a consistent routine between balls and between overs. This helped me to mentally relax between balls to conserve my mental and emotional energy.

My routine allowed me to switch in and out of different levels of concentration (*flexibility*). I developed three levels of concentration: awareness, fine focus and fierce focus.

Awareness. This is a state of being aware of what is happening around you, but is not actually focused on any one thing. I used it while waiting to go in to bat, in between overs and in between balls.

Fine Focus. I switch from awareness to fine focus when the bowler reaches the top of his mark. I then switch my focus on the bowler's face. That gave me an insight into his emotional state as well as his body language. As the bowler reached the delivery point, I switched my focus to the point from which the ball would be delivered and I narrowed my field of fierce focus.

Fierce Focus. This was only used for a very short time (*locking in concentration*) because it required a lot of mental energy. As the ball left the bowler's hand, all I saw was the ball and the bowler's hand. This gave me all the cues I needed to gauge line, length and type of delivery. Once that play was finished, I looked to the crowd momentarily to give my mind a rest, as I switched to a state of awareness. The cue to bring my mind back to the game was to count the fielders and look at the bowler's face as he reached his mark.

I went through this process for every ball I faced. Each time I went through a lean period I was able to trace it back to the fact that I had got away from this routine. As soon as I got back to my routine my output of runs increased.

CHAPTER 5

PRESSURE

Part 1: *What Is Pressure? How Is Pressure Created?*

The mind is its own place and in it, self can make a Heav'n of Hell a Hell of Heav'n.

— John Milton, Paradise Lost

People say a lot of negative things about pressure. Pressure to me is just added responsibility. That is how I look at it. It's not pressure when God gives you an opportunity to be a hero for your team and your country.

— M.S. Dhoni

Pressure helps you to play better but it can be very dangerous. When you put too much emphasis on the word pressure you magnify it in your own mind and make the situation worse. I prefer to talk about dealing with challenging situations.

— Sir Garfield Sobers

HOW DOES PRESSURE AFFECT PERFORMANCE?

Pressure is a self-induced force that is generated in the mind in response to situations you face, remember or imagine. If that force gets out of hand it can cause problems and interfere with your performance, but in the correct proportions it will bring the best out of you. Too little pressure – boredom, lack of interest, under-arousal – can be just as harmful to performance as too much pressure – fear, anxiety, over-arousal. Some people are lifted to superior performance by pressure while others are squashed by it.

People who take pressure lightly and don't plan for it run into trouble when they encounter it because it hits them twice as hard.

You create most of your pressure by the way you evaluate the situations you face and assess your ability to handle them. In pressure situations you tend to magnify the difficulties while underestimating your ability to cope with them. It is that distortion of assessment that creates the pressure. The larger the distortion the greater is the pressure. Some pressure is caused by the actual game but most of it is created by your perception of the game and what you think might happen in it.

For example, walking a two-foot-wide plank across two adjacent rooftops would create a certain amount of fear and pressure because of the possibility of falling and injuring yourself, or worse. But if you had to walk the same plank on the ground you would do so quite easily without worrying about the result or any imaginary dangers.

You create pressure when you get caught up in the future on the result and imaginary catastrophes, or trapped in the past on previous mistakes and failures. When you keep concentration in the present on the task at hand and do the basic things well you won't feel much pressure.

In sport, pressure is also caused by the importance of the moment, the significance of the match, the stage of the match, a make-or-break point or the closeness of the contest. If the situation is not important or if you don't care about the result or what happens to you, you won't feel much pressure.

Some players might handle a pressure situation well at one stage of the match only to mess it up at another. Different challenges in the situation or a different perception of the situation usually cause this. Sinking a two-foot putt is easier on the first green than it is on the last one when the result of the game rests on that putt.

Pressure is dangerous when it produces anxiety. This happens when the brain is overloaded and cannot integrate all the messages it receives. Some of these messages come from the eyes and ears, and others arise in the brain itself in the form of negative thoughts and images.

PRESSURE CAN CAUSE ANXIETY

Anxiety spoils performance by causing:

- Tension and stiffness in the muscles, and heaviness in the limbs and body.
- The impairment of basic motor skills, particularly fine motor skills and hand–eye coordination. It messes up the sequence, tempo, rhythm and coordination of these movements.
- Impaired judgement and poor selection and execution of the basic skills. Once that happens, performance falls apart because the basics form the fabric of your performance.
- Mental tension, negative thinking and self-talk, confusion, impatience, poor concentration, self-doubts, loss of confidence and memory lapses.
- Perceptual distortion, making mountains out of molehills – an inability to see things as they really are without distorting them or getting them out of proportion.
- Fear in all its forms, particularly that of failure, and occasionally that of winning. In some cases the fear is irrational and extreme, out of proportion with the challenges in the situation.
- Emotions like frustration, disappointment, anger, bitterness and despair that sabotage performance. Fear and other bad emotions are to pressure what gasoline is to fire.

Good players know how best to handle the pressures of the day and the situations about to land on them and how to gauge when pressure is being applied to them and when it must be applied to others.

Self-confidence and pressure are closely related. As Peter Thomson says, 'If you know what you are doing and are in control of what you are doing, the pressure, or the sense of crisis – that is what pressure is – will lift you to superior performance. That is the measure of a good player. He is often lifted by pressure. Players with less confidence fall apart under the same conditions.'

GOOD OR BAD PRESSURE: IT DEPENDS ON HOW YOU ASSESS THE SITUATION

Many players describe pressure as a downward force that interferes with their performance. They say that it is like a silent enemy within that does its damage before you know what is happening.

The best players, however, look forward to pressure and handle it in a way that gives them an edge over their opponents. They often label that pressure as good pressure and claim that it sometimes gives them a high, a floating sensation and a feeling of being in the 'zone'. Getting in the zone, however, is elusive. It seems to be limited to those occasions when you are in top form.

Tony Rafferty, an ultra-marathon runner, once said: 'I love pressure. It often lifts me to do great things during the run. That type of pressure gives me an inner feeling that I have never been able to put into words satisfactorily. It is a fantastic feeling. I imagine it is the same sort of feeling that Beethoven and Mozart must have had at certain periods during the creation of a great piece of music.'

Peter Thomson echoed similar comments: 'I used to have a great feeling of floating at times when I was under pressure and was in form and playing well. It didn't happen all the time but I used to look forward to this encounter and eagerly waited for the pressure to come. When it came I used to get a tremendous feeling. It was a great lift or high. Under these conditions, I would almost rise above myself. I have also observed it in other athletes. In the end, there is no pressure to the superior athlete who is in good form. There is no pressure – it is exhilaration. I think pressure is predominantly a downward force and exhilaration is a great lifter or upward force.'

Still, the best players can be messed up by pressure. In an interview with Tony Greig, this is what the 6'7" former England cricket captain, had to say about pressure:

> Pressure can be a devastating or an uplifting force. Can you imagine walking out to bat in a Test match at the Melbourne Cricket Ground with 80,000 hostile Australian spectators screaming for your blood? On the way out your body feels heavy, rigid and tired and you have difficulty walking and breathing. You feel tiny and insignificant. And when you look at the fielders you feel even smaller, because they all look like seven-footers capable of stopping anything. How could you get the ball past these giants?
>
> When you reach the wicket the stumps seem to be twice as big as they really are and the pitch appears to be half its normal length. The ball looks like a tiny red cherry and you wonder how you are possibly going to see it when it is travelling at 150 kilometres per hour. The bowler looks like a supergiant who is capable of crushing you anytime he wants. You become very confused and feel totally inadequate.
>
> However, when a good player faces the moment of truth, he quickly assesses the situation and does something about it. I say to myself, 'Nobody has ever bowled me a ball that I haven't seen. I've made some good scores against these people before and I can do it again. Concentrate on watching the ball and getting into position to play your shot. For all I know, he might be seeing me as a giant and he might be feeling like a dwarf. Get into him and give him hell. Just focus on what you need to do.' This always seems to reduce the pressure and improve my concentration. Suddenly things look very different and you think you can cope. The tension leaves your mind and body and you see things clearly and move freely.
>
> If you start to play well, the pressure that was crushing you earlier now lifts you to superior performance and gives you a wonderful high and an uplifting feeling of pride and achievement.

Tony well describes some of the debilitating signs and symptoms of pressure and the distortion of perception that creates and accompanies it. As soon as he corrects that perceptual distortion, changes the way he talks to himself and focuses on the process he reduces the pressure and eliminates its negative signs and symptoms.

STRESS REACTION

Everyone experiences pressure. The mere act of staying alive is stressful. The stress reaction is a powerful survival programme in the brain that helps you to cope with threatening and dangerous situations in one of three ways: fighting, fleeing, or freezing.

Some people feel that it is an outmoded programme because the threats that kick it off today are very different from those of the distant past. Then, the dangers were mainly physical – attacks by wild animals and other humans or perils from a very harsh and rapidly changing environment. Today's threats are often caused by things like a shortage of money, meeting deadlines, making a living, living up to expectations, peak-hour traffic, interpersonal conflict and a host of fears like fear of failure, winning, rejection, criticism and making a fool of the self.

Excessive stress produces harmful effects in the mind and body. In fact, many of today's illnesses and unusual behaviours are stress-related.

Sportsmen often leave their brains in the dressing room when they go onto the sports field to play the game. Likewise, patients leave their common sense on the doorsteps when they go into hospital for simple tests. These patients put themselves under enormous pressure, not because they are in an unfamiliar environment, but because they worry about what might be wrong with them – cancer or other serious illnesses – or what might happen to them – having an operation.

Under pressure many of these patients do not understand or carry out simple instructions. For example, during an X-ray examination if the patient is lying on his back and you ask him to turn to his left, he might stiffen up and not move, so you repeat the instruction a bit louder and he might apologize and say that he didn't hear your instruction. Then, instead of turning to the left, he might turn to the right, and you tell him that you want him to go to the left and not the right. Again, he might apologize and say that he didn't understand the instruction. But even if he understands and turns correctly he might do so very quickly or very slowly.

Players who are under great pressure before and during the game often experience similar problems. Incoming information usually overloads the athlete's brain and he may not see, hear, or feel things that he should. Even if he is aware of what is happening, he might not understand it. Moreover, if he understands, he might react in the wrong way. And if he behaves correctly, he might speed up or slow down his movements and mess up rhythm and coordination.

Intense pain is a source of enormous pressure that at times can be very difficult to handle.

A young man once came into hospital with excruciating pain in his back and lower abdomen because of a stone in his ureter. He was in great distress and was panicking. 'What's wrong with me doc? I can't stand this pain. It is killing me. Am I going to die?' I informed him that I knew the cause of his pain and would soon rectify the problem.

I told him that I would teach him how to cope with his pain and I explained that his fear and negative thoughts were making his pain worse. Strong emotions such as fear and negative thinking are to pain what gasoline is to fire. I told him that if he could change his thinking and relax his body his pain would diminish and would be manageable. I asked him if he believed me. He gave me a definite yes.

I put him through a simple relaxation procedure to lower his anxiety and get rid of some of his tension, and I coupled it with deep breathing. I then gave him some powerful suggestions that I knew he would be receptive to. I said, 'Pain is often caused by and is always aggravated by tension. The greater your tension the worse your pain will be. This relaxation will get rid of most of your tension, and the less tension you have the less pain you will feel. It won't go away completely but you will be able to tolerate it better.' Those suggestions were repeated a few times.

The relaxation session ended a few minutes later and he picked up a magazine and started to read it. I left the room at that stage but returned five minutes later to check on him. He was still reading the magazine. 'How are you doing?' He turned to me and said, 'I'm fine. The pain is still there but it is not too bad. I'm on top of it, so that is not a problem. I have another problem though. I don't know if I should go to the bathroom to empty my bladder or stay here and continue reading my magazine.' 'That is some problem,' I replied.

Soon afterwards a surprised mother asked me what I had given her son for his pain. I told her that I had helped him to use his mind and inner resources to overcome his pain and distress. She looked puzzled. I don't think she believed me.

This example demonstrates how fear and perceptual distortion of the situation create and intensify pressure and how relaxation, breathing, positive suggestions and positive self-talk reduce it.

REMEMBER

1. You create your own pressure by the way you think and talk to yourself about the situations you face and your ability to cope with them.

2. Just as you create pressure by talking to yourself in a particular way you can turn it off by talking to yourself in a different way.

3. Everyone experiences pressure. The mere act of staying alive is stressful, so you must learn to cope with it.

4. People who take pressure lightly and don't plan for it run into trouble when they encounter it because it hits them twice as hard.

5. Good players are often lifted by pressure and lesser players are frequently squashed by it.

6. A certain amount of pressure helps you to play better but in the wrong proportions it can be very dangerous.

7. Pressure is dangerous when it produces performance anxiety.

8. Anxiety causes the body to become tense and ruins the execution of basic motor as well as mental skills like concentration, thinking, confidence and judgement.

9. Under pressure your concentration is usually focused in the future or the past.

10. If you keep your concentration in the present on the task at hand and do the basic things well you won't feel much pressure.

11. Successful athletes are often lifted by pressure while the lesser athletes are usually squashed by it.

12. Good players know how best to handle the pressures of the day and the situations about to land on them and how to gauge when pressure is being applied to them and when it must be applied to others.

13. Excessive pressure produces harmful effects in the mind and body. In fact, many of today's illnesses and unusual behaviours are stress-related.

14. Under pressure many people have difficulty understanding and carrying out simple instructions and tasks.

15. Fear and other strong negative emotions are to pressure what gasoline is to fire.

Part 2: The Manifestations of Pressure

When the pressure becomes too great, your brain starts to race and everything seems to speed up. If you don't do something about it, it will race around in circles and your body will follow.

— Ian Chappell

THE AUTONOMIC NERVOUS SYSTEM

Most of the signs and symptoms of pressure are mediated through the autonomic nervous system that is made up of two components – the sympathetic and the parasympathetic nervous systems. The sympathetic system produces energy for fight or flight and is like the accelerator in a car. The parasympathetic system helps to conserve and store energy and is like the brakes in a car. If one system becomes too active, the other tries to balance its effects.

The sympathetic system speeds you up, increases your energy and alertness, and makes you impatient and aggressive. You breathe rapidly, your heart beats faster, and your blood pressure rises. Your muscles get primed for action and might become tight and tense and you might sweat, shiver and tremble. Your mouth and throat often become dry.

The parasympathetic system slows you down and helps you to relax. Sometimes it makes you feel drowsy and you might even fall asleep in the dressing room before the game. Before you play you might feel tired and sluggish. You breathe slower and deeper and at times might find it difficult to breathe. You might get 'butterflies' in your stomach and might vomit, get diarrhoea or have stomach pains. Spitting is common.

EFFECTS OF PRESSURE ON THE BODY

Here are a few common signs and symptoms of pressure.

A Racing Heart, Fast Shallow Breathing

These early signs of pressure are usually accompanied by a disruption of the fine motor skills and loss of hand–eye coordination.

Muscle Tension, Tightness and Heaviness

These signs of pressure often mess up performance because they disrupt the tempo, rhythm, and coordination of basic motor skills. These signs are regularly found in the hands, arms, shoulders and neck, and in the face, chest, back and lower limbs.

Under pressure your hands and fingers get tight and you often lose some sensation in them. Most of the time you are not aware of that tension until it is too late. People often twiddle their fingers and do all sorts of things with their hands to relieve that tightness. If you are playing a game in which you have to hold on to a bat, club, racquet or

steering wheel your grip will tighten the moment the pressure starts
to get to you, particularly in the dominant hand. The fine movements
and hand–eye coordination will then suffer as the dominant hand
takes over and the impulse to hit rather than stroke the ball ruins basic
technique. When this happens in golf the swing is often messed up.
The same thing happens in cricket. A golfer once told me, 'When
you are under pressure, relax your thumbs and make love to your
hands. Make gentle love to them.' Functionally, the thumb is half of
the hand and when you relax it, the other fingers seem to follow, and
grip pressure decreases.

Greg Chappell once said that in his younger days he used to get
'cramps' in his forearm muscles when he was batting under pressure.
He didn't realize then that the 'cramps' were the result of his tight
grip of the bat.

Peter Brock the racing car driver once said, 'When I am tense, I
lose a bit of "feel" in my hands and grip the steering wheel too tightly.
Most of the time I am not aware that I am doing so, but when I notice
it I relax my hands, fingers, shoulders and neck to ease the tension
and tightness. At the end of a pressure-packed race I often see little
depressions in the leather of the steering wheel from the pressure of
my thumbs and fingers. Some drivers grip the wheel so tightly that
their arms ache and become tired, and they have to fight the car to
drive it. I have noticed that when I grip the wheel too tightly my
concentration suffers, so there seems to be a connection between grip
pressure and concentration.'

Greg Norman feels the pressure in his shoulders and neck, and in
his legs. He told me, 'I deliberately try to loosen my neck and shoulders
by gently turning my head from side to side and allowing my arms
to fall loosely to my side. When my legs get heavy and tight, I relax
them by walking slowly and taking longer strides. I am not usually
aware of tension in my hands but I try to keep them loose by moving
my fingers and by opening and closing the hands. That tip you gave
me about reducing the tension in my right thumb has helped me a lot,
particularly my putting. It has made a big difference.'

Not all of the players experience those physical signs and symptoms. Sir Garfield Sobers is one of these players. He said, 'I didn't feel any pressure in my body. I felt it in my mind. It was my thinking and concentration that were affected.'

Some people get rid of tension by relaxing the muscles of the face, particularly those of the jaw. Some chew gum while others open their mouths, stick out the tongue, hum, whistle or sing a tune. These simple actions not only reduce pressure but they improve concentration.

Impatience, Over-alertness, Irritability, Restlessness

These are also manifestations of sympathetic nervous system activity. The mind and body are on red alert and players become sensitive to the most trivial stimuli. The slightest noise, the mildest criticism, or the least inconvenience can precipitate an aggressive response. These are often seen in the pre-match period when players are nervous and fidgety.

The period of waiting before the start of a game can be most uncomfortable. Peter Brock thinks that the pressure that is created at the starting line while waiting for the race to begin messes up a lot of the drivers' minds and causes them to become impatient and botch up the start.

In the early part of his career, Viv Richards used to get very nervous in the dressing room while he was awaiting his turn to bat and often took that anxiety with him on to the field and batted poorly. At one stage, Clive Lloyd solved the problem by asking him to open the batting.

Most batsmen are nervous at the start of their innings and make a lot of mistakes early on because of impatience, poor concentration and tension in their bodies. They get heavy legs and have difficulty moving their feet to get into position to play their shots. M.S. Dhoni is very conscious of this problem and says, 'When you go into the nets to practise you should focus on the first twenty deliveries. Once you get over them your heart rate goes back to normal and you become less tense and more relaxed. This net practice will help you to deal with the first twenty deliveries in the match and will enable you to settle down more quickly.'

Drowsiness, Yawning, Difficulty in Breathing and Crying

When the parasympathetic system is active players become calm, quiet and relaxed. Some players become drowsy, yawn incessantly, complain of tiredness in the pre-match period and may even fall asleep in the dressing room before the start of the game. In some people crying is a normal manifestation of pressure but is often regarded as a sign of weakness.

Coaches who are unaware of these signs of pressure get very angry when they see them in their players.

Raelene Boyle, who was one of Austalia's best woman athletes, claimed that under pressure she occasionally had difficulty in breathing. She said, 'During training I used to get what I called mentally induced asthmatic attacks. I used to put a lot of pressure on myself at training and was very emotional about what I was trying to do. When these attacks came I would stop running and hold on to something to relax and get my breath. The wheezing was usually quite bad as my whole body screamed for more oxygen. It was very frightening and occasionally I panicked. But, after a while I learned to cope with it.'

Raelene admitted that under pressure she was also emotionally vulnerable and would cry easily. The slightest things used to upset her, for example, the wrong word, a simple remark or an interruption of her routine. People often see crying as a sign of weakness and instability but she regards it as a normal way to relieve pressure.

Nervousness and Fear

These are regular symptoms of pressure. Common fears are fear of failure, fear of winning, fear of being dropped, fear of embarrassment and humiliation, fear of not being good enough, fear of letting down the coach, teammates or the fans, fear of being hurt, fear of your opponent, fear of disapproval, criticism or punishment and fear of not living up to expectations.

Fear is the enemy of good performance. It usually prevents you from thinking positively, observing properly, making the correct decisions and taking the right action.

Good players see nervousness as a sign of being ready.

Pain

Pain can be a sign of pressure. Headaches, neck ache, back, chest and abdominal pain are often present. On examination, a physical cause for the player's pain is not usually found.

Good practitioners listen carefully to the players' complaints and do an examination knowing that they won't find a physical cause for the pain. The pain often disappears when the players are given reassurance, a massage or a strapping to the affected area. Sometimes a harmless pill does the trick.

A Smile

This is one of the most unfamiliar signs of pressure. Some players smile automatically after making a mistake, when they are in a pressure situation, or during an onslaught from the coach. A few of them unconsciously stick out their tongue as part of this reaction. Coaches get irritated when players exhibit these signs. They think it shows a lack of interest. They believe that under pressure the player should be serious, enthusiastic and focused. A judge once told me that when he sentences guilty people to go to jail they often look at him and smile. He said that used to irritate him until he found out that smiling was a normal coping mechanism for stress.

Andy Roberts, the great West Indies fast bowler, was noted for his poker face and coolness under pressure. He hardly ever smiled on the field and when he did, it was a subject of great discussion among the television commentators. One day Dennis Lillee bowled him a nasty bouncer that almost took off his head. He looked at Dennis and gave him a broad smile and said, 'I have a good memory. I remember everything.' Dennis got the message because Andy was the best exponent of that type of delivery – he had left a trail of broken jaws behind him during his career.

A few days later, some of the players flew to Sydney on an eight-seater aircraft. During the entire trip Andy had a huge smile on his face. At first I thought he was happy about making the trip until I noticed that he was holding on to the arms of his seat with a vice-like grip. I then realized that he was afraid of flying in small planes and that smiling was one of the ways he dealt with his pressure.

REMEMBER

1. Well-known signs and symptoms of pressure are muscle tension, tightness and heaviness; pain – headaches, neck aches and back pain; nervousness and fear; dry mouth; aggression; impatience, irritability and restlessness; 'butterflies' in the stomach, vomiting, diarrhoea and frequent urination. The impulse to hit the ball often overwhelms the desire to stroke it.

2. Less well-known but equally important signs of pressure are smiling, crying, sluggishness, drowsiness, yawning, spitting and difficulty breathing.

3. Fine motor skills, hand–eye coordination, clear positive thinking, and good decision making are some of the first casualties of pressure.

EFFECTS OF PRESSURE ON THE MIND

Too much pressure ruins thinking and motivation and messes up concentration and self-confidence. Your thought patterns change when you are under pressure and clear positive thinking is replaced by muddled and negative thinking. The thoughts in your mind control your attitude, movements, body language and ultimately your performance.

Inability to Observe Objectively

The ability to observe objectively is one of the first casualties of pressure. When this happens you may not be fully aware of the things that are going on around you. But even if you are, you may not understand them or react to them in a sensible way. Your judgement and ability to analyse situations and make sound decisions are often impaired. Under pressure common sense is often a forgotten factor in performance.

Negative Thinking and Self-talk

Thinking is another early casualty of pressure. Negative thinking creates and intensifies pressure. Under pressure your thinking or self-talk can fall into several negative patterns.

- You commonly put yourself down and think about all of your faults and weaknesses at the same time that you magnify the difficulties in the situations you face. 'Poor me, I'm no good, I've never been any good, I can't do it, I'll mess up, he is too good for me, it's too difficult.'

- You put pressure on yourself when you insist that things should happen in a particular way. 'You must… you have got to… this should or ought to…' When things don't happen the way you demand them you get angry and frustrated and place pressure on yourself. It would be nice if things turn out the way you demand them but they don't have to.

- Negative instructions can also produce pressure. 'Don't do this, don't mess up, don't make any mistakes, you mustn't do this, you mustn't fail, you mustn't let down your team….' When you give yourself those negative instructions not only do you put pressure on yourself you often end up doing the very things you tell yourself not to do.

- Players create a lot of pressure by thinking about the result. They think about the things that could possibly go wrong and worry about the things that they don't want to happen. They say things like, 'Wouldn't it be terrible if…? What if…? I wouldn't be able to stand this if…. I hope I don't mess it up like I did last time.'

- The fear of criticism and rejection can create enormous pressure for players who are low in confidence or who like to impress and please other people. Worrying about what other people might think or say about them can place them under great pressure. Common thoughts are: 'What will they think of me if I let them down? I must do well otherwise they might dislike and criticize me. I must impress them.'

Pressure Can Break Concentration

The effects of excessive pressure on concentration have been described in a previous chapter but here is a recap.

Under great pressure concentration suffers when:

- It is incorrectly directed to self and weaknesses instead of the task at hand;
- It is correctly directed to the task but is focused on the wrong aspects of the task;
- It is focused in the wrong time – trapped in the past on previous mistakes and failures or is in the future on the result or the bad things that might happen;
- It loses its flexibility;
- Information and task overload are present; and
- The ability to lock in concentration is impaired.

These concentration errors often cause self-doubts, confusion, indecision and sub-standard execution. You often lose your sense of priorities and give the same significance to trivia as you do to the really important things.

Bill Russell, the basketball player, emphasized the importance of thinking and concentration in dealing with pressure when he said, 'Teams that can keep their collective wits under the greatest pressure will win most of the time. Heart in champions has to do with the depth of motivation and persistence, how well their minds and bodies react to pressure. It is concentration – that is being able to do the best under maximum stress, fatigue and pain.'

EFFECTS OF PRESSURE ON BEHAVIOUR

Pressure affects behaviour in many different ways. Some of these have already been mentioned.

Loss of Patience is a Killer

Impatience is almost instinctive under pressure. Good players value patience very highly because they know that it will help them to stay in the game, handle the pressure and win the contest.

Greg Norman described the terrible price he paid for being impatient at a US Masters Golf Championship at Augusta, Georgia. He said: 'When I am under pressure I sometimes get impatient. I often say to myself, 'Slow down, take a few deep breaths and relax. Walk slowly to the ball.'This stops my mind and body from speeding up too much. It usually works well, but sometimes I fail to recognize the signs of impatience early enough and make mistakes.

'This happened to me in the US Masters in 1981. I was playing with Tom Watson in the final round and I birdied the nineth hole and moved within one shot of the leader, Watson. The tenth tee was about eighty yards away and I had to walk through a very large gallery to reach it. After thirty yards my thighs and legs became very heavy. I was less experienced in those days, so I kept going and walked very quickly to the tee. I hurriedly teed up the ball, played my shot and hooked the ball into the trees. I neglected the warning signs, rushed, broke my routine and paid the price. If I had been thinking at that stage, I would have slowed myself down and who knows what would have happened by the time we got to the final hole.'

Different Types of Behaviour

Under pressure some people become aggressive and confrontational, others placid and supportive. Some take control and lead, others become submissive and follow. Behaviour may be rational or irrational. It may even be paradoxical where the most placid person under normal circumstances becomes very aggressive, or vice versa, under pressure. A very successful racing car driver once said to me, 'When the pressure gets to me before the start of a race, my personality changes from that of a quiet and kind gentleman to a very angry and competitive animal. I hate the opponents and I am very aggressive towards them and I go out there to beat the hell out of them. After the race I become a quiet and kind gentleman again.'

Chronic Pressure and 'Combat Fatigue'

Many people believe that major dramatic changes in life (death, divorce, loss of job) are the most potent producers of stress. But we know this is not so. Most of our pressure is caused by minor setbacks, failures and frustrations and by petty and trivial everyday annoyances and hassles.

Chronic pressure can be a powerful enemy. During World War II, a great deal of research was done on the effects of chronic stress on the performance and health of soldiers exposed to continuous combat. Sir Charles Symonds found that the constant and prolonged tension of battle resulted in a breakdown of performance. It is worth repeating the research findings of Sir Charles. He discovered that every soldier had a breaking point.

In the early part of a campaign most soldiers faced up to their fears and learned to control them. They became competent in battle and developed self-confidence. But, after three or four weeks of constant battle, the signs of combat fatigue occurred. They complained of continuous tiredness that was not relieved by sleep or rest. They could not tell the difference between their own guns and the enemy's. They were easily startled and became tense and confused. They were moody and irritable, and overreacted to trivial stimuli. They concentrated poorly and performed badly. Later on, those symptoms were replaced by dullness, apathy, mental and physical slowness and eventually depression.

Many sportsmen suffer from a form of 'combat fatigue' or mental fragility at some stage of their career.

From the start of his first-class cricket career, Brian Lara was under enormous and unrelenting pressure, not just from his opponents, but also from the cricketing public, team members, administrators, and particularly the press. Breaking the world records for the highest scores in Test cricket and first-class cricket catapulted him to superstardom at a very young and tender age.

Unlike Tiger Woods the golfer, Lara was not prepared or trained to deal with the trappings and the intense and chronic pressures of superstardom, nor did he have the support network around him to protect him from the constant pressures that he faced. Taking on the burden of captaincy did not help. It intensified the pressure.

The continuous battles and chronic stresses that he encountered eventually took their toll and at one stage he showed signs and symptoms of 'combat fatigue'.

He then gave up the captaincy and withdrew from the team for a while to get some rest and recreation and to recharge his physical and psychological batteries.

When he returned to the game later, his mind was rested, fresh and alert, and he played some of the most magnificent innings imaginable.

Although Tiger Woods had extensive training and preparation for his role as a superstar and is the best golfer in the world – a role that he handled competently and admirably – his personal and professional lives collapsed after some off-field indiscretions. The resulting and continuous pressures messed up his mind and his golf game, and at present he is only a shadow of the player he once was. During his development programme, I am sure that he was not trained to deal with those off-field pressures that found his Achilles heel. His golf game will eventually return and he will again become a champion but he will need to do some mental adjusting to get there.

With the heavy workload on today's sportsmen and sportswomen, sports administrators might well have to look closely at the problem of 'combat fatigue' and ensure that the players get quality rest and recreation in order to stay fresh and alert throughout the season. Today's military protect soldiers from the pressures of continuous combat by doing just that.

REMEMBER

1. Impatience can be a killer in sport.
2. When the pressure becomes too great, your brain starts to race and everything speeds up. If you don't do something about it, it will race around in circles and your body will follow.
3. Patience is the strength of every great player.
4. Continuous and unrelenting pressure can cause combat fatigue.
5. Chronic stress and combat fatigue create several mental, behavioural and performance problems.
6. One of the things you lose when you become mentally fatigued is your motivation. You are still aware of your goals and you usually know what you need to do to achieve them, but you just can't be bothered. You lose your drive.
7. Like soldiers who are in continuous combat, sportsmen need quality rest and recreation to recharge their batteries and to stay fresh and alert during their busy and pressure-packed sports schedules.

Part 3: The Management of Pressure

When you understand that pressure is part and parcel of your life and that there are things you can do to control it, you will face up to it in a positive way and use it to your advantage.

— *Rahul Dravid*

> When I am batting and I am under pressure, the moment I
> detect the signs of pressure either in the form of tightness in
> my right hand, negative thinking or impatience, I do something
> about it. I take a few deep breaths, slow down my tempo,
> relax my body and talk to myself sensibly.
>
> — *Ian Chappell*

Coping with pressure is a skill that can be learned and improved
with the right exposure. It requires a lot of practice and training
in conditions that produce pressure. Some of the techniques for
managing pressure have already been discussed in the chapters on
self-confidence and concentration.

FLIGHT OR FIGHT RESPONSE

There are three basic ways to deal with pressure:

1. You can run away from it, mentally and physically, or ignore it
   and hope that it will go away – the flight response.
2. You can face up to it by devising and implementing a plan to
   cope with it – the fight response.
3. You can do something to actively change the situation.

Pressure often causes pain and distress and it is instinctive to run
away from it. In sport, running away is not often a good option, but
on odd occasions it can be. For example in cricket, if a batsman is
having trouble with a particular bowler, he could avoid the situation
by asking his batting partner to take most of the strike against that
bowler. Under pressure it is usually better to resist the flight impulse
and face up to the pressure.

The second option is the fight response – facing up to the pressure.
This can be improved by getting frequent and repeated exposure to
pressure situations, learning the right mental and physical coping skills
and practising them until you can execute them quickly and effectively
in every pressure situation. Depending on the situation, you might have
to be aggressive and attacking or defensive and watchful.

Sir Garfield Sobers says that teaching players how to approach and handle different game and pressure situations is one of the most important lessons you can give them. They will then know what to do when they encounter them.

He adds, 'In cricket you may think that the situation is too desperate to play defensively, so you choose the aggressive approach and attack the bowling. But you have to know how, when and where to attack. You just don't throw the bat indiscriminately at everything. You play the percentages. A lot of people don't understand this.

'At another time a similar situation may require a defensive approach. In some cases, your main concern is just to survive and if you get over the first hurdle, you can then go on to build your innings and take control of the situation.'

Knowing how to deal with the pressure that is being placed on you is important but knowing how and when to put it on others is equally important.

Sir Garfield explains: 'During a Test match at Lord's, the West Indies team was under enormous pressure and we were only about twenty runs ahead of England in the second innings with five wickets down and two days to go. When Holford, our leg-break bowler joined me, I told him that if he stayed with me we would turn around the game. I pointed out that Cowdrey, the England captain would try to put as much pressure as he could on us by crowding us with fielders all around the bat but that would make it easier for me to play a few shots. As soon as I started to attack, Cowdrey went on the defensive. The pressure was then reversed and was placed on him. He never got rid of it. I declared the innings closed at 369 for five. We were both not out. I was 163 and Holford was 105. England almost lost the match. In the last overs of the game they held on by the skin of their teeth.'

Make a Plan and Prepare for the Unexpected

Tony Rafferty highlighted the importance of having a plan and following a routine for dealing with pressure. He said: 'In sport, you can't escape pressure so you must learn to deal with it. As long as I have made a plan I find it relatively easy to cope. The plan allows me to think clearly and sensibly, recognize the signs of pressure early and deal with them before they get out of hand. When you have a plan, you know exactly what you have to do. No matter how tough the situation, your plan will help you to cope with it. As game situations change you might have to modify your plan.'

People who don't plan for the unexpected run into problems when the unexpected arrives. The pressure then overwhelms them. You must always expect the unexpected and be ready for it.

Years ago I was invited to a dinner of the Royal Australasian College of Surgeons at the Melbourne Cricket Ground. At the time the college was conducting its fellowship examinations. In the middle of the second course my host, Professor John Heslop, who was one of my teachers in New Zealand, said to me, 'Incidentally Rudi, you are the guest speaker tonight. I forgot to tell you earlier.' 'What!' I exclaimed, 'You must be joking.' 'I am not,' he replied. 'You're on in about twenty minutes. We want you to talk about performance in sport and about some of the things you do to enhance the performance of your athletes.'

I immediately hit the panic button and said to myself, 'How could he do this to me? I'm going to make a fool of myself in front of all of these exceptionally bright people. What can I say to these surgeons that they don't already know? They are some of the best brains in Australasia. They will laugh at me.' My first impulse was to run out of the room but there was no way out. I had to face the music. I took a few deep breaths to calm myself down and then I remembered something that I used to tell my players about dealing with unexpected pressure, 'Change your perspective and you will change the meaning of the situation; change the meaning of the situation and you will change the way you think, feel and perform.'

The 'little man' inside my head then started to talk to me. As I looked around the room, he said to me, 'They are great professors but they don't know anything about performance in sport. They are novices in this area. You are the only expert in the room. Speak to them the way you would speak to your players. Break down your talk into small segments and make it as clear and as simple as you can.' I kept repeating those thoughts. Soon my mind and body became calm and relaxed and my confidence began to grow. I then started to look forward to the challenge. I was supposed to speak for about twenty minutes but the surgeons asked me to continue for another twenty-five minutes – forty-five minutes in all. They later told me that they were looking for ways to improve their own performance and that of the students.

THE THREE-PHASE METHOD OF COPING WITH PRESSURE

Over the years I have used a three-phase method to teach players how to cope with pressure situations. The phases are:

1. *The phase of education:* I explain how pressure is created and go through its signs and symptoms to help the player recognize them as early as possible. The earlier he can recognize the signs of pressure, the better he will deal with them. I then get him to identify all the situations that put him under pressure. Finally, I show him how simple techniques can regulate pressure.

2. *The skill acquisition and activation phase:* I introduce the player to a range of practical coping skills and I make sure that he practises and rehearses them repeatedly until he can master them and execute them at a moment's notice.

3. *The rehearsal and application phase:* I do simulation training and get the player to practise his coping skills in all the situations that cause him pressure. Exposure to those situations can be real and/or imaginary. In the latter case, he uses visualization and mental rehearsal techniques to create and regulate pressure. Exposure can be gradual or sudden.

As mentioned earlier, there are two models of change that are a cause for concern. The first is the all-at-once model where change is expected to happen right away. The second is the straight-line model where change is expected to be steady and progressive without any deviations. Progress hardly ever follows those two paths.

When coaches and sports specialists teach players how to cope with pressure they should tell the players not to expect sudden all-at-once change or improvement. That is the exception rather than the rule. They should also tell them that improvement will not follow a steady or progressive course – it will always have its ups and downs, and setbacks and failures – so they must be patient and persistent.

REMEMBER

1. To handle pressure you must see pressure situations as they really are without magnifying them in your mind, getting them out of proportion or underestimating your ability to cope with them.

2. To decrease the discrepancy between the perceived difficulty of the situation and your ability to cope, break down the challenges in the situation into small manageable parts and talk to yourself positively to boost your self-image and ability.

3. To familiarize yourself with pressure situations and learn how to handle them you should identify the ones that put you under pressure, get constant exposure to them, and continually practise how to approach and handle them.

4. The three-phase model helps in that respect.

5. There are at least three ways to deal with a pressure situation: You can run away from it – the flight response; you can face up to it and devise a plan to cope with it – the fight response; or you can do something to actively change the situation.

6. You must create a plan to cope with pressure. Having a plan counteracts pressure.

7. Good athletes detect the signs of pressure early and deal with them by (1) Relaxing their mind and body; (2)

Taking slow deep breaths; (3) Clearing up their minds and changing the way they look at the situation; (4) Talking to themselves positively and encouragingly; (5) Slowing down their tempo and rhythm and being patient; (6) Focusing concentration in the present, on the basic tasks; and (7) Breaking down their challenges into small manageable segments.

8.   Stick to your plan, normal routines and style of play.

9.   Like any other skill, learning to cope with pressure takes time, patience and hard work. Progress does not occur all at once or in a straight line; there are always failures and ups and downs along the way.

10. You must learn how and when to put pressure on your opponents.

MANAGING PRE-GAME PRESSURE

Before the game, players and coaches have ample time to prepare for the different situations they are likely to face during the game and to devise plans to deal with them.

But the period of waiting, at home and in the dressing room, can be difficult to handle. During that time the player often worries about his performance and creates unnecessary pressure and anticipatory anxiety. He might then think about all the things that could go wrong or about the things he fears or doesn't want to happen, and it is not unusual for him to start doubting his ability to play well. Instead of staying in the present and concentrating on the process that will lead to a positive result, he is drawn to the future and worries about his performance and the outcome of the game that are days or hours away.

On the field, the player's responses must be quick and effective. His preparation and game plan help in that respect. Good plans negate pressure.

How does a good coach help his players with pre-match pressure and anticipatory anxiety? In general, he focuses on five areas.

First, he gives them a realistic perspective of the game and prevents them from distorting or magnifying the difficulty of the challenge. He often does this by breaking down the challenge into small segments and/or by diminishing the reputation of the opponents. He then directs the players' attention away from the result and focuses it on the process. He might say, 'The situation is not that difficult. He is not that good. The course is treacherous but you can handle it; there's no need to fear it. I am not interested in the result at this stage. We will know the result at the end of the game. All I want you to do now is to take it step by step, focus on the process, and do your job as well as you can.'

When a player's perception of a situation is altered, his thinking and performance change. For example, when players become tired during a game, they often lose confidence and concentration, make simple mistakes and lose the motivation to carry on. This usually happens because of the way they assess their tiredness. If they feel that tiredness is an indication that the body has passed peak performance they might interpret their tiredness as a signal to slow down or stop – an amber light or red light. But if they perceive tiredness as a signal that they are just approaching peak performance, they might see it as a green light and press on to reach their peak. That change of perception acts as a positive stimulant.

Second, he boosts the confidence of the players. He might say, 'You can play well today; you will play well today because you have done so in the past against this team. I have great confidence in you. If things don't go your way in the beginning keep going because the results will come. Just do your job and execute the basics well. You have been well prepared and you have a good plan. Just stick to the process and execute the plan.'

Third, he calms down the players and gets them to relax particularly when he is discussing his game plan and giving instructions. If the players are too tense their minds might not be receptive to his instructions. If that happens, he can use more effective relaxation techniques and get the players to use positive self-statements to improve confidence and self-belief. V.V.S. Laxman says that if the atmosphere in the dressing room is too tense, the players can easily take that tension with them on to the field and into the game.

Fourth, he identifies the first-important priorities in the game, what he wants them to do, how he wants them to play and what he wants them to concentrate on. And he reminds them that mastery of the basics is the key to good performance. He does not overload them with information and instructions because information overload and task overload are killers of performance.

Finally, he gets each player to think about and mentally rehearse or visualize the important things he must do well in the game to defeat his opponents.

During the pre-game period players often cope with the pressures differently; so the coach, captain and the other players should be aware of each other's coping skills. For instance, in Clive Lloyd's team the two great opening batsmen Gordon Greenidge and Desmond Haynes prepared in a different way. Gordon was very quiet and an introvert and did not like to talk to anyone during this crucial period or have his body space invaded. Desmond on the other hand was very outgoing and would talk to everyone. If Desmond was forced to behave like Gordon and Gordon like Desmond during this time their coping skills would be compromised and the pressure would get to them.

REMEMBER

In the pre-match period good coaches prepare their players to deal with the pressures, and challenges of the upcoming game by:

1. Giving them a realistic and undistorted picture of the challenges they face.
2. Boosting their self-image and confidence.
3. Getting them to relax, clear their minds and calm their nerves.

4. Identifying the most important tasks, priorities, goals and responsibilities in the game.

5. Limiting the information and instructions they give to the players to prevent information and task overload.

6. Asking each player to think about and visualize or mentally rehearse the key things he has to do during the game.

7. Programming the player's mind through visualization techniques for action and helping him to relax, building confidence, and concentrating better. There is a natural progression from thinking about it to doing it.

IMAGINATION, SELF-TALK AND PRESSURE: A FLOODING TECHNIQUE

When I tell my Australian Rules footballers that their imagination and self-talk can increase or reduce their pressure, they don't believe me. 'That's impossible,' they would say. 'How can the imagination and self-talk create something that is so real?'

I then inform them that the mind often cannot tell the difference between a real event and one that it vividly imagines. The body will try to operate what you imagine or talk to yourself about. If you imagine negative or disastrous events, or positive or beneficial events, your body will behave as if it is actually experiencing them.

'Don't be ridiculous,' they would utter. 'You are crazy. You mean to tell us that we can trick our mind into believing our body is kicking a football just by imagining it?'

'Yes. Can you remember lying in bed thinking about the girl of your dreams? Your imagination can be very active and creative in those circumstances. All sorts of things happen to your body and sometimes you feel as though you are actually experiencing the relationship.' That example usually rings a bell.

The best way to change those players' belief is to give them a practical demonstration. I ask each footballer to take part in a relaxation session in which he uses his imagination and self-talk to regulate his pressure.

This technique is complex and should only be used by people who have expertise in medicine or psychology.

After the player is comfortably seated I say, 'I want you to relax and allow your imagination to work freely. Please treat this session as a learning exercise and try to enjoy it. Close your eyes now, let your body sink down into the chair and imagine that you are somewhere nice and peaceful.'

When the player is comfortable, a simple relaxation technique coupled with deep breathing is used, and as soon as adequate relaxation is achieved, the next phase begins.

'Relaxation is normal and is quite pleasant. It opens the doors to many parts of your brain, particularly your imagination. You will find that in this relaxed state, your imagination will become very clear and creative. You will be able to create your own images and direct your own movies.

'Now imagine yourself in a pressure-packed situation in the game. Take your time. There is no hurry.'

After a while he describes the situation. You then ask him to imagine that it is becoming worse. While this is happening you ask him to tune into his mind and body to see what is taking place there.

'Whatever you are experiencing let them get stronger. Feel the effects of the pressure and let them grow.'

After a few minutes he is asked to describe what is taking place.

'My heart is racing. I am breathing quickly. My throat is dry and I feel as if there is a lump in it. My muscles are tense and my body is heavy and rigid.'

'Where do you feel the tension?'

'In my hands, arms, shoulders, neck, head and legs. I have a bad headache and I feel as if I have a great load on my shoulders. I don't like this. It is a very unpleasant feeling.'

'What is going on in your mind?'

'I am confused. Everything is blurred. I am bloody scared and I don't know why.'

What is your confidence like?

It isn't too good. I don't think I can handle what is going on. I feel trapped, like a captive who cannot escape. I feel so small and insignificant and my opponents look so large and powerful.

'Why do you say that?'

'They look like giants and they are in total control. They are looking down at me as if to say,'We can destroy you anytime we want.' I can't understand why I feel like this or why I should be in this mess.'

'Do you know how to handle this situation?'

'I would like to run away and hide but there is no place to run to. I wish the game would end right now.'

'What is your concentration like?'

'Terrible. I can't concentrate on anything for any length of time. I am confused and my mind is flitting from one thing to the other.'

'That's great. Now pay attention to the feelings deep down in your body and the thoughts in your mind, and let them get stronger. Allow the pressure to increase, let it grow. That's good. You are doing fine.'

At this stage the physical evidence of pressure is clearly visible. The fists are clenched, the jaw is tight, the body is rigid, and fear is written all over his face. He has difficulty talking and expressing himself clearly.

'How do you feel now?'

'Bloody awful. I don't know if I can bear this pressure much longer. I feel as though I might panic at any moment.'

'Have you ever felt like this before?'

'Never. I feel totally useless. My body is so heavy that I can hardly move. I don't know what the hell I am supposed to be doing.'

'Can you see your teammates? Can you hear them?'

'Everything is blurred. I can see people but I am not sure who they are. I can't hear anything. I can see myself though.'

'What do you look like?'

'Bloody awful and useless.'

'What would you like to do now?'

'I would like the ground to swallow me up. I can't run away and hide because everyone is watching me. I am not able to run anyway because I am too stiff and tired. I hope the coach takes me off the field because right now I am an embarrassment.'

'What else is going through your mind?'

'All sorts of crazy thoughts. Most of them are unrelated to the game. My mind is far away from the game.'

'What is your job on the field? What did the coach instruct you to do?'

'That is the maddening thing. I don't know what I should be doing? I don't know what the coach told me. I am all confused.'

'Did you make a plan before the game? Did you make a list of the important things you had to do?'

'I don't know.'

'What would you like to do now?'

'Get to hell out of here.'

'OK. We'll do that. Let's turn down the pressure. I will show you how to reduce it. You will do so by talking to yourself at the same time that you are taking some slow deep breaths, in and out.

'I want you to breathe in and out very slowly through your mouth and let your neck and shoulders relax. While you are breathing in say to yourself, "C'mon, I'm in control." At the end of your inspiration pause for a second or two and say, "So," and as you breathe out say, "Relax and let it happen." Remember the statement, "C'mon, I'm in control, so, relax and let it happen." With each breath you take and statement you make your pressure will decrease. Turn it down to the level you wish.'

While he is doing this you see the signs of pressure actually disappearing from his face and body. After a few more deep breaths I ask, 'How are you feeling?'

'Great. The headache has gone and my body feels light and relaxed. The pressure has disappeared!'

The difference in his speech is obvious. He now speaks with confidence and self-assurance.

'What is your confidence like?'

'It's great. I am in control now. I know what I have to do and I know

I can do it. My opponents are not that strong. I can deal with them and beat them. I am running freely and I am enjoying the game.'

'What about your concentration? Is it better?'

'Yes. Everything is clear and I know what my job is and what I have to concentrate on.'

'Are you still afraid?'

'No.'

'Why are you so confident that you can do the job now? The conditions on the field are still the same.'

'Yes, but my attitude and thinking have changed. My thoughts are now clear and I am in control of my emotions and the situation. I know what I have to do and I am confident I can do it.'

'That was very good. Now open your eyes.'

'That was amazing! It was so real and I did it just with my imagination.'

'You will probably never experience this level of pressure in a real-life situation, except in the case of a disaster. You created and built up your pressure and then you turned it down. You just saw what negative images and negative self-talk do to your mind and body. And you also saw how you could reduce pressure with breathing and positive self-statements. If you can create pressure you can also turn it down. You just did that.

'If you practise this technique you will get good at it and you will be able to control your pressure in any situation. The moment you encounter a pressure situation you will automatically be able to cope with it. That is what good players do. Do you still doubt the power of your imagination and your self-talk?'

'No!'

This method – induced affect – is a mental flooding technique that I have used very successfully to teach athletes how to manage pressure. The player is thrown into the deep end and learns how to swim.

Another Example of Flooding Technique

Many years ago in Australia, Sir Garfield Sobers used this technique in a real-life situation to help one of his players cope with his fear and pressure.

In the early part of his career, Roy Fredericks, the West Indies opening batsman, had great difficulty playing the short-pitched ball. On a West Indies cricket tour to Australia he was constantly struck on his body and in his head when he was batting and was clearly under a lot of pressure. After a while, the captain decided to take matters into his own hands to help him overcome his problem. He did so by throwing him in at the deep end.

He invited him into the practice nets in Adelaide to face the four fast bowlers in the team who were given instructions to bowl short, attack his head and body and give him the works. Helmets and body protective gear were not around in those days. Fredericks was told to stand up and face the music and was instructed not to retreat mentally or physically in any way. At first he struggled against some very fast and hostile bowling and it was quite frightening to watch him. But after a while, he started to cope and by the end of the net session seemed comfortable and in control of his batting. That baptism by fire triggered off something within him because soon after he became one of the world's best and most exciting players of short-pitched bowling.

A few years later, in a Test match in Perth against Australia, he destroyed the bowling of Dennis Lillee and Jeff Thompson, the two fastest and most dangerous bowlers in the game, on a wicket that was regarded as the fastest and bounciest in the world. He made 169 magnificent runs, most of which came from hook, pull and cut shots, against very fast bouncers and short-pitched deliveries.

He scored those runs off 145 balls and raced to his hundred in seventy-one! Lindsay Hassett, the Australian batsman, who played alongside Bradman and had seen Don do many amazing things said on ABC radio that Frederick's 169 was the greatest innings he had seen in Australia. Soon after, Sir Robert Menzies, a great cricket lover and the then prime minister of Australia, said the same thing to me at a luncheon at the Carlton Football Club in Melbourne during which he marveled at the brilliance of that innings.

GETTING RID OF NEGATIVE THOUGHTS AND SELF-TALK

'How can we get rid of our negative thoughts?' players often ask. Many of them complain that the harder they try to get rid of them the worse they become. Coaches often tell them to forget their negative thoughts and put them out of their minds, but that doesn't work either.

You cannot get rid of negative thoughts by telling yourself to forget them.

Try this exercise. Repeat the numbers 1, 3, 5, 7 and 9 for a minute or so. Now forget them. It is very difficult. Isn't it? Now think of those numbers again and instead of telling yourself to forget them, repeat the numbers 2, 4, 6, 8 and 10. As soon as you do so you will forget the first set of numbers or put them to the back of your mind.

Good players don't make a fuss about negative thoughts. They say that it is normal to have them. Instead of telling themselves to forget them they replace them with positive thoughts. When they get a negative thought they often say, 'STOP' and then think of something else.

The very good players get rid of negative thoughts or relegate them to the back of their mind by taking a few deep breaths and refocusing their concentration on three simple questions: 'Where is my mind? Where should it be? What should I be concentrating on and doing right now?' They might then follow up with, 'What is my goal? What are my priorities? What is the next step?'

When the best players get negative thoughts, they take note of them and then let them quietly pass out of their minds.

POSITIVE THOUGHTS AND SELF-STATEMENTS

Earlier we saw how negative thinking and self-talk create pressure and how positive thinking and self-talk reduce it.

There are many positive things you can say to yourself to manage and capitalize on your pressure. You should experiment with various self-statements to see what works best for you. Here are a few simple ones that many athletes use in pressure situations:

- Take a few deep breaths, relax and get control.
- Concentrate on the basics and stick to your plan.
- Stay in the moment and enjoy the process.
- You can do it. It's not that difficult.
- You have done it several times before.
- It's normal to be nervous. You play well when you are nervous.
- Slow down, relax and focus on your job.
- Stick to your routine.
- Relax, let it flow and get your rhythm going.
- Take one step at a time. Keep your concentration in the present.
- Focus on the process not the result.
- I don't like it but I can stand it, so relax and let it happen.
- Enjoy yourself and let it happen.
- What do I have to do now? What do I want to achieve?

Sense of Humour

The more pressure players experience the more serious and worried they become. But the ability to laugh at yourself or your predicament is a good way to reduce pressure. Humour is a great antidote for pressure but some people find it difficult to keep a sense of humour when they are under pressure.

Years ago, I arrived at a golf course in a country town in Victoria, Australia, and had to make a desperate dash to the bathroom to empty my bladder. I rushed through the first door and by the time I got through the second one I was ready for action. I took a deep breath and was just about to start relieving myself when I noticed a curled-up black object about nine inches away from my right foot. My body instantly went rigid and everything stopped midstream. Time seemed to go very slowly as I said to myself. 'No. This can't be. Somebody is playing a trick on me. It must be a toy or a dead one.'

While those thoughts were going through my mind, the object

started to move and lifted its head off the floor. It was a black snake. I don't know which one of us was more scared and I didn't wait to find out. I literally flew out of the room and crashed through the doors. I didn't have time to make myself respectable and was in full view of a couple of old ladies who were just about to tee off on the first hole. I shouted, 'There is a black snake in the bathroom.' One of the ladies who was obviously Scottish looked up at me and replied, 'Aye Laddie, and there seems to be one out here too.'

At this stage my mind and body went on red alert. As soon as I realized what the good lady had said, I started to see the funny side of the situation and laughed uncontrollably for about five minutes. Soon after, I started my round, still with a full bladder, and went on to play one of my best rounds ever. About thirty minutes later, I was able to ease the pressure in my bladder in a safe and peaceful place.

When I was manager of the West Indies cricket team during Kerry Packer's World Series in Australia, a humorous but extremely important incident occurred during a team meeting at the Old Melbourne Hotel in Melbourne before the start of the first Supertest.

It was an incident that altered the self-image and self-belief of the West Indies players and changed their thinking and performance. I don't think the players up to this day understand the significance of what really happened in that meeting.

Until then, the West Indies team had never won a series in Australia. Frank Worrell's team came close but couldn't pull it off. Many of the other talented West Indies teams that toured Australia succumbed to the pressure and were never able to perform to their potential. Yet, Lloyd's team felt confident that they could beat Australia because they thought they were a talented and professional team. But I was able to detect a few self-doubts in the players and some chinks in their mental armour. This is always the case when you are trying to establish a first.

Near the end of the meeting I said, 'Gentlemen, these Australian cricketers are pretty tough and they are hard to beat. They will insult you and call you black bastards, and worse. They will do this to make you angry, break your concentration and mess up your game.' There was a moment's silence and then one of the players said, 'Doc, that's no problem. We are used to that and we can cope with it.'

I continued, 'The last time they played England they threw lots of insults at the England players and constantly referred to them as "Pommie bastards". The English kept quiet for a while and then came up with a very clever reply, as only the English could, to hit back at the Aussies. Each time the Aussies abused them on the field, they would raise both hands high in the air and alternately place one hand over each wrist. This was meant to convey the word handcuffs to remind the Aussies of their convict background. When the Aussies got the message they were livid.'

This produced great laughter in the room and when it died down, a voice was heard in the corner of the room. It said, 'Mr Manager, we can't do that.' There was immediate silence because Albert Padmore had just spoken – he only spoke every two weeks. Everyone waited with great anticipation to hear what he was going to say. He went on, 'If we do that those buggers would look us straight in the eyes and place their hands around their ankles.'

Everyone fell about in fits of laughter. Some of us were laughing and crying at the same time. Albert was telling us that if we reminded the Australians of their convict background they would have no hesitation in reminding us of our slave background. The laughter was so loud that hotel guests rushed down the corridor to the meeting room to see what on earth was going on.

I detected a change in the players' attitude soon after and I went to Kerry Packer and said to him. 'We are going to beat the hell out of you.' He laughed at me and replied, 'That's a joke. You don't know how to win. You are weak mentally and will crumble under pressure.'

I then said to Kerry, 'Something took place in our last team meeting that will change all that. The players went through a process of self-acceptance and have come to terms with something that has been bugging them for a long time. I now expect them to go through a mental transformation. They are not even aware of the significance of what really happened in that meeting and probably never will, but soon their self-image will change and they will become different players.

The team will be tougher mentally and will win the mental battle with the Australian players.' Kerry gave me one of his famous looks and told me I was talking garbage and a lot of psychological gibberish.

We won the first game and eventually the series. After our first win Kerry admitted, 'This is very dangerous for us. You buggers have just learned how to win against us. It will now be very difficult to beat you.' How right he was. It took Australia more than sixteen years to beat us again.

EXERCISE AND ANGER

Exercise is a very good way to reduce stress. Today, people are flocking to gymnasia to get rid of everyday pressures and improve their health. Even though athletes get a lot of exercise, they get tremendous satisfaction and relaxation when they play other sports or take up other recreational activities.

Players have different objectives when they go to train in the gym. Some of the football players with whom I worked used to go there to get rid of their anger, frustrations and pressure. They would go to the punching bag and beat the hell out of it, all the time imagining that the bag was their coach or the person who was pissing them off. That session always got rid of their tension and pressure.

Anger is a good stress reliever if it is well directed and is not allowed to last for too long. John McEnroe, the great tennis player, used to reduce his pressure during the game by getting angry and quarrelling with match officials or anyone else he would encounter. His outbursts were short, and immediately afterwards he would redirect and refocus his concentration like a laser on the next point. Anger often messes up players' performance because they allow it to go on for too long and fail to redirect and refocus their concentration on the next play.

A SUPPORT NETWORK

In a group, a sense of identity, a feeling of belonging and a feeling of being needed are important in generating confidence and enhancing the ability to cope with pressure.

When faced with danger, monkeys behave more confidently in a group and cope with pressure situations better than when they are alone. In one study, the mice that were injected with cancer cells coped better and lived longer when in a group but not as much when in isolation.

Today, doctors discharge patients from the hospital much earlier than before. They claim that when patients go home they heal and recover faster because of the love, care and support they get in the family environment.

In sport, team support in times of pressure strengthens the will to fight on. The pressure seems to be less disruptive when it is jointly shared in the group. But when unity weakens or when support groups are removed the pressure intensifies.

REMEMBER

1. You can't get rid of negative thoughts by telling yourself to forget them. You eliminate or suppress them by focusing on something else. Remember the 1, 3, 5, 7 and 9 and the 2, 4, 6, 8 and 10 exercise?

2. One of the ways to suppress negative thoughts is to say, 'STOP' as soon as you notice them and replace them with a positive thought or statement.

3. Good players don't make a fuss about negative thoughts. They say it is normal for them to come and when they do so the players just allow them to pass out of their heads.

4. You can direct concentration away from negatives and focus them on the positive by taking a few deep breaths and then asking three simple questions: 'Where is my mind? Where should it be? What should I be focusing on and doing right now?'

5. Experiment with positive thoughts and self-statements when you are under pressure and see which ones work best for you. Couple them with your in and out breathing. For example say 'C'mon I'm in control' during inspiration then

pause at the end of inspiration and say 'So' and as you breathe out slowly say, 'Relax and let it happen.' This often changes your perspective and relieves your pressure.

6. The flooding technique is a quick and effective way to teach players how to deal with pressure but some people feel that the stress inoculation technique where players are exposed to gradual increases in pressure is kinder and gentler and is just as effective.

7. Humour is a great antidote for pressure.

8. Exercise is a good way to prevent and reduce pressure.

9. When correctly directed, short bursts of anger get rid of steam and improve concentration, especially when attention is refocused on the task immediately after.

10. Support networks build confidence and help to reduce pressure, on and off the field.

RELAXATION: THE FIRST STEP IN HANDLING PRESSURE

During the relaxation response arousal is lowered, breathing is slowed down, tension in the mind and the body is reduced, thinking becomes clear and simple and is focused on solutions rather than problems. Relaxation is an essential ingredient while handling pressure. But it is only a first step. You must then focus your thinking and concentration on finding and implementing solutions.

Some players find it difficult to relax when they are under pressure. In fact, many of them actually become tenser when they tell themselves to relax. Knowing when to relax is equally important. If players allow the pressure to get out of hand before they start to relax they will run into trouble.

Players should train themselves to initiate the relaxation response as soon as they detect the early symptoms and signs of pressure – the earlier the better. They should also experiment with various techniques to see what works best for them. Repeated practice will improve their coping skills.

RELAXATION TECHNIQUES

Some of the relaxation techniques are quite easy to learn but others are more complicated and may require guidance from an expert.

One of the simplest methods consists of:

- Taking some slow, deep breaths.
- Relaxing the muscles, particularly those of the hands, fingers, neck and shoulders and in the forehead, cheeks and jaw. Opening the mouth, chewing gum, sticking out the tongue, humming, smiling or whistling help those muscles to relax.
- Talking to yourself positively, for example, 'Slow down and relax, take a few deep breaths, relax and get control,' or 'C'mon, I'm in control, so relax and let it happen.'
- Keeping concentration in the present on the task at hand.

MANNERISMS AND MICRO-MOVEMENTS

Players often display certain mannerisms and go through particular routines and rituals in the dressing room before the start of the game. To onlookers these actions might appear senseless and irrational but they are very important because they help the players to relax. If they are prevented from going through these rituals, they might become irritable and tense. For example, stopping people from humming, doodling, daydreaming, and walking around etc., during their day-to-day activities often give them headaches and make them nervous. These seemingly senseless activities help them to relax and reduce pressure.

During the game, players display certain mannerisms that are an important part of their routine. These mannerisms or micro-movements have a particular sequence and tempo and are some of the first movements to be affected by pressure. When this happens hand–eye coordination and motor skills usually suffer. These mannerisms seem to prime the mind and body to initiate the correct technical movements.

Researchers claim that micro-movements and routines (1) keep you alert but relaxed; (2) are part of your pressure-regulating mechanism; (3) help your balance, stability, tempo and rhythm; (4) are trigger movements for the major technical movements; and (5) improve confidence and concentration.

When some batsmen are told to concentrate on the ball they become so transfixed by it that they get tense and rigid and lose the micro-movements that normally enhance performance.

In the first chapter, I related a story about psychotherapist Milton Erickson's interaction with the US Army rifle team. It has such a powerful lesson that it is worth repeating. He was asked to help prepare the US Army rifle team for its contest against the Russians whom they had never beaten. In teaching them, he first got them to relax their feet, knees, hips and entire body. He asked them to allow their hands to be comfortably placed and the rifle butt to rest against the shoulder in just the right way. Then he asked them to slowly lean their cheeks against the butt until it felt comfortable and let the gun nozzle focus on the target, wander up and down, back and forth across it, and gently press the trigger when the right moment arrives.

Erickson did not ask them to fix their eyes on the target. He explained that doing so would interfere with the micro-movements of the body and would put the person under some strain and tension. He wanted them to keep their body in natural movement with a sense of comfort and relaxation. Instead of selecting just one part of the total picture – the target – he took the entire picture of the total body functioning. That year, the army rifle team beat the Russians for the first time.

When a basketball player is about to take a free throw or when a tennis player is about to serve, he goes through a routine of bouncing the ball a certain number of times. Under pressure he often changes that number and invariably misses his throw or serves poorly. In cricket some batsmen go through certain rituals between deliveries and between overs. Dhoni, for example, fiddles with his batting gloves. Interrupting that ritual or mannerism or altering its tempo and rhythm might make him uncomfortable and put him under pressure.

BREATHING

Slow deep breathing promotes relaxation of the body and mind but many athletes do not understand the mechanics of efficient breathing.

During normal breathing the lungs and chest expand during inhalation. The diaphragm moves downwards and the abdomen relaxes and moves outwards. And during exhalation the process is reversed – the lungs and chest contract, the diaphragm moves upward and the abdomen moves inwards.

But if you ask a player to take slow deep breaths, the in-and-out movement of the abdomen is often reversed – it moves in during inhalation and out during exhalation. This is the wrong way to breathe. With this type of breathing the player's shoulders are elevated and tense at the top of inspiration. He also feels tension in the neck and chest and there is a sensation that his upper body is being lifted up as his neck straightens and his head rises. As he breathes out slowly his neck relaxes and his head moves down a bit. His chest and shoulders relax and his shoulders fall. Suggestions to relax work best when they are given during exhalation.

When the player allows his abdomen to move correctly, he feels less tension in his neck, shoulders and upper body during inhalation and is more relaxed and grounded during exhalation. But under pressure many players find abdominal breathing difficult. Breathing through the mouth helps in that respect.

In pressure situations players' shoulders are kept in an elevated position and they often complain of stiffness in the neck and shoulders and a feeling of having a great load on their shoulders. When that happens the tempo and rhythm of their movement change and the execution of their basic skills suffers. Slow deep breaths through the mouth reduces that tension and stiffness and improves balance and movement.

Greg Norman says when he is under pressure he feels a lot of tension in his neck and shoulders and this messes up his swing. He reduces the tension by taking slow deep breaths, loosening his neck and shoulder muscles by turning his head from side to side and allowing his arms fall loosely by his side. In a Dunlop Masters tournament in England he had to play three good shots to birdie the last hole and win the tournament. Before each shot, he rolled his head around, loosened up the neck and shoulders and relaxed his hands and fingers. After he won, a BBC reporter asked, 'Why do you move your head around before you address the ball?' Norman told him that it relieves tension, and helps him to swing smoothly and hit the ball better.

Here is a simple breathing technique that I teach players. I say to them. 'I am going to ask you to take ten deep breaths with your mouth slightly open. Allow your lower chest and abdomen to move out during inspiration and move in during expiration. As you breathe in, notice the movement of air over your lower lip and tongue and the relaxation in the jaw and facial muscles. Hold each breath for a second or two at the end of each inspiration and let it out slowly through your mouth. Each time you breathe out, say or think the word relax. With each breath you take you will feel the tension leaving your body as you become more and more relaxed. Just take ten deep breaths now.'

Other relaxation techniques include progressive muscular relaxation, visualization and mental rehearsal, centring, the rapid relaxer, balanced breathing, systemic desensitization and other behaviour modification methods, meditation, biofeedback, autogenic training, hypnosis and self-hypnosis, yoga, stress inoculation and induced affect methods.

PROGRESSIVE MUSCULAR RELAXATION

Relaxation of some parts of the body is more important than in others. For example, the face and hands represented by sizeable areas in the brain are more important than the back that has lesser representation in the brain.

The relaxation of the facial muscles is very important in reducing stress. As you relax these muscles, tension goes from the cheeks, the jaw relaxes, the jawbone droops, the lips relax and part a little, and the forehead loses its wrinkles. This smoothing out of the forehead muscles has a calming effect on the mind.

In the progressive muscular relaxation technique, I ask the person to lie down, close his eyes, take a few deep breaths and imagine that he is in a pleasant and peaceful place. I then start the relaxation: 'Pay attention to the muscles around your eyes. Let them relax and let that relaxation spread to the rest of your face allowing the wrinkles in your forehead to disappear. Let your jaw relax and notice how your lips part a little and how your tongue relaxes. Feel the relaxation in your neck and allow your shoulders to go loose and limp… your arms are also relaxing and this sensation is flowing down to your hands and fingers. Let them go loose. This relaxation is now going to pass down your body to your buttocks and pelvis… as it does so, notice how relaxed the muscles in your chest and the small of your back have become… notice also that as you breathe out your feeling of relaxation increases. Let the relaxation pass down your thighs to the muscles of your legs, feet and toes… just let them go limp… and enjoy this beautiful relaxing feeling.'

THE RAPID RELAXER

Described by Peter Lambrau and George Pratt, this technique is a very quick and effective way to relax. It takes about thirty seconds. It combines tapping on the back of the hand with eye movements, humming and counting. Humming stimulates right-brain activity, while counting enhances left-brain activity. Eye movements activate regions in the visual cortex and integrate both hemispheres of the brain. And tapping adds energy to the meridian sites.

Locate a spot between your fourth and fifth left metacarpals about an inch above your knuckles and tap that spot repeatedly with the tips of your second and third right fingers.

While you are tapping, look straight ahead, keep your head steady and moving your eyes only look down and trace an imaginary line along the floor, up the wall to the ceiling and then back to the floor where you began.

Continue tapping. Looking straight ahead and keeping your head steady, glance down to the left and then to the right. Rotate your eyes full circle in a clockwise and then in an anticlockwise direction. Then hum a few notes of your favourite song, count from one to five, and hum a few notes again.

Still tapping, look straight ahead and keeping your head steady look down and draw an imaginary line along the floor, up the wall to the ceiling and then back down to the floor where you began.

This exercise at first appears complex but once you get the hang of it, it becomes very simple.

MEDITATION AND CENTERING

These have already been discussed in the chapter on concentration.

HYPNOSIS AND SELF-HYPNOSIS

Hypnosis and self-hypnosis are not only good relaxation and pressure management techniques but are also excellent performance enhancing procedures.

Today, there are still many people who mistakenly think that hypnosis is a healing sleep or a magical force or power. Hypnosis is a special but normal type of behaviour that occurs when concentration is focused on an experience, object, thought, image or process. You experience it many times during the course of a day.

Hypnosis cannot create new abilities in the athlete but it can help him to make better use of what he has and to tap in to abilities that he doesn't think he possesses. It also gives him confidence and frees him from the limiting beliefs, negative thoughts, self-doubts and fears that sabotage performance.

Hypnotic techniques have been used with great success over the years by a variety of practitioners. Interested athletes should consult specialists in this field to learn how to use these methods to control their physical and mental skills and improve performance. A few of these techniques were described briefly in the chapter on concentration.

INDUCED AFFECT

Induced affect was described earlier in this chapter. It is a flooding technique in which the player is exposed to the full intensity of the pressure without any preparation, relaxation or anxiety-reducing training. The person is thrown into the deep end and is told to swim. The stress inoculation technique is a variation of this method but is gentler and helps the player to learn to cope with gradual and incremental increases of pressure.

REMEMBER

1. Relaxation is only the first step in handling pressure. You must then direct your thoughts, concentration and actions to the task at hand.

2. Under pressure some players become tenser when they try to relax.

3. Learning how to initiate the relaxation response quickly and effectively in the heat of battle should be a top priority.

4. Knowing when to relax is equally important. If you allow the pressure to get out of hand before you start to relax, you will run into trouble.

5. You should initiate the relaxation response as soon as you detect the early symptoms and signs of pressure – the earlier the better.

6. You should experiment with various relaxation techniques to see what works best for you and practise them repeatedly.

7. Handling pressure is a skill that can be learned and improved by constant exposure and repetitive practice in pressure-producing situations.

8. Just because you possess good pressure-coping skills does not guarantee that you choose or execute the right ones during the contest.

9.   In competition, you must not just know how to handle your own pressure but also how and when to put pressure on your opponents.

INTERVIEWS

RAHUL DRAVID

Rudi. What is pressure and how does it affect your performance?

Rahul. I think a certain amount of pressure or nervousness is good. It means that you care about what you are doing and are priming your instincts to be ready to react. Obviously, you cannot let the pressure get to a point where it is counterproductive. There is a fine line and balance there. You shouldn't allow the pressure to get to a stage where your legs become heavy, your hands become tired, and your mouth becomes dry. If that happens you are in trouble.

Pressure will always be there; it is something that all international sportsmen have to deal with. Running away from it or hoping that it will just go away is unrealistic. You must face up to it. When you accept it as a natural part of life and understand that there are things you can do to control it, you will face up to it in a positive way and use it to your advantage.

Rudi. A lot of players fear pressure.

Rahul. Yes, that is true. One of the first instincts of facing pressure is to avoid it or run away from it. The good players, however, face up to it and look at it as a challenge and opportunity to show how good they are, something that they spend their whole life wanting to do. Sometimes you think that you are the only one feeling the pressure, but your opponent feels it too. The bowler who is running in to bowl at you or the batsman that you are bowling to also feels the pressure. And if you cope with it better than he does, you will beat him.

Life is pressure. Pressure is part and parcel of life. Everyone faces it. You must learn how to get it to work for you instead of against you.

Rudi. Some athletes claim that at times pressure lifts them to superior performance and gives them a wonderful feeling that they find difficult to explain. Many of them describe it as being in the 'zone'.

Rahul. I have occasionally had those feelings. It is very hard to create them and that is why getting in to the zone is so elusive and happens so rarely. Striving to get into the zone does not get you there. Mastering the basics, enjoying the process and relaxing and letting things happen give you a better chance of getting close to it. I wish I could get there more often.

I do get nervous and tense under pressure and I do have negative thoughts at times. But I am now better equipped to handle them.

Whenever I get negative thoughts or find my mind wandering, instead of deliberately trying to remove them, I focus on my breathing, and that somehow calms my mind and removes some of them but it doesn't eliminate them completely.

You are always under pressure at the start of your innings. Early on, I try to get my feet moving freely and if I go forward to a ball that I should go forward to, and go back to a ball that I should go back to and not get caught in the crease, I get a lot of confidence, knowing that I am in control of my batting.

When I get negative thoughts, lose confidence, get a bit worried about being hurt, or have a feeling that I might not be able to cope, my feet get lazy and heavy and my body becomes stiff.

Rudi. What kind of negative thoughts do you get when you are under pressure?

Rahul. A few of them are: 'What will happen now? That bowling is too good for me. I mustn't get out, I have to score runs for my team. I don't know if I will be able to cope. This wicket is turning and bouncing and I am not equipped to play this type of bowling. I'm too tired. It's a long way to go and I don't know if I will get there.'

Sometimes the thoughts are irrelevant and irrational and do not match the reality of the situation.

Rudi. Under great pressure you tend to distort reality. You magnify the difficulty of the situation and the reputation of your opponent and at the same time put yourself down and doubt your ability to cope. One of the best ways to reduce that distortion is to break down your challenge into small manageable segments, talk to yourself positively and focus on the task at hand.

Rahul. That is a good way of putting it.

Rudi. Players often lose patience when they are under pressure. Everything speeds up and they become impulsive and impatient.

Rahul. Patience is a great asset particularly when you are under pressure. Impatience is one of the main causes of failure when things get tough. We are way too impatient with ourselves and sometimes we do not understand that everything takes time. There are no short cuts to success. We usually get angry with ourselves when we make mistakes or have setbacks. It is difficult to have success without failures along the way. They are part and parcel of success.

We live in a world of speed and instant gratification but the basic principles of success, at least in cricket as far as I know, have not changed. Success is a journey that takes time. You must be patient with yourself, stay in the moment and focus on the process. We must also be patient with younger players. They pick up our impatience when we are dealing with them and become stressed by it.

V.V.S. LAXMAN

Rudi. What is pressure and how does it affect you?

Laxman. Pressure for me is going into tough and intense situations where things are not going your way and the odds are stacked against you. Whenever I am in those situations I rise to the occasion and get the best out of myself.

Rudi. Where does the pressure come from?

Laxman. The mind creates and reduces pressure – how you assess the situation and react to it. If there are too many negative thoughts going through your mind about yourself and the game situation, you will probably succumb to the pressure. But if you have a different attitude and see the situation as an opportunity to do something special and become a hero for your team, you won't feel much pressure. I am driven by opportunities that give me a chance to do something extraordinary. If you worry about the pressure while you are in the situation you will make it worse.

In pressure situations, one positive thought or one good shot like a straight drive can turn things around and change the way you look at the situation. If you have the right attitude your mind might tell you that there is no pressure even when others are feeling it. So the way you talk to yourself is a critical factor in pressure situations.

Rudi. Sir Garfield Sobers hardly ever mentions the word pressure. He talks about dealing with challenging situations. He says that one of the best lessons you can give to a player is to teach him how to recognize and manage the many different game situations he is likely to face in the game. Then he will know how to recognize them quickly and deal with them when he faces them.

Laxman. I totally agree with him. That is why experienced players handle pressure better than the inexperienced players; they have had the exposure to pressure and know what to do when they encounter it.

Rudi. Some players become very impatient under pressure. How important is patience to you in pressure situations?

Laxman. Patience is critical. Pressure situations don't last forever and are never constant throughout the match; they are always changing. In challenging situations patience should be one of your top priorities. Opponents are very clever and are always tempting you to lose your patience because they know that when you do so you will make simple mistakes that will benefit them. Impatience can interfere with your judgement and sabotage your performance.

If you stay patient when the pressure is on you, and you keep your wicket intact, you will bounce back as soon as the pressure eases. If you remain patient when your opponents are trying to break your patience, they will eventually lose theirs and start to make simple mistakes and the momentum and dynamics of the game would then change.

When we won that Test match against Australia in Mohali, Chandigarh, we kept our patience but the Australians lost theirs. We were in a very tough situation, needing eighty runs with just the last two wickets in hand. Ishant Sharma and I held on for a while and Australia got frustrated and started to make mistakes. As we kept our patience and built a partnership, the Australians lost theirs, forgot their plan, and bowled a lot of loose balls that we were happy to receive.

Rudi. What would you like to do when you finish playing cricket?

Laxman. I don't want to rely on what I have achieved in cricket. I want to do something that will be of service to society. I don't know what it is yet. But whatever it is, I must have the zeal and the passion for it. If you are not passionate about what you are doing you will start and then quit somewhere along the way. I have lasted a long time in cricket because of my love for the game and my desire to represent my country. So when I finish playing cricket I will look for something that I am truly passionate about.

M.S. DHONI

Rudi. In sport, pressure is a force that all players must confront. In some cases it spoils their performance and in other cases it improves it.

Dhoni. I see pressure as an opportunity to do well but there are times when I would rather not have it. If you are under pressure, you should not see it as a danger and give in to it. You should see it as a challenge that will give you a chance to excel and be a hero for your team and country. I prefer to look at it as an opportunity rather than a threat.

People say a lot of negative things about pressure. Pressure to me is just added responsibility. That is how I look at it. It's not pressure when God gives you an opportunity to be a hero for your team and your country.

Pressure can be dangerous if you have a weak attitude towards it, if you don't recognize it when it comes, and if you don't deal with it properly. It will then ruin your performance.

If you expect pressure and have a plan to deal with it you will know exactly what to do when it comes, and more often than not you will handle it in a positive and productive way.

The best way to deal with pressure is to stay in the moment. Don't get trapped in the past or caught up in the future on the result or on what might happen. If you stay in the moment and focus on the process you won't feel much pressure.

Rudi. What is it like having a superhero like Sachin Tendulkar in your team?

Dhoni. I never dreamt of playing with Sachin. Playing with him is like having a God coming into this world and blessing you. I am honoured to share the same dressing room. The kind of character he is and the way he has conducted himself on and off the field over a period of twenty or twenty-one years is really amazing. In his first year he became a superstar and in the next twenty years his life was like that of a demigod. He has been an inspiration and role model to everyone in the Indian team.

Sachin is a true professional and it is very interesting to see him prepare himself for a game. His preparation for a Test match is no different from that in a club game. His practice sessions are usually the same each and every day and his passion and love for the game has remained unchanged over the years.

I have learnt a lot from him, and his advice and opinions are always highly valued. Not only has he helped the younger players in the team but also the senior ones.

Rudi. Dravid and Laxman, the seniors in the team, seem to be getting better with age.

Dhoni. That is what is special about them. They still have a great passion and love for the game and everyday they try to become better players. They are an inspiration to the team.

Rudi. What does life after cricket hold for M.S. Dhoni?

Dhoni. I don't know what the future holds for me but there are two things that I have already lined up. The first is to work with the Indian defence forces. We have the second largest army in the world and very soon I will be joining them. I have just accepted an honorary rank (lieutenant colonel) in the Territorial Army. I just don't want this to be a ceremonial rank. I want to be active and participate and interact with them.

I draw a lot of inspiration from the defence forces. It is a tough job serving and defending your country. Many of my friends are in the army. I am definitely looking forward to joining them after I finish cricket. I believe that I will accept my rank later this year. That will be the happiest day of my life – the day I see myself in uniform.

The second thing I have lined up is starting a sports institute or sports academy in my city. When I was growing up I never had the luxury of a having an excellent coach but I had facilities where I could practise, and gear that I could use during training. I believe that at the lower levels of sport, facilities are very important. As you know cricket has become an expensive sport and every year it is getting more and more expensive.

I will provide the infrastructure and create a learning environment to speed up the development of young players. I will then leave it to those youngsters to discover where they are, where they want to go, and to find out if they have the grit to improve and go to the highest level of the game, like I did.

IAN CHAPPELL

Ian. Pressure is a force that is mainly generated in the mind. If it gets out of hand it can present problems and interfere with your performance, but in the correct proportions, it will bring the best out of you.

Rudi. How does it affect you?

Ian. When the pressure becomes too great, your brain starts to race and everything seems to speed up. If you don't do something about it, it will race around in circles and your body will follow.

At the end of a day's play, I used to get this tightness in my head when I went back to the dressing room. It wasn't a headache, just tightness. It usually took me two hours to unwind. If the pressure came when I was batting, I would feel the tension in my hands, particularly my right hand. I then gripped the bat very tightly.

After getting out I would have a cooling off period of half an hour. It was an irrational period and everyone knew that they had to stay out of my way. They approached me only when an important team decision had to be made. I used to get rid of my anger in a vocal manner and took it out on the soap in the bath.

Rudi. Do you have trouble with thinking when you are under pressure?

Ian. Yes. When you are under pressure, there are two ways in which you can think: (1) You can think about all the things that could possibly go wrong and worry about all the things you don't want to happen to you, or (2) You can think about the things you want to achieve and how to go about achieving them. A lot of people use the first type of thinking and become very negative. This creates more pressure and they worry more. They think in terms of don'ts, must nots and what would happen if… They lose sight of their targets and goals and their thoughts lose clarity. Clear rational thinking controls pressure. You should always remind yourself of your goal and ask yourself the questions, 'What do I want to happen? What am I trying to achieve?'

You should also think in a way that will place the odds in your favour. You must play the percentages.

No matter what sport you play, you should always have a plan, and develop and follow some kind of routine. These negate pressure. When you have a plan your thinking falls into a rational pattern but if you don't have one, it often becomes irrational and negative. You must stick to your plan but as situations change you might have to change it.

Rudi. How did you cope with pressure?

Ian. I will talk about the after-match pressure first. I stayed around the dressing room for at least two hours after the game. I can't understand how today's players come off the field, get dressed and then leave the dressing room in half an hour. The post game period is very important. It allowed me to unwind, get rid of my tension, and relax over a couple of beers. It is a great learning period because you can talk to your team-mates about things that occurred during the game while they are still fresh in your mind.

Rudi. I agree with you. That is when debriefing, one of the most potent weapons of performance, should take place.

Ian. When I am batting and I am under pressure, the moment I detect the signs of pressure either in the form of tightness in my right hand, negative thinking or impatience, I do something about it. I take a few deep breaths and then say to myself, 'Slow down Ian, slow down.' This almost always clears my mind and helps me to think logically. When I find that I am gripping the bat too tightly with my bottom hand, I use it as a trigger to talk to myself. I would say, 'Relax your right hand, relax and concentrate on what you are doing.'

My routine for turning off pressure consists of taking a few deep breaths, relaxing my body and talking to myself. My thoughts are usually, 'What do I have to do now? What do I want to achieve? Slow down, there is no hurry. Take a few deep breaths and relax. Relax your right hand. Stick to your plan and follow your routine. Play the percentages.'

Rudi. What advice would you give to players about coping with pressure?

Ian. Each player is different and he must work out his own routine. He must:

- Find out the situations that are likely to put him under pressure.
- Find out how pressure affects his performance and his game.
- Find out where the signs of pressure manifest themselves in his mind and body.
- Detect these signs as early as possible.

- Learn about the techniques for overcoming pressure. He must practise them because in the game he will be alone and might not have anyone to help him.

- He must work out a routine that will work for him and he must stick to it.

- In team sport, each player should know exactly what is expected of him and the role he has to play.

Rudi. Where did most of your pressure come from?

Ian. It came from sources outside the game like the press, TV, the administration and fans. They are never satisfied and the more you give, the more they demand. If you don't deliver the goods they become very critical. There is an easy way to handle this type of pressure. You can always tell them to get stuffed.

Captaincy is a very taxing job. I think that a four or five-year period is just about the limit for most captains because the pressure sometimes gets to them after that, dampens their initiative and creativity and interferes with their motivational and leadership skills.

SIR GARFIELD SOBERS

Sir Garfield. Pressure helps you to play better but it can be a very dangerous thing. You must know yourself really well to cope with it. You must know what you can and cannot do.

I don't like to use the word pressure. I prefer to talk about dealing with challenging situations. When you put too much emphasis on handling pressure you magnify it in your own mind and make the situation worse. Pressure is produced by the situations you encounter. If you learn to cope with these situations, you won't feel the pressure. Once you have acquired a reasonable level of skill, you should be taught about situations, particularly how to approach them and deal with them. Situations change every moment and what is important at any one stage of the match may not be so at another. So you have to know what is important about each situation and how to deal with it. You must tailor your skills to meet the requirements of each situation.

When I am playing a friendly game in golf, I don't feel any pressure because the result isn't very important. If I am trying to make a three-foot putt, it doesn't worry me. However, if I am playing in a serious competition, like playing for Barbados, it is a different situation. The same putt would then place me under pressure because the situation is now an important one. You suddenly become concerned about missing it, so there is more pressure on you to sink it.

Rudi. So you think that the importance of the situation generates pressure.

Sir Garfield. Of course. If the situation isn't important or challenging you don't feel pressure. The pressure arises as a result of the importance you attach to the situation. In a high-pressure situation you tend to place too much emphasis on the result instead of trying to cope with the problems at hand.

Rudi. Why do so many batsmen get out in the nervous nineties? Why do they feel the pressure at this stage?

Sir Garfield. Because they concentrate on 100 instead of the next ball. When they reach ninety the most important thing for them is to reach 100 and the closer they get to it, the more pressure they feel. Some of them become very impatient and try to hit each ball for ten! Others become scared of getting out and literally become paralysed, so they prod at the ball and block it. They forget to hit the ball. Instead of continuing with their normal game they change their style of play and put unnecessary pressure on themselves.

When you are faced with a tough situation you must believe in yourself and trust your skills. If you doubt yourself and your ability, you will be severely handicapped. You must talk to yourself sensibly, approach the situation calmly and try to apply the appropriate skills to deal with the problem areas. If you do this, you are likely to get the best out of yourself.

During that innings at Lords in 1966 when Holford and I played so well, we were in a very tough situation early on. I said to myself, 'I can handle this. This is no problem. All I need is someone at the other end to stay with me. The bowlers are good but I don't think they will give me any problems today.' In the early stage, Cowdrey brought in the field and tried to apply more pressure on us... As far as I was concerned the first-important priority in the situation was the wicket, and after playing a few balls I realized it was a good one. I then went down to the other end to speak to David and I told him, 'This is a very good wicket. It is like our wickets at home. Just think about batting on a Kensington wicket in Barbados and imagine yourself batting well. How could they get you out? The only way they could get you out is if you do something stupid. They are not going to get me out today because I don't see any problems in this situation. Cowdrey is trying to crowd us but this is going to make it easier for me to play a few shots.' As soon as I started to attack, Cowdrey went defensive. The pressure was then reversed and it was placed on him. He was never able to get rid of it. I wouldn't have coped well if I had gone out there and said, 'Geez, this is going to be difficult. This is real pressure. How am I going to survive it? If I make any mistakes, it will be disastrous for the team. What will happen if I don't get on top of the bowling...?'

Those thoughts never crossed my mind. I always found that if I was challenged and I spoke to myself sensibly and approached the challenge calmly, I didn't feel pressure. I knew that I had the skills to handle any situation, so if my thinking was positive, I didn't have any problems.

Rudi. Where did you feel the pressure? Did you feel it in your body?

Sir Garfield. No. I didn't have any problems with my body. I felt it in my mind. Occasionally, my pulse would race but I wasn't aware of any real problems in my body. It was my thinking and concentration that were affected. Good players are able to control these changes and get back to normal quickly.

Rudi. Where did most of your pressure come from?

Sir Garfield. It came from the crowd. Once you acquire a reputation there is always pressure on you to live up to it. I always tried to please the crowd because I knew that most of them used to come to see me bat. After a while I found it difficult to turn it on for them.

Pressure from the opposition never worried me. I always responded well to their challenges and invariably played better.

I found it almost impossible to handle the pressure that came from within my own team or the administration. When there was dissension in the team it used to upset me. I couldn't cope with petty jealousies and silly arguments. Anything that came from within the team and threatened to disrupt its unity placed me under pressure. This was because almost all of my motivation to do well came from the team. I always wanted to do well for the team, not myself. The team came first. I was never interested in my own score. If I had been I would have scored a hell of a lot more runs.

GREG CHAPPELL

Rudi. What do you feel about pressure?

Greg. I love it. It improves my concentration and brings the best out of me. If I have a challenge I respond in a positive way. When there is no pressure, I get mentally lazy and I don't play well. I must have pressure to fire up.

Rudi. How do you know when you are under pressure and where do you feel the pressure in your body?

Greg. My thinking becomes muddled and negative and I find it hard to stop it. I get funny feelings in my stomach. My hands and arms get very tight when I am batting. At school I used to get cramps in my arms but I thought that was normal. I also thought that the 'butterflies' in my stomach were a normal part of being ready for action.

Rudi. Did you ever feel that your opponent was too good for you?

Greg. Not really. I always respect my opponents but I didn't think that they were too good for me. I always give myself a chance of getting out of tough spots. I've done so on several occasions. I might change my approach or alter my tactics, but I don't lose confidence in myself. I must admit though that during my big slump, I probably lost it and probably rated that quartet of West Indian fast bowlers too highly.

Rudi. What are the things that put you under pressure? Was it the captaincy or your batting? Having the Australian innings revolve around you must have placed you under pressure.

Greg. I loved the responsibility of being the best batsman in the team. It put a bit of pressure on me but it brought out the best in me. It made me concentrate better.

Most of my pressure came from sources off the field – public relations exercises, the press, the TV, the fans and my business interests. Going on to the cricket field was a relief at times. The captaincy didn't place too much pressure on me. I knew I could always cope with it.

Rudi. What about the underarm incident against New Zealand?

Greg. The series against New Zealand was a frustrating one. I was fed up with the Melbourne pitches and I was tired of complaining about them. I was annoyed about the attitude of the people in charge of the game as well as the apathetic attitude of my players. All these things added up and the underarm incident was just my way of protesting about everything. It really stirred up a storm.

For three or four weeks I coped with the pressure quite well but after that it started to get to me. I was copping it from everyone. It started to drain me and I became mentally tired in the end.

Rudi. This is similar to the battle fatigue that soldiers experienced during World War II. When they were exposed to the constant pressure of battle they broke down after three to five weeks. Practically everyone suffered if they were subjected to it for a long enough period. Its onset was heralded by tiredness and by difficulty in concentrating. The soldiers became tense, irritable and lost confidence. This state was followed by a group of symptoms that constituted emotional exhaustion. They became dull and listless, and suffered from indifference, apathy and mental and physical slowness. I am sure that sportsmen go through some of those changes when they become mentally fatigued.

Greg. One of the things you lose when you become mentally fatigued is your motivation. You are still aware of your goals and you usually know what is required to achieve them, but you just can't be bothered. You lose your hunger.

The easiest thing for me to do at that stage would have been to run away and hide, but that was not my style. I decided to face the pressure head on. We had to go to New Zealand to play a series soon after, and I knew I had to face the music. I knew how strong the anti-Australian, and in particular the anti-Chappell, feeling was, so I knew what was awaiting me. I thought the best way to handle the situation was to get totally involved in doing what I was best at – batting. I played extremely well during the series. The antagonism and harassment turned to applause and admiration for the batting skill that I displayed.

GREG NORMAN

Greg. Pressure affects my mind and my body. They both get tense when I am under great pressure. In my body, I notice it mainly in my legs and thighs and to a lesser degree in my neck and shoulders. At the Victorian Open, I was in a winning position on the seventeenth hole when my legs suddenly became very tight and stiff. I couldn't walk properly. I felt as though I was dragging legs and I thought, 'Gosh, these people might think I am stupid walking like this, but I can't move my legs feely.'

When I feel tight, I walk quickly and take short strides. To cope with the tension, I deliberately try to walk slowly and take long strides. If the legs are tight and stiff when you address the ball, you feel uncomfortable and often swing badly.

Rudi. Do your legs feel heavy as well?

Greg. Yes. Very heavy. That happened yesterday during the third round of the Australian Masters when I played with Seve Ballesteros and had a disastrous seventy-eight. I got a triple bogey on the fourteenth hole and my legs suddenly felt very heavy and tired as I walked to the fifteenth tee. Again I found it hard to walk.

When I am under pressure I sometimes get impatient. I often say to myself, 'Slow down, take a few deep breaths and relax. Walk slowly to the ball.' This stops my mind and body from speeding up too much. It usually works well but sometimes I fail to recognize the signs of impatience early enough and I make mistakes.

This happened to me in the US Masters in 1981. I was playing with Tom Watson in the final round and I birdied the nineth hole and moved within one shot of the leader, Watson. The tenth tee was about 80 yards away and I had to walk through a very large gallery to reach it. After 30 yards my thighs and legs became very heavy. I was less experienced in those days, so I kept going and walked very quickly to the tee. I hurriedly teed up the ball, played my shot and hooked the ball into the trees. I neglected the warning signs, rushed, broke my routine and paid the price. If I had been thinking at that stage, I would have slowed myself down. Had I done so, who knows what would have happened by the time we got to the final hole?

My neck and shoulders also get tense and I deliberately try to loosen them by turning my head form side to side and allowing my arms to fall loosely to my side.

Last year, when I made that desperate phone call to you from Birmingham, England, I was in a very bad way. You reminded me about the importance of having loose, relaxed shoulders and neck muscles. That half-hour conversation helped me enormously and was largely responsible for the reversal of my very bad form. I won the next two tournaments, one of them the Dunlop Masters, with a record score. I had to birdie the last hole to win, so I had to play three good shots. Before I played each shot, I rolled my head around and loosened up the neck and shoulders. After the tournament I was interviewed by a BBC television reporter and was asked, 'Why do you move your head around before you address the ball?' I said, 'It relieves the tension, relaxes me and helps me to hit the ball better.'

Rudi. What about your hands and fingers?

Greg. My hands don't usually get too tight. At least I don't think so. Perhaps they do and I am not aware of it. I try to keep them loose by moving them around and opening and closing my hands. This probably stops them from becoming too tight. The advice you gave me about reducing the tension in my right thumb has helped me a lot, particularly with my putting. It has made a big difference.

Rudi. What happens to your thinking when you are under pressure?

Greg. If I can keep a clear head and think in a simple way, I handle the pressure well. In fact, I don't feel it if I do this. However, if I am thinking negatively, the pressure usually gets the better of me. So the way I think more or less determines whether I feel the pressure – whether I control it or it controls me.

If I am leading a tournament and I am under pressure, in 90 per cent of cases I would think positively. I say to myself, 'There is the target, there is where I want the ball to go, so put it there. Get a good rhythm going and let the club do the rest.' It's only when I am playing badly and my swing isn't as good as it should be, that I start to think negatively. I say to myself, 'Don't hit it there. You mustn't do this and you mustn't do that, etc.' This is precisely the time when I get into trouble. This is when you should be thinking positively, but it is very difficult to keep out those negative thoughts. They take over.

Rudi. What are other bad thoughts that you get?

Greg. When the result of the match is uppermost in my mind and I am saying things like, 'Don't blow it now. Don't hit the ball into the rough. If you lose now you will look very stupid. Everyone will laugh at you. Don't bogey these holes.' Normally I stick to my routine, select a target and aim for it. But sometimes I forget those things.

Rudi. This is where your caddy can be of great help. He can remind you of those things and clear your mind of those negative thoughts. What else happens to your mind at times like these?

Greg. My attitude changes and I get very conservative. Instead of trying to win, I try not to lose so my shots become tentative.

Rudi. What about breathing at times like these?

Greg. Breathing is very important. The crucial factor for me when I am putting, especially on fast greens, is to breathe properly. Whenever I putt well, I always follow a routine of taking two deep breaths. This is the length of time I spend over the ball, until I stroke it. I take a deep breath looking at the hole and I breathe out slowly as I look back at the ball. I then take another deep breath when I look at the hole again and I breathe out slowly and completely as I focus on the ball. Then I wait for a fraction of a second. At this stage I feel solid and relaxed. I then stroke the ball to the hole. If I break this routine I usually hit a bad shot. The faster the greens the more important this is because the relaxed feeling in your body and hands is more critical. If I hit the ball when I am breathing in chances are that my body will move.

Rudi. You breathe out when you are hitting the ball, do you?

Greg. No. I have no breath in me at all. I hit the ball after I've blown out all the air in my lungs.

Rudi. When did you first learn that breathing got rid of tension?

Greg. I knew a bit about it but I never used it properly. I became aware of its importance during my wife's pregnancy. I went to antenatal classes and practised all the breathing exercises with her. After I started to do that, I realized how quickly I was able to relax myself. Sometimes I was so relaxed that I felt like falling asleep. I then decided to try it out on the golf course.

BIBLIOGRAPHY

Amen, Daniel G. *Magnificent Mind at Any Age*. New York: Harmony Books, 2008.

Ariely, Dan. *Predictably Irrational: The Hidden Forces That Shape Our Decisions*. New York: HarperCollins Publishers, 2008.

Bennis, Warren, Jagdish Parikh and Ronnie Lessem. *Beyond Leadership: Balancing Economics, Ethics and Ecology*. Massachusetts: Blackwell Publishers, 1994.

Brafman, Ori and Ron Brafman. *SWAY: The Irresistible Pull of Irrational Behavior*. New York: Broadway Books, 2008.

Branden, N. *The Psychology of Self-Esteem*. Los Angeles: Bantam Books, 1981.

Carron, A.V. *Social Psychology of Sport*. New York: Mouvement Publications, 1980.

Chappell, Greg. *CRICKET: The Making of Champions*. Melbourne: Thomas C. Lothian Pty Ltd, 2004.

Clarke, Christopher J. and Arthur J. Jackson. *Hypnosis and Behavior Therapy*. New York: Springer Publishing Company Inc., 1983.

Clemmer, Jim. *Pathways to Performance*. California: Prima Publishing, 1995.

Copley, Gregory R. *The Art of Victory: Strategies For Personal Success and Global Survival In a Changing World*. New York: Threshold Editions, 2006.

Csikszentmihalyi, M. *Beyond Boredom and Anxiety*. San Francisco: Jossy-Bass Publishers, 1977.

De Bono, Edward. *Conflicts: A Better Way To Resolve Them*. London: Harrap Publishers Limited, 1985.

Ellis, A. and R. Grieger. *Handbook of Rational Emotive Therapy*. New York: Springer Publishing Company, 1977.

Erickson, Milton H. *Innovative Hypnotherapy*. New York: Irvington Publishers Inc., 1980.

Gallwey, Timothy W. *The Inner Game of Golf*. New York: Random House, 1981.

Golf magazine, 'How to Put The Wheels back On.' July 1978.

Hall, Jay. *The Executive Trap: How to Play Your Personal Best on the Golf Course and on the Job*. New York: Simon and Schuster, 1992.

Harari, Oren. *The Leadership Secrets of Colin Powell*. New York: McGraw-Hill, 1992.

Hartland, J. *Medical and Dental Hypnosis*. London: Balliere Tindall Publishers, 1973.

Hirai, T. *Zen and the Mind*. Tokyo: Japan Publications Inc., 1978.

Heggie, Jack. *Running With the Whole Body*. California: North Atlantic Books, 1996.

Hemery, David. *Sporting Excellence*. Toronto: Willow Books, 1986.

Hoffman, D.A., R.R. Jacobs and J.E. Baratta. 'Dynamic criteria and the measurement of change,' *Journal of Applied Psychology*, Vol. 78, 1993.

Hunt, John W. *Managing People at Work: A Managers Guide To Behaviour in Organizations*. London: McGraw-Hill Book Company Limited, 1986.

Kotter, John P. *The Leadership Factor*. New York: Free Press Macmillan Inc., 1988.

Kroger, William and William Fezler. *Hypnosis and Behavior Modification*. Philadelphia: J.B. Lippincott Company, 1976.

Landy, Frank J. and Jeffrey M. Conte. *Work in The 21st Century*. Massachusetts: Blackwell Publishers, 2007.

Lambrou, Peter and George Pratt. *Instant Emotional Healing*. New York: Broadway Books, 2000.

Lavallee, David, John Kremer, Adrian P. Moran and Mark Williams. *Sport Psychology: Contemporary Themes*. New York: Palgrave MacMillan, 2004.

Liggett, Donald R. *Sport Hypnosis*, Human Kinetics, Illinois, 2000.

Lipton, Bruce H. *The Biology of Belief*. California: Hay House Inc., 2008.

Meares, A. *Relief Without Drugs*. Great Britain: Fontana/Collins, 1970.

Meares, A. *Wealth Within*. Melbourne: Hill of Content Publishing Company Pty Ltd, 1979.

Murphy, James D. *Flawless Execution*. New York: Reagan Books, 2005.

Niddeffer, R. M. *The Inner Athlete: Mind Plus Muscle For Winning*. New York: Thomas Y. Crowell Publishers, 1976.

O'Connor, Joseph. *NLP and Sports*. London: Thorsons, 2001.

Parent, Joseph. *Zen Golf: Mastering the Mental Game*. New York: Doubleday, 2002.

Scaglione, Robert and William Cummins. *Karate of Okinawa: Building Warrior Spirit with Gan Soku Tandem Riki*. New York: Person to Person Publishing Inc., 1993

Rossi, E. L. *The Collected Papers of Milton H. Erickson on Hypnosis*. New York: Irvington Publishers Inc., 1980.

Russell, B. and T. Branch. *The Memoirs of an Opinionated Man*. New York: Ballantyne Books, 1979.

Sargant, W. *Battle For the Mind*. London: Heinemann, 1957.

Smith, R. *Induced Affect*. Personal Communication.

Simpson, Bob. *The Reason Why*. Sydney: Harper Sport, 1996.

Stellar, James R. and Eliot Stellar. *The Neurobiology of Motivation and Reward*. New York: Springer–Verlag, 1985.

Straub, William F. *Sport Psychology: An Analysis of Athlete Behavior*. New York: Mouvement Publications, 1978.

Tice, Louis E. *Smart Talk For Achieving Your Potential*. Seattle: Pacific Institute Publishing, 1995.

Webster, Rudi V. *Winning Ways: In Search of Your Best Performance*. Sydney: Collins/Fontana, 1984.

Yarbus, A.L. *Eye Movements and Vision*. New York: Plenum Press, 1967.

Young, J.Z. *Programs of the Brain*. Oxford: Oxford University Press, 1978.

Zaffron, Steve and Dave Logan. *The Three Laws of Performance*. California: Jossey-Bass, 2009.